A MIRROR FOR RUFFIANS

A MIRROR FOR
RUFFIANS

By

PHILIP LINDSAY

Essay Index Reprint Series

BOOKS FOR LIBRARIES PRESS
FREEPORT, NEW YORK

First Published 1939
Reprinted 1972

Library of Congress Cataloging in Publication Data

Lindsay, Philip, 1906-
   A mirror for ruffians.

   (Essay index reprint series)
   Reprint of the 1939 ed.
   1. Adventure and adventurers. I. Title.
CT105.L5 1972   920'.02   72-303
ISBN 0-8369-2799-0

PRINTED IN THE UNITED STATES OF AMERICA
BY
NEW WORLD BOOK MANUFACTURING CO., INC.
HALLANDALE, FLORIDA 33009

Contents

Illustrations

DEDICATION FOR

W. L. Hanchant

My Dear Wilfred,

Inevitably this book is yours, you were indeed the "onlie begetter" of it, way back in 1931. Merely seven or eight years ago! It seems eternities away, so many are the adventures we have faced since then, together and alone. And how young we were in spirit! so arrogantly young and so assured of ourselves and of the heroic future that lay ahead! It is true that you had an air of maturity which I envied, a sophistication which I never possessed and never will possess, but now often I wonder if behind that calm Byronic mask of yours you had not been almost as simple and possibly sometimes quite as frightened as I before a future that might hold anything and which certainly did hold starvation and many worse tribulations than an empty belly. One thing at least we can say with pride, we never flinched before what came, no matter how often a malicious world crumbled at our too-eager explorations, no matter how the schemes matured outside the British Museum—at least it was warm in the reading room, but the passion to talk and smoke drove us continually into the cold—or, when we could rake up pence enough, in the romantic gloom of the old Plough Tavern, never seemed to materialise. There was that magazine about antiques which you started and of which I was officially sub-editor without pay, and my knowledge then of antiques was about equal to my understanding of the Einstein theory; there were the various private publishing ventures, and the anthologies we mapped out. Troubled times, certainly, but there was

9

always ambition to send us home cosily at night, even though we had to sprawl many a wasted afternoon away on Hampstead Heath while nearby the Spaniards remained hospitably open to those with wealth enough to buy at least a glass of mild. We have stepped now beyond that world and should be content, but it is not only the nostalgia which most of us feel towards our youth that makes me, in a way, sentimentally regret the passing of those days. It is grand fun when there are noble unfulfilled ambitions in you and you have good friends with whom to talk the days and nights away, even though there be no food in the larder or coals in the grate or even the entrance-fee into a pub.

This book springs from those times. I have no need to remind you that you commissioned a work from me, then entirely unknown, when you were in charge of the now defunct Desmond Harmsworth Press; you will also not need reminding that the entire book was written frenziedly in about a fortnight spent scuttling from your office in Great Russell Street to the B. M. until at night, drunk with phrases and excitement, I tramped to my underground room in St. John's Wood, a room so damp that mushrooms literally grew under the bed. You gave to me possibly the greatest thrill of my life when I saw your list of publications with my name boldly placed under the title RUFFIANS' HALL with a rousing blurb to make me shiver and blush. Jeanne and I sat in the Express Dairy behind your office, toasting the future in a pot of tea, fingering those pages with awe, quite certain that our fortunes were made and that I was going to become a very famous man within a month or so. What did it matter if you could afford no larger an advance than £15? The royalties, we were certain, would add many a nought to that sum. Therefore I was astounded and bewildered and

very scared by the violence with which many of the critics
pounced on me, and my despair was heightened by the
realisation that those attacks were mainly justified. Seeing
the book with new eyes, with the eyes particularly of Mr.
Compton Mackenzie in the *Daily Mail* and Mr. Howard
Spring in the *Evening Standard*, I saw how hopelessly
irresponsible and bombastic it was. But whatever pain
those men gave me, teaching me a much needed lesson
which I hope I have never forgotten, whatever gloom they
spread in our strictly eighteenth-century Hampstead
room that was delightful in winter but invaded by incalculable armies of ferocious insects in summer, they fully
compensated for it all by the too-kind words they wrote
later of my first novel. I am proud to know that in so
swift a time I earned their commendation and I still keep
the encouraging letters they sent me when I plucked up
courage enough to tell them—after they had spoken
kindlily of the novel—under what strain of poverty and
how quickly that previous book had been written.

It was called, you will remember, *Ruffians' Hall*, and has
been out of print for years and will for ever remain out of
print. Yet the planning we made together still sticks in
my mind and I have often longed to do more justice to the
idea. This is the result. Little indeed of *Ruffians' Hall*
remains. *Morgan* has been altered very slightly, for I discovered after a thorough rewriting that I killed its crude
vitality, that youthful enthusiasm which one can never
repeat. The *Prince Regent* and *Walker* are the only two
other remnants of *Ruffians' Hall*, practically all else is new,
and *Walker* has had enough new material added to give
it an entirely different bias. *Kelly* I deleted because it was
so appallingly bad that I couldn't bear to re-read it, and
the same may be said of the *Hildebrand*. With gusto I
discarded them both. *Colombus* also has gone, for after

the publication of my friend Charles Duff's book, I revised my opinion of the man a little ; *Bligh* too has disappeared because nowadays there has been far too much written about him for me to add even a few lines.

This new book you will find so different from *Ruffians' Hall* in material, outlook, design and construction that with a good conscience I can offer it to you as an entirely new work. Nor do I offer it because you are the " onlie begetter," nor because of memories of painful yet happy days, but because your name must stand before at least one of my books as a symbol of affection, as a kind of seal on our old friendship.

PHILIP LINDSAY

London, N.W. 8

. . . will needs carouse, conspire, and quarrell,
that they may make Ruffians' Hall of Hell.

NASHE

I
Trepanning the Ruffian

He is a splendid creature, the ruffian. Splendid at least in his own eyes, he can see little beyond the glory that surrounds him; all is puny beside his strength, mankind but fodder for his lusts. His belief in himself, the chosen of God, is such that he can face the most tremendous perils and pass through unharmed. For there is a magic about him so that even death itself seems to stand aside before his unconquerable courage; yet it is not truly courage because the ruffian knows that he has nothing to fear. Being under the wings of dark angels, guided by protective stars, he feels that until he has taken all that life can give, all that he justly demands, he cannot die except by some strange accident. Can one applaud Achilles slashing down the Trojans when his heel is armoured? Somewhere in every ruffian lurks this little chink that leaves him open to a wound, but it is so hidden, so small a thing that if he can but mask it he is safe. We ordinary frightened creatures, elbowing aside a multitude of terrors, can but watch, puzzled and scared, the heroic ones who smile in battle and, calmly insolent, argue with income-tax collectors or shut the doors of their spirits on the fury of an outraged wife. We slink by genial policemen, resentfully accept what evil pomatums the barber may force on us, we are the predestined prey of ruffians, we are the suckers of the world. I know that I have always been a sucker, hypnotised by the ruffian's will, cringing and weakly surrendering before his arrogance. A sucker is not inevitably a fool, he is not always deceived, but as a rabbit stands paralysed before a stoat so do I automatically produce my small change when some smiling ruffian strides into the bar. What is this magic, this irresistible power they have which paralyses one? The confidence tricks one reads about in papers seem puerile, things that a half-blind idiot would laugh at, yet every day clever men succumb to the most outrageous lies and almost eagerly finger pen and cheque-book. The ruffian's eye is upon them, that quick determined eye; his cunning tongue has netted them and there is no escape. Like a lover who knows his mistress's duplicity yet worships her, we, the suckers, realise that we are cheated yet give way in homage before such art.

But the confidence trickster is by no means the only type of ruffian, he is of the lesser breed, a petty forager of that army. Let us dismiss him with his few miserable hard-worked-for pounds and seek the adytum of Ruffians' Hall where sit the great ones of the earth, men's gods. First, however, before we enter this dangerous world, we must strive for a definition, for some touchstone that will reveal the ruffian under whatever coat he chooses to wear—coat of a soldier, mantle of a king, rags of a beggar or vestment of a priest. It is useless asking the dictionary. Inquiry within even the vast covers of the N.E.D. leaves one as baffled as ever, running blindly through a maze of words. For the dictionary is concerned with facts and never with abstractions, it treats ruffianism not as a state of mind but as a violent expression of—well, of violence, let us say, confusing the obvious effect with the subtle cause. The N.E.D.—which, as usual, stuns one with a variety of examples about entirely irrelevant matters—gives as its first definition of *Ruffian*: "A man of low and brutal character; one habitually given to acts of violence or crime; a cut-throat

villain." I have pondered laboriously over this with no
result whatever. To call a dog a canine ruffles one's
æsthetic palate, but to hear it called the Friend of Man
is justification for literary homicide. And that is the
dictionary's trick of sidling away from a straightforward
definition.

No, the dictionary will not help. It but gives you an
abstract noun in place of your concrete one and throws
in a few adjectives to dazzle you, much as the conjuror
patters while he slides the chicken from his sleeve. We
have to create our own terms to explain anything of a
moral character. It is useless to talk of the effects of
that character, glibly chattering of " low and brutal "
types and " acts of violence and crime ", like a politician
pivoting around the truth. These are the effects, not the
cause. The same may be said of " the cut-throat villain ",
one of the most despised breeds of ruffianism, and surely
no passport into Nashe's brazen Hall? Most cut-throats
are but murderous louts or poltroons too inexpert to earn
a living by some more subtle method. To become a
ruffian in the true sense of the word—anyhow, in my
sense of the word—you must rise far above the crudity
of slitting throats or jabbing a broken bottle into a man's
face. Such things are done only by the apprentices of
Ruffians' Hall, or by bungling over-zealous amateurs.

Too often do we consider a state of mind as something
distinct from the acts of the body, for after all the body
is the instrument of the will, discarded when the spirit
tires of it, or let to die when the spirit is weary of the
conflict that we call life. Flesh is the servant of the
mind; when one's fist strikes, it is as impersonal as a
sword or a gun. To differentiate act from act we must
understand the impulses that guided each act. Every
killer is not a murderer. Despite the clamour of pacifists,

B

soldiers cannot be classed as murderers, their impulses to kill being vastly different from that of the anti-social lunatic, just as the anti-social lunatic's reflexes are different from those of the man who slays in self-defence. Even the law's spectacles can see that far. If the act itself meant anything, our code should hang the hangman immediately after hanging the victim. We are all likely killers, but very few of us are likely murderers. For example, there is a great difference between butcher Haarmann and philandering Landru. Haarmann used to kill young men in Hanover shortly after the war and would then sell their cooked carcases in pies; Landru's interest in his clients was so mercenary that when he conducted them to the operating couch at Gambais he always bought one return and one single ticket. In a petty fashion, I would classify Landru as a ruffian, but I would keep Haarmann locked out of the Hall, for Landru possessed that essential of ruffianism, the belief that his own existence was of such importance that he could burn a few worthless wandering females with a good conscience; but Haarmann was confused by sexual impulses and did not kill purely for self-preservation, he killed sadistically. Men such as Landru then, and Smith of the bath-tub, we will take as our first examples, they give us a little light into the secret of ruffianism. They slew to live.

To define ruffianism more fully we must throw aside all preconceived conceptions of murderers, assassins, bullies, cut-throats, and such. We must seek for a common denominator, for a denominator that does not state that a man is a ruffian because he is a bully, but one that proves he is a bully because he is a ruffian. And there is one word that helps greatly, that will link the drug-crazed gangster with many an honest soldier and priest, locking them together in Ruffians' Hall: that word is Arrogance. It naturally does not cover all shades of ruffianism, but it is the nearest I believe that we will come to a clear definition, if we accept arrogance as meaning the mental state of one blind to everything but himself and his own ambitions. Under such a ruling we will find ruffians who would despise the slitting of a throat unless it were absolutely necessary, men who would never even speak an unkind word; men such as the mighty Brigham Young leading his exhausted exultant followers over the deserts to the Salt Lakes, even geniuses like Moses can enter this Hall. Noble creatures many of these ruffians might be, the inspiration for centuries, but it is their unswervable belief in themselves, their gigantic arrogance, that gives to them the strength not only to stand upon their own feet but to lift up the feet of others. They are ever undaunted, undauntable, they can lead armies or break the Stock Exchange, they can write great poetry, paint great pictures, or they can guide man- kind to the ecstasy of some spiritual joy. And they can hit you with a sandbag, or ask you to look up at the moon while they slide a razor over your throat.

Let us forget our moral alphabet, that creation of timid souls striving desperately to control the ruffian. We must look with new eyes, with stronger gaze, upon a fierce brave world. These men, these ruffians, are the titans of earth, gods imprisoned in flesh, they are the leaders, the iconoclasts, whom we may detest, whom we may try to shuffle into prison, or to whom rever- ently we may offer an earthly crown or a wreath of deathless laurels. While they live and are dangerous, we may think to escape their magic by jeering at them or, in desperation, by stringing them to the end of a rope, but when they are safely tucked away under our feet we

can breathe once more and even canonise them. We do
not realise that often we canonise the dead for those
very qualities we detest most in the living; we worship
Napoleon, we would shudder from the man, we speak
with condescending affection of poets like Shelley, but
we would swiftly lock away our wives and daughters
were he to come knocking at the door and we would
shut our appalled ears to his atheistic and communistic
gibes. Being dead, these men are safe, and smugly we
can canonise them for what they created or destroyed,
while we quickly push into our minds' attics all
memories of what we feared in them when they were
alive—their ruthlessness, their dominating egoism. That
is the great jest of ruffianism: like a saint, the ruffian
rarely gets his halo until after he is dead.

Perhaps our sneaking veneration for these giants is
mainly envy, they possess what we strive to possess, they
are the incarnation of our daydreams. Shamefully, in
secret, man sees himself surrounded by adoring females
or leading triumphant armies or knocking cricket-balls
over the pavilion at Lord's. In each of us flickers this
yearning for greatness, for the respect and admiration of
our fellows, and this can be attained most easily by creating fear in others. To make men tremble at your glance is
power whether you sit upon a throne or juggle in Wall
Street. Within each of us, within even the mildest, there
is a speck of ruffianism, of the jewel that shines through
the triumphant eyes of the great. We hide it, with terror
we smudge its blinding colour, cowardlike we train the
muscles of our faces into amiable grinning masks. But
the ruffians wear no masks, they disdain to be tolerant
of others' weaknesses, they uncover the jewel of arrogance and dazzle even themselves with its fire, this jewel
that, like the eye of Vathek, makes all collapse before it.

And who more arrogant than Vathek, a dreamer who
for the sake of petty knowledge flings human lives into
the tumultuous fire of his Babel? Vathek, one might
almost say, is the most perfect ruffian conceived in literature; he is, in fact, too perfect to be convincing.
It is this arrogance, a kind of diminishing glass, that
guides the ruffian steadfastly towards his purpose. He
sees everything around him small in comparison with his
own greatness. Nothing human can hurt him because
he is practically a god; and peculiarly, very little ever
does hurt him if the magic is powerful enough. He
stands in battle with shot falling about him, yet himself
remains unscathed. He does not die because he knows
he cannot die. So mighty is the will, the necessity to
live to achieve some purpose, that it seems that even
inanimate things must obey it. Wellington at Waterloo,
although never out of danger, came through untouched
while there was not one of his staff left without at least
some wound. Grenville, Cæsar, Rufus, Paul of Tarsus,
Marlborough, Calvin, Titus Oates, Charles XII, the names
of mighty ruffians, heroes and villains of flesh or spirit;
they walk boldly unarmoured or with drawn swords,
and cannot die. Only age, treachery or an accident can
get them, a stab in the back, a falling brick, a disrespectful germ, or a gangrened wound such as knocked King
Richard I into his bed: so certain of his own divinity
was Richard that in his impatience he tried to drag the
crossbow-shaft from his flesh and snapped off the barb.
The bolt did not kill him, it was his own defiant arrogance that did the deed. And William I, too—it needed
the pommel of a saddle to jab into his ponderous belly to
lay him low; dysentery struck down Edward I and
Henry V, ptomaine got Henry I, overeating and drinking tore King John's bowels to bleeding agony. Such

is the way of the ruffian. He will earn a V.C., tackling machine-gun nests single-handed, but a bus in Piccadilly will probably squash him into pulp. Napoleon rode through battle after battle, untouched, while thousands died because of his huge ambitions; a cancer ate him to corruption on St. Helena where he lay in irritable glory, bullied by that turnkey Sir Hudson Lowe, and peered at by tourists. Bucklered in arrogance, fiery with determination, nothing human can destroy the ruffian. Drake could sail into Cadiz and burn the armada and could sail out again. Sometimes in a mêlée, perhaps, the ruffian is killed—like Gustavus Adolphus slain by we know not whom—only an accidental hit may reach them, although even that is rare. When face to face with an enemy, the enemy inevitably dies. Again and again, in histories and romances, we find this miracle of ruffians' invulnerability repeated. Occasionally they fling themselves on to the spears of death, like the Emperor Julian taking off his armour in a moment of terrible despair, sometimes they are cunningly murdered like Christopher Marlowe, but usually they die in their beds, old and querulous like Sir John Hawkins and Sir Francis Drake on their last most pathetically tragic voyage together. Treachery is the great enemy they have always to watch, the man who steals on them from behind. Take Pizarro, conqueror of Peru. His death is one of the most sudden, yet one of the noblest in history, he died with a gesture, although he was a rogue, a murderer, a liar, and a traitor who betrayed the noble Balboa.

He had been warned of the conspiracy but in his arrogance he scoffed at what small men could do to him, and his contempt scared the plotters. Almost they crept away but one, more desperate than his comrades, flung open the door and cried that either they followed him

or he would shout their names loudly in the street. They
rushed out then, yelling the traditional catchcry of
political murderers—" Long live the king! death to the
tyrant! " And they caught Pizarro before he could buckle
on his steel—with only a cloak wrapped about his sword-
arm he held the rabble off, shouting, " Ha! traitors! so
you've come to kill me in my own house! " With but
that sword, his old body unprotected, the mighty ruffian
kept his enemies at bay by the sheer power of his will,
by the glare of the jewel through his eyes, as the great
Thomas Becket kept the assassins off in the gloom of
Canterbury. Then the leader of the conspiracy, one
Rada, growing impatient, cried, " Why are you so long
about it? Down with the traitor," and with admirable
presence of mind, picked up one of his comrades and
threw the poor wretch at Pizarro. Pizarro caught the
human missile on his sword-point, but before he could
draw out the weapon, an enemy slashed him across the
throat, and slowly he crumpled to his knees. Sword
after sword was plunged into him. " Jesu! " he moaned,
" Jesu! " and, sprawling, twisting on the floor, witeh
trembling fingers he painted a cross in his own blood.
As he bent to kiss it, one man hit him on the neck, and
he died.

But the Spaniards know well how to die, they have
proved that magnificently against all the might of
Italians, fascists, Moors and Germans in their struggle
for democracy. A magnificent nation, the proudest
in the world, as Borrow says, and he knew them
well. Their pride has given us probably the finest
gallery of ruffians on earth. The conquistadores, that
glorious rabble, conquered great nations, they were the
White Gods, fearless, heroic. Cortés indeed seems a god;
driven from the captured city of Mexico by the stupidity

of his friend Alvarado, he yet could find courage to return with a handful of dispirited, defeated men and
retake all that he had lost. What gave these Spaniards
their strength, what bred the arrogant power within them,
was their unbounded faith in God. They murdered for
the greater glory of God, destroying works of superlative
art to melt into gold and silver, tearing down temples
of sculptured dignity with which to build churches.
Cortés's letters are dotted with references to God: it was
God Who did this, and God Who did that, the soldiers
seeming but automatic pawns in the fingers of the deity.
When at Otumba, outnumbered by about twenty to one,
the Spaniards were struggling to retreat, Cortés himself
with one or two comrades charged the Mexican Eagle
waving above a palanquin; he slew the chiefs surround-
ing it and dragged the symbol to the dirt. Yet in his
humility before heaven, he calmly writes of the deed,
" It pleased God that one of the enemy should be killed
who must have been so important a chief that on his
death all fighting straightway ceased." In his mind,
himself and God seem confused, as is often the case
with the true ruffian: King Henry V was perhaps the
finest example of this, he was in his own eyes a kind of
crusader and therefore when the French naturally resisted
his utterly unjustified invasion he considered them as
rebels, almost as blasphemers. The conquistadores were
obsessed by their divine mission. Cortés, most tactful
and cunning of politicians, might intend to treat the
Mexican religion with tolerance, but at the first sight of
a bloodstained temple, he shouted furiously, " I'll take
no small joy in fighting for my God against your gods
that are no gods! " And unable in his horror to wait
even until his friends came to support him, he picked
up an iron bar and with his own hands battered the

stone idols. "On my word as a gentleman," writes one who watched, Andres de Tapia, "even now I seem to see him looming hugely above us as he leaped forward and balanced for a moment, holding the bar by its middle, before bringing it down with a crash on the topmost eye of the idol, tearing the whole gilded mask from its face." Because of this supreme faith in the greatness of their destiny, these Spaniards could not be defeated; the worried Montezuma was as if hypnotised by Cortés. Emperor of a great and powerful nation, of a nation of merciless and barbaric warriors, his will was yet surrendered utterly to the will of Cortés, for how can you withstand a man so sure of himself that he translates his motives into the motives of his God? And not only Cortés, but his men too were driven by the same high purpose, bathing their wounds in holy oil after battle, "and a soldier named Juan Catlan," writes Bernal Diaz, "blessed them for us and made charms, and truly we found that our Lord Jesus Christ was pleased to give us strength in addition to the many mercies he vouchsafed us every day, for the wounds healed rapidly." It was this same Bernal Diaz—cunning, brave and simple soldier—who summed up the purpose of the conquistadores. "Where are now my companions?" he asks, "they have fallen in battle or been devoured by the cannibal, or been thrown to fatten the wild beasts in their cages! they whose remains should rather have been gathered under monuments emblazoned with their achievements, which deserve to be commemorated in letters of gold; for they died in the service of God and of His Majesty, and to give light to those who sat in darkness—and also to acquire that wealth which most men covet." This would have been a thoroughly just summing up if the pious soldier had not forgotten to include the Indian girls, for there was almost a mutiny when the king's tax collectors began to collect the girls as well as the gold, stamping them in the faces with hot iron to proclaim them slaves, " so that many of us soldiers when we captured good-looking Indian women hid them away and did not take them to be branded, but gave out that they had escaped; or if we were favourites of Cortés we took them secretly by night to be branded, and they were valued at their worth, the royal fifth paid and they were marked with the iron."

God is more than popular with the ruffian. These Spaniards while squabbling because the king wished to enslave their women, striving to cheat his Majesty of the royal fifth, slaughtering Indians who preferred death to torture—" Seeing that by fire and sword," writes Alvarado from Guatemala, " I might bring these people to the service of His Majesty, I determined to burn the chiefs, and they themselves said at the time that they wished to be burnt "—destroying works of beauty, knew no such thing as a bad conscience save perhaps when dying. " Where does your highness suffer most? " they asked Alvarado on his death-bed, and he whispered, " In my soul." But it is notorious that the better the Christian, usually the more agonizing and tortured is his end because he fears to face his jealous God.

Practically all these heroic Spaniards were fired by lust of God. The first of them, Cristobal Colón, called Colombus—although no Spaniard, more probably a Genoese—was a fanatic about God. An outrageous liar, penniless, with no asset but his own stupendous faith in himself, he nevertheless convinced not only important grandees of Spain but even Queen Isabella herself, that shrewd, religious woman, that he would bring back untold gold if they would only give him a ship to sail westwards to India. And he was no seaman. When at last he got his ship and with the help of the great sailor, Pinzón, set out for his dream, he soon lost his nerve in violent storms and when his crew threatened mutiny, he suggested that the expedition return to Spain. Pinzón shouted, "Forward! forward! even though it takes a year to reach the land we seek! We'll reach it—or die!" and when Colombus muttered about his crew, Pinzón told him to hang half a dozen of them or fling them into the sea. For that one moment faded the lunatic inspiration that had fired Columbus ever since he first saw Toscanelli's chart proving that the world was round, for that one moment he saw with clear eyes the endless horizon and perhaps feared that the ship would tumble over the edge of the sea. It was a quickly passing phase, however, for soon again he strode the poop—drunk with the stars, as his crew put it—until on the night of Thursday, October 11, 1492, Juan Rodrigeuz Bermejo, a seaman, sitting in the crosstrees of Pinzón's ship, the *Pinta,* saw a dark blur sway on the skyline. The Queen had promised ten thousand maravedis to the first man to sight land, and swiftly Bermejo slithered to the deck and rushed to a cannon. He seized the linstock that was kept always burning for this moment, and shoved it into the touchhole. But Bermejo never got his ten thousand maravedis: the next day, Columbus blandly told him that he had seen the land hours before. The extraordinary part is that Columbus was probably not lying. So intense is the ruffian's absorption within himself that he deceives without intention, as women so easily do when taxed with infidelity. By some queer twist of the mind the accusation of a lie will justify a lie; the fact that you do not believe a woman is to her an insult and therefore deserves with a thorough good conscience to be repudiated. The ruffian is queerly feminine on this point. His acts are always automatically justified, he feels quite certain that he is incapable of being wrong. Therefore, according to Columbus's creed that he was the divinely appointed discoverer of India, it was to him incredible that God could have slipped in letting another get in first. God having marked him out, it was only fair to God that he claim the intended honour; it was not only the money he desired—although gold is always important to the ruffian—it was the prestige, the power to keep his own faith in himself inviolate. Besides, he hoped to discover Paradise, being certain that it was where India touched the equator. " It has the form of a mountain," he wrote, " or rather it lies upon a mountain-top that resembles the thin end of a pear, or a ball topped with the nipple of a female breast; and the hard earth swells up into this nipple. These are the sure signs of Paradise." How could the divinely appointed discoverer of such a land be cheated by a common seaman?

Always the Indies lured the ruffian, for here was gold to be had for the mere trouble of murdering a few Indians who were, on the whole, a harmless race that, as Columbus noted, "would make good servants, of very good characters, and I also think they could be turned into Christians without difficulty." But the men who followed the early conquistadores were not quite so obsessed by God, they were more frankly obsessed by gold, whether they sought to earn it by selling slaves in the fashion of Hawkins or by stealing it in Drake's manner. Hawkins certainly started one of the ruffian's favourite trades when he sailed in about 1562 with his black cargo. The men who in later years stole the negroes from Africa must have been on the whole incapable of a single decent feeling, which is true ruffianism. Nothing is sacred to the ruffian except himself and his personal property. To read the testimony on the slave trade given before parliament in 1789 and 1790 is a sure antidote to any sentiment one may have about the nobility of the human race. There was a certain Captain Hildebrand who, getting a negro drunk, bought his wife, and when the poor devil grew sober next day, refused to return her; no matter what profit the frenzied husband offered, Hildebrand would not listen, although he might have made a better bargain by selling her then than by hazarding the dangerous voyage to the Indies, for numerous slaves died of disease during every trip. They were packed below-decks exactly like sardines, some even manacled, and all stark naked as it was feared their clothes might carry plague. And there, cramped, unable to move, in the stink of their own unwashed bodies, they stayed the night, while every morning one or two corpses would be dragged out and thrown to the expectant sharks. In the already mentioned parliamentary testimony, one witness told of a certain captain whose habit was "on the receipt of a woman slave—especially a young one—to send for her to come to his cabin so that he might lie with her. Sometimes they would refuse to comply with his desires and would be severely beaten by him and sent below. There was one young girl that he retained for some time as his favourite and kept her in his cabin, until one day when she was playing with his son, she accidentally tore his shirt. When the captain learned of it, he whipped her unmercifully with the cat, and beat her up with his fists until she threw herself from him against the pumps and in doing so injured her head so severely that she died three days after." On reaching their destination and on being sold as "Prime Gold Coast Negroes," the negroes' fate was often even more abominable should they fall to some sadistic master, of whom there were many. I have in my possession a pamphlet of 1828, *The Memoirs of Charles Campbell at Present Prisoner in the Jail of Glasgow* who, during the early part of his narrative, gives some revolting descriptions of the treatment of slaves in the West Indies. Campbell himself was no ruffian, as the Glasgow jury decided when they sentenced him to jail for the term of his natural life instead of having him hanged. He suffered from spasms of insanity during one of which, in an abrupt moment of jealousy, he murdered his wife: a justifiable enough act, for she seems to have been a whorish creature and was slain while kissing another man at a dance. What he killed her with remains a mystery, " some sort of instrument," seems the nearest description we can get of the weapon, which " had a clear shining light." This, however, is more than irrelevant, about as irrelevant to my main thesis as the present digression on slavery, but the cruelty of the overseer whom Campbell met in Jamaica is worth recording. His name was Morgan and he " had punished an old female slave with thirty-nine lashes of the cart whip," after which she was ordered to hospital, but after a few days, her wounds not being properly dressed, she wandered off to seek a doctor. " The overseer, on hearing her complaint, burst into a fit of laughter. ' O,' says he to the doctor, ' leave her to me, I will soon cure her.' Previous to this, the doctor and he had examined her wounds, and found they were what is commonly called fly-blown. Morgan then called for some gunpowder, and making it into a paste, ordered a slave to rub it into her sores. This being done, he called for a match, and lighting it with a segar, set fire to the wetted powder." The woman died, but Morgan suffered nothing worse than the loss of his job. The attractive negresses were, of course, lucky, and many had quite a jolly time with amorous planters.

But women are rarely of importance to the true ruffian. The lover must be prepared to surrender himself physically and spiritually to the beloved, and such a sacrifice is beyond the ruffian's understanding. When passion does enter his life through some unguarded weakness, too often it proves his entire undoing: the conflict of two loves, of love for himself against love for the woman, betrays him, leaves him open to exposure as an ordinary human being. About the only time that women take on serious proportions to the ruffian is when by some amazing aberration they fail to succumb to his superlative fascination; thus we can see the breakdown of Casanova's character when in London he met the cold contemptuous Charpillon with her "sweet, open face " that " was the soul of candour, and seemed to promise all the delicacy of feeling and exquisite sensibility which are ever irresistible weapons for the fair sex." He soon learned otherwise. She enticed money from him and went to extraordinary means deliberately to torture him, to lure him on only to resist him with lascivious delight. London—or the Charpillon—spelled Casanova's end as a ruffian, in 1763. " Truly," he wrote, " it is from this time that I felt myself aged. But I was only thirty-eight."

A very dirty pirate, Charles Gibbs, in a boasting whining autobiography tells us freely that his one lapse into weakness was the result of love. " I fell in with a woman," he writes, " who I thought was all virtue, but she deceived me, and I am sorry to say that a heart that never felt abashed at scenes of carnage and blood, was made a child of for a time by her, and I gave way to

a dissipation to drown the torment." The arrogance of
that is almost horrible. It is as though God took one famili-
arly aside to confess to a little failing. A lying rogue was
this Gibbs. When his mob of cut-throats captured a Dutch
ship in which there was a pretty girl of seventeen or
eighteen, they calmly butchered her parents before her
eyes, then carried her off to their private fort to the west
of Cuba. Here, Gibbs smugly informs us, while pre-
tending innocence of the whole affair, " she received such
treatment, the bare recollection of which causes me to
shudder." After this interlude, tiring of the lady, the
pirates were at least gentlemen enough to poison instead
of slaughtering her. I confess that my chief interest in
Gibbs lies in a letter written by him to a wench in the
same jail before he was hanged for a particularly brutal
mutiny and murder. It is too long to quote fully, but a
few phrases will help to bring the ruffian more clearly
before us, such documents being the most valuable of
our data.

" It is with regret," he writes, " that I take my pen
in hand to address you with these few lines, under the
great embarrassment of my feelings placed within these
gloomy walls, my body bound with chains, and under
the awful sentence of death! It is enough to throw the
strongest mind into gloomy prospects; but I find that
Jesus Christ is sufficient to give consolation to the most
despairing soul. . . . But I look forward to that serene
calm when I shall sleep with kings and councillors of
the earth. There the wicked cease from troubling and
the weary are at rest! There the prisoners rest together—
they hear not the voice of the oppressor; and I trust that
there my breast will not be ruffled by the storm of sin—
for the thing which I greatly feared has come upon me.
I was not in safety, neither had I rest; yet trouble came

. . . I have had a fair prospect in the world, at last it budded, and brought forth the gallows. I am shortly to mount that scaffold, and to bid adieu to this world, and all that was ever dear to my breast. But I trust when my body is mounted on the gallows high, the heavens above will smile and pity me. I hope that you will reflect on your past life, and fly to Jesus who stands to receive you. Your character is lost, it is true. . . . I shall now close my letter with a few words which I hope you will receive as from a dying man; and I hope that every important truth of this letter may sink deep in your heart, and be a lesson to you through life.

> Rising griefs distress my soul,
> and tears on tears successive roll—
> for many an evil voice is near,
> to chide my woes and mock my fear;
> and silent memory weeps alone,
> o'er hours of peace and gladness known.
> I still remain your sincere friend,
> CHARLES GIBBS."

Really, this letter is superb, oily with good conscience, penned obviously for posthumous publication. He writes with regret to say that he is to be hanged and is embarrassed by his situation: these are the natural feelings of a gentleman of the period—the date is 1831—stolen from some cheap novelette. Even the strongest mind, he adds, might turn gloomy in such a predicament, throwing himself a delightful compliment, for after all he is smug enough to notice that he is not so very gloomy; besides, he has Jesus Christ to help him and talks with a certain familiarity about the Crucified, gently reassuring the incarcerated Miss that Jesus will help her too if she's good—although, it is true, her character is lost—just as one might promise to intercede on another's behalf with an influential friend. Altogether, this letter is of extreme

c

interest, a lie from beginning to end, but a lie that deceives nobody but the liar himself. The ruffian is an actor and needs an audience, which justifies the abolition of public hangings; there would a great many more murders if murderers could strut their last moments away before an admiring people. I remember some years ago in Sydney, a moustached bald-headed murderer cut the throats of his three small daughters, placed newspapers under the bed to stop the blood from spoiling the carpet, then lay beside the still-warm bodies and calmly slept through the night as if weary after great labour; on being arrested his simple explanation, which to him apparently justified any act, was that he wished to see his name in the papers, and a kindly press obliged with mighty headlines. It was the same impulse that dictated Gibbs's letter, that caused Gentleman Harry Simms to pen his incredible autobiography which I have used extensively elsewhere, and that made slim-fingered David Haggart, the Switcher, in Calton Hill Jail compose a long elegy and make a drawing of himself hanging in chains. Some of his verses are quite amusing in their way, revealing the inevitable smugness of the ruffian,

> " Now all you ramblers in mourning go,
> for the Prince of Ramblers is lying low;
> and all you maidens, that love the game,
> put on your mourning veils again."

Of more interest to us, however, is Haggart's own estimate of his abilities and qualities. A few days before his trial, on May 29, 1821, a phrenologist called to examine Haggart's bumps, and when he wrote down his discoveries he asked his subject to scribble a few notes on each deduction, and again the ruffian faithfully reveals himself. He was " not much given to quarrelling excepting when I was insulted," Haggart tells us, " but if it did come to a fight I seldom left the field till covered with wounds," and he adds—typical ruffian characteristic—that from childhood he loathed authority, continually disobeying his parents and being unable to " endure being ordered, even by my superiors. I need not describe my cleverness when I became a young man, as that is well known to the public already. There were few that ever knew my secrets . . . To work and be a slave of mankind I could never think of. Money was never my object to make myself rich; but the love of dress and company was my motive. I thought I was no worse than others who had been before me and would come after me. I knew that mankind were over-reaching each other, but thought they could never over-reach me in their formal style of proceeding. Cruel to my inferiors I never was; but I rejoiced to pull the lofty down, to make them on a fair level with their own brethren in the world. Whatever I did, I never looked back to my former crimes with regret. It was my greatest failing that I had a great inclination to the fair sex; not, however, of those called prostitutes; for I never could bear the thought of a whore, although I was the means of leading away and betraying the innocence of young women, and then leaving them to the freedom of their own will. I believe I was a master of that art more than, any other I followed."

We find here an intrusion of sex, but it is the sex of the ruffian, the superior contemptuous attitude of the peacock towards drab hens. No mention of love, you will notice, merely a sly grin at the thought of girls betrayed—or in truth, most likely of girls far more clever than David, for he seems to have been a rather gawky red-headed lout. Of his other failing, liquor, he gives but a casual mention in the phrenologist's list, saying that although "a little spirits were always a necessity," he could abstain if needs be and "when in drink I was very quiet, and would think twice before I spoke once." Altogether, David's summing up of himself is a fine estimate of the good ruffian: slow-tempered, being aloof from the petty quarrels of lesser men, and yet no coward; a hater of authority; a boaster of his cunning at his craft of picking pockets; proud of his secrecy, for a ruffian necessarily lives much within himself; needing money for ostentation, to show outwardly his own uniqueness, demanding adulation, ready even to pay for it; certain that he could out-trick all men; tolerantly kind to his "inferiors," yet jealous of those above him, resenting their power and longing always to drag them down; without conscience about theft or murder; gloating upon his power over women, but disdaining cheap flesh that others too could buy. The famous lawyer, Lord Cockburn, scribbled on the flyleaf of Haggart's *Life*: "This youngster was my client when he was tried and convicted. He was a great villain. This life is almost all lies, and its chief curiosity consists in the strange spirit of lying, the indulgence of which formed his chief pleasure to the very last."

Again we find this reference to the liar in the ruffian, and it is an essential part of his make-up. The ruffian lives before a mirror, he acts continually, but his only real audience is himself. To that applauding sycophant, his soul, he postures in a thousand chivalrous situations, sees himself always as one harried by fate, a noble, generous, courageous and misunderstood gentleman, one far above his fellows, one with enormous cleverness that few are intelligent enough to appreciate. His world is often fantasy. He is an idealist, spurred on by the fury of his own arrogance, reckless of whom or what he destroys in his climb upwards. Whether the goal be some great benefit for humankind or merely the parasitical determination to exist without work, it dominates every thought and action of his life. And this desire to escape work is rather curious, for a ruffian will go to the most tremendous pains to earn a few pounds dishonestly rather than make hundreds by respectable means.

In the previously mentioned Gibbs's trial there is another example that we can well add to our chart of ruffianism. Arraigned with Gibbs was a rogue called Thomas J. Wansley who gave resentful evidence before being sentenced to a merited death. When asked that stupid question whether he had anything to say why sentence should not be passed, he revealed the mind of one labouring under a heavy grievance: two thoughts were uppermost—the informers were not to be hanged and they had cheated him of the proceeds of the murders. " I will say a few words," he growled, " but it is perhaps of no use. . . . Notwithstanding my participating, they have sworn falsely for the purpose of taking my life; they had the biggest part of the money, and have sworn falsely for the purpose of taking my life; they would not even inform the court how I gave information of money being on board; they had the biggest part of the money, and have sworn falsely. I have said enough. I will say no more." To the very last the cheat rankled in his mind; he was to be hanged, but he could not forget that these informers had grabbed the largest share of the proceeds; he might even have forgiven them peaching on him, but to rob him of his hard-murdered-for gains was unforgivable. Nevertheless, Wansley was not a true ruffian, for he later said, " I have committed murder, and I know I must die for it." Far too honest a statement for that automatic liar, the ruffian, to make; Gibbs was more in the tradition when with expostulations to his God he swore his innocence of murder, although he remarked casually that " the captain was struck, and, I suppose, killed, and I lent a hand to throw him overboard." When a ruffian confesses his crimes it is not in the abrupt manner of Wansley, it is to boast of his supreme villainy or to exhort humanity to beware his example, it is to act a part of some description. But far more often he walks calmly to the gallows, declaring his innocence to the very end. There are many reasons for this. Most ruffians have such faith in their god that each feels certain that like Macheath he will be rescued even when the rope begins to tighten around his neck; also, they are so obsessed by a sense of man's ingratitude, by the peculiar malice of their own fate which has hounded them to an unmerited death, that they often actually believe in their own innocence. They have committed murder, certainly, but that is of trifling importance, of no importance whatever compared to their own existence. In their own eyes they are innocent because what they have done is justified; they cannot be blamed for a slit throat any more than God can be blamed for throwing a thunderbolt or blasting a tree with lightning. Such accidents are God's prerogative. Therefore, firmly on the gallows stands the ruffian, swearing faithfully to his innocence and thoroughly believing in it, knowing that God will understand what man is far too blind to recognise.

This brings us back to the God-complex of the ruffian, the obvious expression of which is not far to seek to-day when contemplating the totalitarian states. But in many ruffians it is not quite so simply revealed. A dictator naturally exposes it fully, becoming a second Jehovah in his determination to force the people to obey his fanatical supremacy. The conquistadores were more humble, they considered themselves merely the instruments of God, while other ruffians have translated their godhead into a sense of superiority. Yet there are ruffians of even simpler make not bothered by such subtleties, they boldly set out to attain gold, and with unconquerable arrogance get what they seek. The buccaneers, for example: fiends like Lolonnais who could chew a man's heart raw and warmly bleeding to terrify his other prisoners. They followed the conquistadores without any rant of religion. Most of them—and they were mainly British—went to the opposite extreme, jeering at Roman pomp, such as the pirate-breaker, Woodes Rogers's men joining in a religious procession and solemnly playing *Hey, boys, up go we!* to the singing of the monks. The Sieur Ravenau de Lussan, one of the most gallant of buccaneers and a good Catholic, records with horror how he and the other Frenchmen would rescue paintings and statues of saints in captured towns on the Main " that they might not be exposed to the rage and burning of the English, who were not much pleased with these sorts of precautions; they being men that took more satisfaction and pleasure to see one church burnt, than all the houses of America put together." Sir Henry Morgan, greatest of all buccaneers, certainly had no regard for the religious when he burned the cities of the Main. And he had small cause to like them, for they were most adroit at concealing what he looked upon as his rightful earnings after so much bloody labour. A cunning general, a brave man, yet one so unscrupulous that he would cheat his own followers of their dividends, Morgan, like a good ruffian ended with a knighthood and the Lieutenant Governorship of Jamaica, and only because of his uncontrollable arrogance was he deprived of his honours a very short while before he suddenly died.

II

Sir Henry Morgan

AFTER so splendid a life—to come to this! He, Harry Morgan of Panama, who with his own hand had squeezed the life from many a Spaniard's throat! This hand, sir, thin though it may be now—God drown this devil in his chest!—was feared in every Spanish port as Harry Morgan's hand that brought death with it. It's Morgan's hand, Harry Morgan's hand, he who took Panama and raged his way over sea and earth until the consumption of that cursed England nipped him in the lungs. This hand has touched King Charlie's hand, this shoulder felt his sword-tap. Sir Harry Morgan to be kicked out of the Assembly by a pack of cowardly merchants and farmers! Not that he was hard on farmers. By God, his father had been a farmer way back in Llanrhymni in Monmouthshire. He could still remember, when maudlin drunk, the slow green hills of Monmouthshire, the valleys soft as plush, moaning of cows in a mist, and his mother calling to him from a lighted doorway that dinner was ready.

It would certainly have been more than peculiar if he had failed to remember such details, for he had fled the security of home when he was twenty-seven years of age. From Bristol, amid the rich smells of American goods—bales like murdered sheep where the cotton burst its covering, monkey-chattering of black servants, shrieking bundles of colour called macaws—he had sailed for Jamaica.

When he spoke of this, the colour glowed to copper on Sir Henry's nose and glistened through his eyeballs.

Rage would make him thump the table or batter his pewter against the wall. For the lie still went, nothing could throttle it, not the two hundred pounds libel from the publisher, Crook, nor his grovelling apology, not all the threats and denials that rumbled menacingly in Sir Henry's own chest, could kill that lie. To call him a slave! To say that he had worked like a negro or some spunkless white bond-slave in the fields for three years to earn the miserable pence of his freedom! It was that rat Esquemeling who'd started it with his stinking book. And who was Esquemeling? A Dutchy! By God, all he could remember of the rogue was a thin insect-face, lean nose and finicky fingers pecking at a soldier's wound. He was rotten any way. And to write such a book! how could people think of such wicked lies? A slave! By God, his uncle, Colonel Edward, was Lieutenant-Governor when he arrived. He came of a right good family. The Morgans of Glamorganshire. Everybody knows them. Everybody should know them. They've got nothing to hide, only things to be proud of, by God.

Then he would grow pugnacious, rant, and dare his boozy comrades to call him slave until at last they pushed him back into his chair and shouted for more rum-punch with which to cool his choler—for kill-devil, as they called it. It was gulped down, and they waited while Morgan crouched back, twisted, squirming in his fight against the bubbling coughs that brimmed his mouth with blood.

Byndloss was usually with him, a planter, one-time ship's surgeon, but now settled down ashore some twenty miles from Port Royal; Bob Byndloss, Morgan's brother, for he'd married Morgan's wife's sister, Anne Petronella. Elletson, too, was often there, the lawyer with his quick wit whom the Assembly had also kicked out, mainly because of that quick wit. He was the cunning behind the political faction of which Sir Henry constituted the noise and strength. But now even he was out, although they'd tried hard to get him re-elected in a distant part of the island where there were but few electors, and they ignorant, although not quite so ignorant as had been hoped. Fat Craddock was sometimes with the group—suspended with Ellotson—the parson Longwood, and before he was ejected violently from the colony, Sir Henry's brother-in-law, Charles, his wife's brother, Sir Henry's cousin. They called themselves the Loyal Club, and drank and cursed that bloody Lynch, the Governor.

Those were great days in Jamaica. Days of thrilled expectancy when the verbose fire of politics replaced the thundering of guns against Spanish walls. There was also money in it, if worked well. And they had worked it well until that lousy Lynch . . . But at the very mention of the name, the veins would swell like leeches in Sir Harry's throat, the massive fist would tighten, the arm jerk up, and another pewter would bounce against the wall followed, like a ball with the crash of powder, with a burst of violent coughing. This Lynch had started everything. He was a Puritan, a scurvy-throated dissenter apeing the politician. To make such a poltroon Governor of Jamaica was more than stupid, it was suicidal: of Jamaica, a land of whispering stab-in-the-back factions, of earth richened with blood of slaves, of a few isolated towns hemmed in by forest peopled with those murderous runaway blacks, the Maroons. They needed a soldier at their head, someone not scared to hang a dozen—ten dozen—rogues, if necessary. Suppose he were a Spanish privateer now as once he'd been a British, he'd soon scare Lynch out of that pompous wig of his. He'd start on the coast and burn every plantation in sight. Yet perhaps that'd be bad policy, for it'd bring the English out against Spain and leave room for the Frenchies to hop in. But he'd do something. He'd turn French, by God!

Yes, those undoubtedly were great days in Jamaica. Nobody knew with which faction to side. Perhaps the next Governor which that complacently blind old grandmother England would send out might be another Lord Carlisle. And if you were an anti-Morganite then—well, God help you, that's all. God didn't help most of them when England in its old fatuous way sent out Albemarle, Monk's son, to follow Lynch. Then there were ructions. Morgan and Byndloss were up again and the Assembly was fought to bring them back to power. Elletson got the job of Chief Justice, and because snub-nosed Johnny Bourden refused to be one of the Assistant Judges under him he was suspended from the Council. And serve him right.

Up and down. This party in. This party out. Next month they would be back again. What could the planters do? Whom could they bribe? What was the use of giving a bribe when before you'd scarcely left the building there was another strange palm itching for gold? There was nothing they could do except put their trust in God, but as old England seemed to have taken the business out of God's hands, this was rather unsatisfactory. It must be confessed that public opinion was against Sir Harry. Lynch had a good plank in the Assiento, the trade in negroes with Spain, and Sir Harry's efforts to upset this plank with bellowings about the French scare seemed a mere mewing in comparison. Assiento meant gold coming into the colony; the French scare meant it going out in building forts and raising militia, and as raising militia meant every white man carrying a musket and being hit in the face by Charlie Morgan—Sir Henry's cousin and brother-in-law—the prospect was scarcely enticing. The very whisper of Charlie's name in the garrison threatened mutiny. Before he'd been flung out of the colony, when he was still Governor of Charles's Fort, no soldier had been safe. He'd almost killed innumerable sergeants by beating them and kicking them after he'd beaten them—even when they weren't in pay. There was a strong rumour that he'd murdered some woman's husband, but this was difficult to substantiate as husbands were continually disappearing from Jamaica, usually after a ship sailed for England. Officers avoided the Castle, sergeants hid, half the army deserted. It was Charlie's habit not to appear on duty until midday when he'd drunk himself into a choleric state of indignation at having to leave the puncheon for duty. In this state he was capable of practically anything diabolic; chasing sergeants—who seemed his legitimate prey—and the common trash of privates round and round the barrack square, although it was usually decided that it was safer to take the first hit and be done with it, for running in this tropic heat only worked up his choler—if that were possible. Martin, the Receiver General, had a gruesome tale to tell of the day that Charlie asked him for more money. Charlie got no money, but Martin ended up in hospital.

The night before he left, they'd had a great time of it, boozing and cursing Lynch. Then into the streets, out of the lighted tavern, down the rutted byways of Port Royal for a last game of sergeant-hunting, with Parson Longworth in his dusty coat dancing on ahead. Sir Harry still chuckled creakingly at the memory of

SIR HENRY MORGAN

that night. Charlie was such a lad with his bull-voice
and his tremendous laugh that shook the very flames in
the lamps along the streets. Such times! Now that
Albemarle was in they'd come again. He must get
Charlie back. Charlie was the boy.

If only he could cough this devil out of his lungs!
He had a feeling that some day if he coughed hard and
long enough he'd see that devil come raging out, half-
drowned in blood and phlegm. Then he'd be right
again. He'd be the old Harry Morgan of Panama.

Panama. Hot days of marching through sand and
flies. Endless stretches of jungle with snakes like living
branches coiling out flat heads, bright-eyed, to see the
buccaneers march past. It was good to look back on
the adventure. It had been hell at the time. He would
sometimes almost give up hope when he gazed at the
hungry faces of his men as they sprawled, gasping, in
puddles of shade. Those lean bodies, could they march
another step? Those wellnigh fleshless arms, mere skeins
of muscle, could they lift a gun? Could the skeleton-
fingers pull a trigger? Surely not. Morgan was tired
himself, as hungry as they, but he did not think of
himself. It was his men he watched, their faces painted
by a gaudy sun, bright with the reflection of sharp
tropical green, their cheeks caved in as if the flesh had
been scooped from between the bones, eyes almost lost
in hollows, their hair gluey with sweat. And about
them—life. Life of the jungle that is felt rather than
seen or heard in the murmur of leaves brushing together,
the faint humming of hidden insects, abrupt screaming
of birds, and somewhere, distantly, the hollow cries of
animals. These men alone were dead. They were corpses
that cut their way along, fighting aside the dew-flies and
mosquitoes, too tired sometimes even for that, but

passively letting them suck what little blood moved in their veins, too tired even to pluck the ticks and leeches from their naked legs, or to scrape away the lice. Some fell and lay in the shade, listening as if to something infinitely remote and unimportant, to the thudding of their comrades staggering on ahead through the shrubs and lianas, slipping against trees; listened until the noise grew fainter, became merged with the unceasing threnody of jungle-life. They waited calmly then for the snakes to loosen their fat bodies from the trees, for the floppy sound of big cats padding near, or for the myriad ants to gnaw the skin from their living bones; waited until sudden night fell like solid ebony scarred with the glowworm eyes of patient animals. Their comrades floundered, panting, forward, boiling their boots and accoutrements for food. Once they found a pack of hides left by the Dons, and these they wolfed as if they were a banquet of guinea-fowl or partridge. They had thought the trip would be so easy in the canoes left far behind now on the shallow Rio Chagres. They had not bargained on starvation and on these endless days of tramping through metallic vegetation, feet ripped by thorns and blistered by hot earth. But there was no turning back. It must be Panama or death. And most probably, Panama itself was death.

Morgan marched at their head. There was no phthisis then in his lungs, his great chest breathed enormously; his eyes, though bloodshot, could see further than any man's. There wasn't much to see. Sometimes there wasn't even any sky to see, for the trees bunched together, were tied in a hundred knots of writhing creeper. The buccaneers were walled in with leaves and trunks of trees as if caged forever. Yet they struggled on, tongues swollen, minds incapable even of resentment.

That was until they found the barn of maize. Such a little food, gulped almost raw, but it brought life with it. Morgan had watched, lying in the shade while a negro cooked his share, and had wondered to see life return so swiftly, to see those expressionless eyes widen and gleam as if the maize were light that flamed within them, to see gestures return, hear human voices, even a faint heroic laughter. Their tattered banners were lifted up, unfurled; they smiled at this symbol of victory, fingering the cloth with love and pride. Knives were pulled from belts, and the sap of trees wiped carefully from the blades until the steel blinded you when the sun tinselled its edge; guns were oiled, cocked and fired, a little precious powder wasted trying to shoot a bird glimpsed through foliage; teeth gleamed behind beards, hands were clasped; mockery and jests gave strength. It was far better after that. The taste of food brought desire for more, and soon the desire was satisfied. A herd of bulls was found pasturing, and limbs that were almost nerveless became suddenly alive, voices were lifted in triumph, and throwing down their guns, those half-naked skeletons darted into the flock. Their old train-ing on Hispaniola found its use now. . . .

When telling this story, Morgan would pause at that moment, his sharp dirty teeth would show through his dark lips as if he caressed the memory on his palate, savouring it as one does the aftertaste of some sweet food. He would pause, and slowly, methodically drink his rum, smiling; for that at last was the end of the journey. After, it was fighting. And such fighting! Have you ever stood alone against a murderous gang and realised that there was nothing for it but to fight or die? That was how those buccaneers fought. The Spaniards blun-dered. They charged instead of waiting for the assault. It was their blunder, and Morgan instantly grabbed the chance. He left the road that he knew was fortified and crept through the woods to the savannahs before the city. The fools sent bulls against them! As if buccaneers feared bulls! They had earned their name from catching the wild beasts on Hispaniola and boucaning, smoking, the meat to sell to ships. Now they just shouted at the clumsy herd, and the frightened bulls scampered back and gored their own masters. The fight took exactly two hours. That little band of buccaneers, less than a thousand strong, starved, exhausted, their banners dripping in ribbons from the poles, utterly outnumbered, with rusty guns and chipped swords, fought two hours against an army. Lean devils that nothing, it seemed, could kill; swords and pikes were thrust amongst them, but to the stupefied Spaniards it was as if no man fell before the steel; there was blood about them, but it was Spanish blood; they slipped on blood and entrails, tumbled over bodies, feet kicking on dying and dead flesh . . . but it was always Spanish blood, Spanish flesh. Santiago! these men were devils! Banners fell, were wrenched from hands, almost wrenching the hands from wrists, but they were always Spanish banners; those old weather-rotted banners, the cords rusted, cloth in strips like pennants, never fell: they were ever on high, ever in the press of battle, waving triumphant over Morgan's curls. The Spaniards fell back, yelling *Santiago!* tripped over their comrades, struggled together, shouting to give courage to each other, to recapture the spirit of Cortés and Pizarro, before this handful of men maddened by rage and hunger out of all humanity. Two hours of bloody battle before the Dons gave way and scuttled back behind the walls of Panama. But the buccaneers did not follow. They were tired. Now that fight was over, weariness seemed to hit them a violent physical blow, and they fell where they were, resting exhausted limbs, still quivering with the fever of battle, upon the dead and wounded.

Morgan realised that if he let them rest too long, the almost sensuous relief would grow too delicious to break, so he suddenly gave the order to march, lifted on high again those bloodied strips of cloth nailed to poles, roused the men with drum, bugle and fife, blew out the shattering blast of trumpets, and slowly those scarecrows rose like corpses at the last trump, red with the blood of Dons. They wiped their swords, cocked guns and pistols, and with gritted teeth, made the advance on that walled city of Panama. Panama, with your spires rattling great bells in clanging fear, with your pretty gardens and huge-eyed señoritas, gayest city of the New World, Pearl of the Pacific . . . Panama, the devil was at your gate! Girls hugged themselves in terror, for had they not been told of these cannibal-toothed buccaneers? Panama, ring your bells of silly noise, throw furniture into the streets for barricades, prepare the guns. For they were coming, the dreaded demons of the Indies led by that devil Morgan; they were at your gate, merely a handful flung at your gate; all their tattered banners could have been folded a dozen times in one of your huge flags; they were starved, they were tired, they had marched for days without food; why did you fear, Panama? Why did you ring your great, foolish bells? Why did you crowd the women into churches and bar the doors? What did you have to dread in these few exhausted men?

It was the very madness of their adventure, it was utter desperation, that turned these buccaneers to devils. They smashed in the gates with what appeared inhuman strength, they seemed to throw stone walls aside like

D

paper bricks. Barricades were swept over in one rush, and little bands of Spaniards were forced against the walls to gurgle through their slitted throats. Within three hours the buccaneers had cleared the city, the great flags, the blood and gold of Spain, were hauled down from the battlements and scraggy British banners took their places. Three hours of close fighting, three hours during which guns were practically useless even had there been time to reload, when only knives, axes and swords were used. Morgan was in the thick of it. His sword was slimy with blood, his great chest breathed in sharp jerks of exultant rage, teeth dazzled like foam through blackened lips. His kinsman, Bledry of the rear-guard, was next to him now. Two Morgans! They alone were enough to clear a city chockablock with Spaniards! The feeling that they were two of a family against the world beat the hot blood inside their skulls. Now and then they grinned at each other in a momentary pause, and nodded their heads as if just recognising each other after years of parting. Two Morgans against Panama!

But even after the last Spanish throat was slit, as they sat on the chairs and beds that had been flung for barri-cades across the streets, Morgan's task was not over. His trumpets called the men together in the main plaza, and when they had all dragged their tired way to him, he raised himself upon a table to speak a few words. He spoke of their courage and of his love for them. Then he paused. They waited for his words in the sunlight, within blood-splashed walls, under a sky cloudless and grey with heat. Then they stiffened as they heard, mouths shut, some groaned as if in pain. The wine was poisoned. They mustn't touch a drop.

Morgan was extremely proud of that ruse. He was over-fond of telling it, and whenever the conversation turned towards wine—which was often enough—his friends would show great cunning in trying to switch him from the inevitable yarn. They failed because it was inevitable. And after all it wasn't such a clever trick. It was rather obvious. Obvious and nasty. But nobody ever dared tell him that.

He couldn't risk the buccaneers drinking themselves into somnolence so that they could be slaughtered should the Dons rally, therefore he said that the wine was poisoned, and with those few words robbed his men of half the joy of battle. They had only women left with which to console themselves. And many of those were probably poisoned too: it was difficult to tell the golfa from the high-born señorita when they were packed, an indiscriminate muddle of femininity, inside a dark cathedral; and many a man boasted later in Port Royal stews that he'd grappled a princess when actually he had tasted the result of hundreds of gallants' labours of love.

Then some youngster in the tavern would pipe up: "Women, Sir Harry! Wish I'd been with you! I'd have shown myself off prime, I would! How many did you get, Sir Harry?" And Morgan would look glumly at him from over his pot, for wasn't he a respectable man, by God! None. He'd never touch the bitches. He'd important things to think about. Even that lying stinkard Esquemeling hadn't dared accuse him of that. There was, of course, the Panama Lady . . . Esquemeling made up a long yarn about her, damn him, but it wasn't true; and even Esquemeling had had to admit that Morgan never got her. The truth of that? Mayhap he'd tell. Yes, he'd given her a rough time. That was true. Yes. Yes. But it was only for treasure. He never looked on that as treasure which she tucked so complacently under her gown. He meant real treasure . . . money, jewels. Besides, she was a spy. He proved that. Even Esquemeling wrote that he'd called her a spy. If Esquemeling hadn't written it, he should have any how, curse his liver. But when Esquemeling said he offered her jewels for a night, Esquemeling lied like the dog he was. Give her pearls! Who ever knew Sir Harry Morgan give a woman pearls? A bloody insult, by God! Yes, he stripped her. That was true. Um. But he thought she might have a plan written on her skin. He'd heard of that. He'd done more too, but he'd only done it thinking she might be hiding something. Women had more chances, being squeakingly modest, of hiding things than men. But he'd made certain of all her chances. You wouldn't believe the things you'd some-times find after a little patient search. But she'd nothing but ordinary things hidden. So he shoved her into a dark cellar amongst rats, scorpions and black-beetles, but even then she wouldn't confess, although she said that she hated nasty crawly things, especially buccaneers. He starved some of the mutton off her, not only with kicks but with bread and water. Then just to show what an honourable man he was, he let her go without a stain on body or character, even without ransom, when he learned that some knavish priests had robbed her. He was a just man, although only a Colonel in those days. You knew that when you got to know him. Justice even before gain. Justice every time.

On and on he gabbled when coughing let him. Of how he tricked his men at Chagres after the return from Panama, gave them ten pounds apiece and slipped off in the night with a few cronies to Port Royal. He chuckled at that for clever sport; and if ever any audacious drunk dared mumble about it being mean,

Sir Harry would bounce in his seat with rage and would shout and throw his mug on the floor—if the mug were empty. He gave them ten pounds each, God blast your rotten soul! and he needn't have given them that. It was the better man who wins, and he—by Christ, he'd prove it to you, swords or pistols, fists or boots—always was and always would be the better man. Even when they dragged him off as a pirate to England with Governor Modyford, he was the better man. They hadn't dared do a thing to him, although he'd been privateering a year after peace was declared with Spain at Ryswick. King Charles—God bless His Sweetness—had admired the cut of his red velvet coat, and Lady Castlemaine had swept her great eyes over his stocky form and had casually enquired if Portuguese ladies lived in Panama, and whether they were as sweet-marrowed as rumour said they were—with a sidelong glance at His Majesty. Morgan blushed and bit his moustache to hear such words, even from a woman, for they smacked of treason.

Yet for all the glory and fame it brought him, he could not forgive fate for that imprisonment. Although it brought a knighthood and the Lieutenant-Governorship of Jamaica, it also brought the devil into his chest. That devil lurking in the fogs and smells of London had suddenly pinched his lungs, and there was blood in Morgan's mouth, his own rich blood adulterated with phlegm. And it had cost money. He'd paid heavily for every moment of the two years wasted in that smutty land of fog and rain. That was not to speak of bribery too. Yes, it was in England that the devil put his pincers on Morgan's lungs. Sir Harry would curse mightily whenever the country was mentioned, and he would shout in violent rage, " God damn the place and every-

body in it except the King—God bless him—and Lord
Carlisle! for here am I coughing like a crocodile because
of its dirty water. But I'll drown the bastard yet!'" No.
Even rum couldn't drown that devil. Harry Morgan was
always flung back, beaten, in his chair, always flung
back, spluttering, damning, with crying eyes and a scarlet face. The devil was the one person who could
punch old Harry Morgan back. Old! He wasn't old!
He was in his prime, the age when men do their boldest
deeds. What liar would call fifty-three old? Here,
tear the handkerchief off this scarred scalp and blind
yourself in finding a grey hair! He dared them, glaring
truculently around the table with bloodshot eyes, lower-
lip out with its dab of beard, the scarlet bandana clutched
in his monstrous fist.

He always wore a handkerchief about his head—as
was the Jamaican custom—except on Sundays and Court-
days when he donned a wig and appeared very gay in
silk coat and waistcoat trimmed with silver. But his
usual costume—drinking costume, he called it jovially,
which came to the same thing—was the scarlet handkerchief knotted on his skull, thread stockings, linen
breeches and waistcoat, sometimes a coat—although that
was rare—and, of course, the hat. He wore the hat with
either wig or handkerchief underneath, and even when
inside Church or Court he carried it in his hand or rested
it on his knee. It gave him confidence, replaced the
pistol. When he drove to see Lynch or the Council at the
island capital, Spanish Town—or at St. Jago de la Vega,
as Lynch insisted on calling it in his mincing voice—
through the cemetery-like palisades that choked the
square, he carried his hat and coughed into it when he
couldn't find his handkerchief. There were bloodstains
inside it: his own blood.

He loathed calling on Lynch, for he felt that that
giant house was his by right. The lofty portico shadow-
ing the drowsy sentry, the dozen Ionic pillars and the
marble steps . . . to be Lynch's! the Governor's! He'd
never felt like that in the good old days of Carlisle when
he'd trotted along for a yarn about the privateersmen and
for a discreet paring of booty. He always felt respectful
towards Carlisle, the true Lord who had fought with his
own dainty hand in the Civil War—fought against the
King certainly: but that was over now and forgotten. No
one had any right to drag up a man's past. But even
Carlisle, Lord though he was and haughty in his ways,
could not stifle the voice of envious calumny. Sam Long,
the stinkard, had peached when he saw the buccaneer
Pindre yarning to them at Carlisle's house—that was at
Port Royal—and had said openly that if Sir Harry and
Carlisle had at several times shut their doors they
might have catched most of the chief pirates and privateers in their own houses. To speak like that of a Lord!
Sir Harry could pass the insult, being a mere knight—
but a Lord! No wonder he sometimes longed to go privateering again, with Sam Long in the forecastle, and
not only with Sam Long, but with Johnny Bathurst too,
the rat! To beard Carlisle in his own chamber about that
likely young scoundrel Sawkins, and to tell him to his
Lordly Face that the Assembly was against him and his
ways! Yes, even in the happiest of times there was too
often a weevil in the biscuit. And what happy times
they'd had under Lord Carlisle! When Sam Nash sued
Sir Harry at common law for a few years old debt, Carlisle had stood up like the gallant gentleman he was and
told Nash to go and drown himself before he dared
bring such an action against his old friend, Sir Henry
Morgan. Officious Wilson when he found a hundred

bags of cocoa in the *Primrose* and ran to tell Carlisle, only lost his job for his haste. That was the way to govern a Colony. None of this snooping Lynch way of going about it.

But ill health—they called it—sent Carlisle back to England, and for a short while Morgan reigned, until Lynch got the job again, and kept it. And since Lynch got the job, the country had gone to hell. To hell. Then there was this Mingham business. It was all rather complicated, this Mingham business. It happened some years back when Mingham sailed into Port Royal in his *Francis*, trying to smuggle liquor. Morgan later insisted that he was smuggling two butts of brandy and twenty casks of black cherry-brandy, but Mingham always said that he'd had no more than two casks of brandy. No matter what he had, Morgan grabbed the lot, then confiscated the *Francis*, shoved Mingham into jail, and fined him £2,000 damages for defamation of character, for Mingham had a sailor's tongue and soon let Port Royal know what he thought of Sir Harry's behaviour. Defamation, by God! He couldn't get away with that! Sir Harry bolted him into the common jail that stank so abominably that most of the prisoners died within a few days, shoved him in amongst murderers, debtors and negroes, and told him that if he wanted a better room he'd have to pay for it. Mingham paid. Sixteen pounds. The sale of the *Francis* brought in £600, divided between Martin as Chief Justice and Sir Harry as prosecutor. There the whole affair would have ended decently if Mingham hadn't been a revengeful man and gone back foaming to England. Nobody could call Sir Harry revengeful. Hadn't he written sweetly to Mingham, agreeing to forget both insult and fine if he'd only apologise and buy Lady Morgan the coach and horses her heart bled to possess? But being of a vengeful nature, a sailor and no gentleman, Mingham had replied with an oath and refused the offer. Sir Harry promptly forgot all about it. Imagine his surprise then, his surprise, his indignation, and his horror, when he heard that Mingham was blackguarding him in England, and that the King —yea, even His Sweetness!—in Council had ordered him to refund the money and had told Mingham that he could take whatever legal remedies he liked! Was ever such a verdict heard before, such an outrage? But being a meek man—as he always insisted with swords and oaths—and of no vengeful nature, Morgan quietly returned the money. But Mingham was a vengeful man. He came back to Port Royal, pert and cockety; he swaggered about the town and grinned in Sir Harry's very face. Sir Harry did nothing, he bowed and passed on with empurpling cheeks. Yet Mingham's very sauciness brought his own downfall. Even pope-holy Lynch had to take action at last.

It happened this way. Mingham's cooper lost his job and went to see if Churchill of the R.N. wanted a man aboard his frigate the *Falcon*, and Churchill seeing him to be a brisk likely fellow, offered to sign him on if Mingham agreed. Mingham answered Churchill's polite note asking him to step aboard for a yarn, with an insolent one, telling him to look for him if he wanted him, and adding the name of the tavern where he was always to be found. On receipt of this, Churchill sent for the cooper's chest, but Mingham's mate sent him to the devil with hard words. Churchill was no man to take this gently, and he pressed five of Mingham's aboard the *Falcon*. In a howling fury, Mingham's son and a Captain Wild's mate started cursing up and down the port, swearing mighty lies of revenge and murder, which being bellowed in front of the *Falcon's* coxswain, he hurried to the frigate and reported the slander to Churchill. " By God," said Churchill, heaving his chest, sweat on his forehead, " I'll not stand for this! " and he sent for Mingham's mate, caught him, stripped him Adam-naked and hoisted him as high as the gunbill for all the port to see and snigger at, leaving him there for a full hour, in agonized preparation for a ducking. Meantime, Wild's rowdy mate, Bill Flood, was daffy enough to come aboard the *Falcon*, whereupon they grabbed him too and ducked him three times from the yardarm, firing a gun off over his head after each ducking. And because he cursed and blasphemed more than was right in a King's ship, they flogged that treason out of him with twenty lashes on the bare back.

This stirred Mingham from his boasting, and he and his mate and the interfering Captain Wild dashed off to see Lynch. But Lynch, always a poltroon, waved them aside with vagaries, saying that Churchill was beyond his jurisdiction, being homeward bound, but that the Admiralty might give them justice if they cared to write. So they scribbled affidavits with the Judge Admiral who pigeonholed them and dozed back into his siesta. That, however, didn't satisfy the noisy villains, they woke him up and demanded a warrant against Churchill. The Judge Admiral opened one eye and told them to see Lynch about that. They left him to his sleep and bolted back to Lynch who was mighty furious at being disturbed a second time and told them to take themselves to the devil, for they deserved all they got and worse for having been rude to a King's Captain, and the best thing that they could do was to go to Churchill, apologise like gentlemen—if they could—and then they might get their men back, if they were as lucky as they were troublesome.

Such wisdom drove them wild as monkeys and they tumbled into the street, arguing and shouting for all Port Royal to see and hear. Then of a sudden, up they made their minds, dashed to the jetty, and after much quarrelling and cursing, forced Mingham's mate to row over to the *Falcon*.

Churchill met him on deck and, grinning, asked if it were a ducking he wanted.

"No, by God," said Mingham's mate, "for Bill Flood's dying of one now."

Churchill blanched a bit at that, but he kept his head and asked, "If it's no ducking, what is it you want?"

"My men," said Mingham's mate, "Lynch commands you to give them up."

"And tell Lynch," said Churchill, "that he may be Governor ashore but I'm Governor aboard this ship."

So off darted the mate, back to the jetty, to tell the two captains what had happened, which made their eyes bulge with rage, and they all rushed off to wake Lynch up again with the treasonable speeches of Churchill of the King's Navy. Lynch kicked them out, and they ran to the Judge Admiral, woke him, and gave depositions swearing to Churchill's words, and drew up a petition to the Assembly craving justice et cetera. The Assembly would have nothing to do with it and very discreetly passed it on to Lynch as Admiral, and Lynch almost raved himself out of his gout when it came back to him, and he gave Churchill the wink to clear out, which Churchill couldn't do, owing to the tide. So Lynch, not knowing what better to do with it, passed the petition on to the Council, who blinked at it and passed it on to the courts martial of England.

Mingham, not caring for West Indian justice, started trouble on the Point where trouble always started at

Port Royal, that being the gathering-place of seamen, loafers, whores, and merchants. Not satisfied with this, when he met his old cooper one day, Mingham grabbed him and carried him before Judge White to get a warrant against him as a refractory seaman, and poor old White, not knowing the truth, issued the warrant. Mingham with a big stick was protecting the constable who had hold of the cooper when a crowd from the *Falcon* chanced along and started a glorious brawl. They rescued the cooper, but most of the rescuers, with a representative collection of onlookers, found themselves in jail for rioting.

All this time, Flood was jerking about in bed, bright with fever and close to death, when all of a sudden he gives a howl, and he does die. Wild, who'd been fidgetting around for the last four days since the ducking, waiting and praying for this, dashed off immediately to Lynch and almost wept in front of him. "Why," asked the fuddled Lynch, dratting the whole affair, "do you say now that your mate was murdered?" But Wild wasn't being trapped that way. He insisted that Churchill be stopped from sailing until after the inquest, and Sir Harry, who was there at the time, wiping a little of the warmth from his copper nose with his big bandana, was sent by Lynch to do what he thought right and legal, as he was then commander of the Fort and Regiment. The inquest came on soon enough, and it took the jury seven hellish hours under Sir Harry's bully to decide that Flood died a natural death from fever. Immediately the inquest was over, the treacherous jury rubbed their skulls together and four of them sped to Lynch to tell him of Sir Harry's insulting behaviour, of how the evidence was transposed and depositions not fairly taken, of how fifteen jurors were sworn and three sent away after-

wards. Lynch tried to brush the matter aside, telling
them that it was nothing to do with him, that as they'd
brought in their verdict they'd have to stick by it, which
didn't please the jurors, their consciences being curiously
troubled. But Lynch would say nothing definite, remark-
ing only that Sir Henry and Captain Musgrave were in
court merely to prompt the coroner, Mr. Wingfield, on
points of law, he being rather weak on the subject; but,
added Lynch, if they wanted to inform against Sir Henry
they could do so at the next Grand Court, or if they preferred the Council to hear it, he offered to bring all
parties together that very day. But the jury didn't dare
risk such open antagonism to Sir Harry, and they left
him, grumbling. Then Lynch made one of his usual
faux pas and, instead of Tennent, let Churchill set the
Port Watch, which made the Point blind mad with rage,
none of the captains taking the slightest notice of his
orders.

A wild dissenter called Coward who was also snooping about the Point, looking for some excuse to make a
row, seized this chance and started giving speeches and
callings on God to blow Churchill's ship out of the water,
which God very wisely didn't trouble His head in doing.
Here was Sir Harry's chance, and he and his Loyal Club,
taking Churchill's part, kicked Coward up and down
the streets, and whispered long tales of Lynch's subtle
villainy into the distracted Churchill's large ear. Churchill rushed to Lynch, who was sick at the time, and sat
down in a chair beside the bed, his face drawn and white.
"God help me," he moaned, "but Penhallow and his
gang are after murdering me. They were to do it on the
Day of Thanksgiving for the King's Recovery but I
stayed aboard the frigate. They'd a gang waiting and
were going for me when one of them sung a song they'd

decided on." Lynch groaned from his bed in pain that
Penhallow was one of Jamaica's most respected merchants and no murderer, but Churchill wouldn't listen
to him, and he afterwards repeated the whole plot before Council, affirming it with many oaths and adding
that they were after murdering him because of his name
and because his family depended on the Duke. " Oh,"
he cried, beating his temples, " the Point is worse than
Algiers! Sir Henry told me everything, and he's a man
of honour." Sir Harry, who was sitting gravely in the
Council, nodded at this and glanced at his fellow-
councillors who looked solemn and dubious—all except
Byndloss and others of the Club. Catching Lynch's eye,
Sir Harry heaved himself out of his chair, walked importantly up to the Governor and, taking his arm, led
him into the parlour. There he pinned him against the
wall and said slowly, with a tremendous frown, " That's
truth what Churchill says; and what's more, there's a
plot against my brother-in-law, Captain Morgan, for fear
you'll make him major after Bach goes." The wretched
Lynch squirmed from the bearish grip and fled back to
the Council Hall, and Sir Harry buttonholed Sir Francis
Watson in another corner and told him the same lies.
Sir Francis, not being able to keep a secret, instantly repeated everything in Council, which rather embarrassed
Sir Harry who tried vaguely to deny having said it, being
unable to show any proofs of the accusations.

To show that there actually was a murderous plot
afoot, the Loyal Club gathered one night, drank itself
into a suitable state of fury, and chased Penhallow, who
was sober, and almost killed him. Sir Harry, outraged at
this, sent Penhallow to jail for breaking the peace and
bound him and his friends over for the sessions. In rage
and extravagant words, he swore roundly up and down

the Point that the people were a pack of Duke-killing rogues who had meant to murder Churchill, and that the villains hadn't killed Captain Charles Morgan the other night because Churchill wasn't with him, just as the rats in England hadn't murdered the King because the Duke of York wasn't there.

That started all the uproar in Jamaica, and because that chitty-faced Lynch wrote whining letters home to England, Morgan was suspended from the Council, Charlie was forced to leave the colony, Elletson wandered back to desultory law, and Byndloss was charged with disrespectful carriage before the Assembly, with striking Thomas Martin, and with using provoking language when discussing the riot with Colonel Molesworth, and was suspended from the Council and ordered to leave the town within an hour's time. Once the dogs saw Morgan down they all darted out to snap at him. That queasy bitch Mrs. Wellin crept forward to say that she'd heard Sir Harry use the awful words, "God damn the Assembly," and the Assembly was duly shocked. He was charged with Disorder, Passions and Miscarriage at Port Royal. Lynch sneaked forth to denounce him as a Turbulent, Uneasy and Insolent Fellow, he called his Loyal Club a Little Drunken Silly Club whose debaucheries went on night and day, and added that Byndloss was easily the Worst Man he Ever Knew.

No wonder then that Sir Harry cursed at the mere mention of Lynch's name, or dented his pewter furiously on the table; no wonder the slaves on his plantation shuddered when they saw him reel out after siesta, his face swollen with rum and Madeira. But when, coughing and damning, he had blasted Lynch to a midget of unimportance, his eyes would sometimes blur with the memory of Panama. He'd gulp his rum and the listeners would lean forward, avid to hear again the story of that splendid fight. They never lost, at every repetition, the thrill of that moment when Morgan gazed down from the hills on to Panama with its spires, its sluggish flags, and the ships putting out to sea. They stood tense, those few hundred ruffian-scarecrows; they leaned forward with caught breath, hands tightening on guns and sword-grips, gazing upon Panama, doomed Panama, with towers soon to be burnt to dust, its gardens to be trampled, its women bloodied with rape, its gold and its jewels all gone; doomed to follow the way of Porto Bello, of Puerto Principe and Maracaibo, for Morgan with his band of half-naked vultures was staring with hollow eyes upon that garden by the seas, the loveliest city of the Americas, was staring upon Panama.

Those were the days. Sir Harry would laugh and show his teeth and take a long pull at his pipe, puffing out storms of smoke and coughs as if the tobacco exploded inside him. Good days, indeed! And to show that God meant him to live and become the saviour of Jamaica, there was that miracle which took place aboard the *Oxford* before the Carthagena attack that never came off. Morgan gave a dinner in his flagship which instantly blew up and killed every man on the opposite side of the table. Only his side of the table remained unhurt except for a little scorching. If that, by God, wasn't a miracle, just show him one!

Lynch . . . How could he revenge himself on Lynch? If only his brother-in-law Charlie was here, he'd think of a way. That was a good jest Charlie played when Lynch's scrawny wife died: he immediately ordered a suit of white and was the only man in the Colony not dressed in black. Yes, Charlie was the man. But Charlie didn't come back. He'd disappeared in a storm of sergeant-hunting, of hiccuping shouts and volcanoes of laughter; had disappeared, no one knew where.

Although Charlie didn't return, that patient old grand-mother England sent out Albemarle in his stead. Sir Harry liked Albemarle, and Albemarle liked Sir Harry and he wrote urgently to the King desiring Sir Harry's reinstatement; and the King, not bothering a great deal about what was happening on that funny little island of his, granted the request. But he granted it too late.

On August the twenty-fifth, sixteen hundred and eighty-eight, Sir Harry Morgan, at the age of fifty-three, managed to cough that devil out of his lungs with a titanic effort. But the devil had a firm grip on Morgan's soul, so that Morgan coughed them both out together. He died with a puzzled look on his face, and was buried with all pomp and honour. Captain Lawrence Wright of H.M.S. *Assistance* scrawled in his log that night: "This day about eleven hours noone Sir Henry Morgan died, and on the 26th day was brought over from Passage-fort to the King's House at Port Royall, from thence to the Church, and after a sermon was carried to the Palli-sadoes and there buried. All the forts fired an equal number of guns, wee fired two and twenty and after wee and the *Drake* had fired, all the merchantmen fired."

That was indeed an honour, for twenty-two guns was one above the regulation salute for celebrating Guy Fawkes' Day, St. George's Day, or any other public holiday, which meant that Sir Harry's death was another extra public holiday. God rest his soul. He died as he had lived, fighting; and fighting a braver battle than ever he had fought before—against that treacherous devil in his lungs.

E

III

They Dwell in High Places

A BRAVE and simple ruffian, Henry Morgan must stand as one of the finest of our examples: a splendid soldier, a man who never seemed to suffer from physical weaknesses when in action, one dominated entirely by two ambitions—honour and gold. It is true that in his later days he indulged in graft wherever possible, but there is no evidence that he did so to harm the good of Jamaica; he invested in privateers and did a little smuggling, that was all. His conflict with Lynch was inevitable, the conflict of the impatient man-of-action with the cautious politician. Morgan could never understand the petty morality that condemned any-one for looking after himself. In that, he was the true ruffian, as also in his treatment of Mingham and the vindictiveness with which he took Churchill's side over a petty dispute that developed practically into a riot. This Mingham business, by the way, throws up one treasure for our delight, a note from Morgan to the Lords of Trade and Plantations. " I left school," he tells us, " too young to be a great proficient in either that or other laws, and have been much more used to the pike than the book; and as for the profit there is no porter in this town but can get more money in the time than I got by this trial. But I was truly put in to maintain the honour of the court for His Majesty's service. Without this the act of navigation cannot be enforced for it is hard to find unbiased juries in the plantations for such cases. For in-stance, a ship from Ireland came here with several casks of Irish soap, and was seized by His Majesty's receiver.

The case was tried in the Court of Common Pleas, and the jury found for the defendant with costs. One witness swore that soap was vittles and that one might live upon it for a month, which the jury readily believed and found the aforesaid verdict. I beg your Lordships to believe that if I have erred at all in this matter it has been of judgment only. May God love me no longer than I love justice." A charming and almost convincing letter, showing that Sir Henry could be a tactician in politics as well as in the field, while the concluding sentence is a masterstroke; the only thing wrong with it is that it failed to work.

Against Morgan, only one really bad act can be proved, his sneaking off from Chagres with most of the booty, leaving his comrades with but a few pounds each. Otherwise we do not find him cruel or miserly except in the way of business—ruffian's business, getting money. His treatment of the Panama Lady was rather brutal, but by no means so brutal as it could have been; nor does Esquemeling—who obviously disliked Morgan, perhaps he was one of these left at Chagres—say that Morgan raped the lady, as most buccaneers would certainly have done. The unfortunate women of the Main lived in continual dread of the coming of the buccaneers, although, according to gallant de Lussan, on meeting the enemy they swiftly changed their opinion " and have given us frequent instances of so violent a passion as proceeded sometimes even to a degree of folly," as de Lussan himself learned from personal experience, one captured lady imploring him to marry her and turn Spaniard. These senoritas would probably have dismissed the thought of rape as one of their lesser fears, for they had been taught that buccaneers had the bodies of monkeys and that they loved to crunch up girlish bones and guzzle girlish flesh.

The unnamed Lady in Morgan's hands suffered nothing worse than a brief starvation and imprisonment—small charge indeed to lay against a man who held her life and body entirely in his power. On the question of Morgan's cruelty towards prisoners in general we must remain undecided. Esquemeling makes definite charges, but we can no more accept them than we can the publisher's apology that " it is not credible that he would suffer either any such Cruelties or Debaucheries to be done. Neither (as I am told) was there any such Cruelty committed, as the Wrecking of a Fool or the Torturing of a Rich Portugezen, or the causing a Negro to kill several Spanish prisoners thereby to create an hatred of the Spaniards against him, and with intent to prevent his returning unto them. Or, the hanging up any Person by the Testicles. No more Truth was there in that Story, that many Religious were pistolled; for, no such Persons were killed, unless they were found in Arms."

Anyhow, it is entirely irrelevant ; I don't for one moment doubt that Morgan would have squeezed out a prisoner's eyeballs with a knotted cord had that been necessary to discover buried treasure. Nor was his cruelty unusual for the age. We have but to remember Cromwell in Ireland and James II's treatment of Monmouth's friends to consider Morgan quite angelic. Being a ruffian, however, of the highest order, life in others would never appear to him to be of paramount importance. He was, nevertheless, sane enough to realise that cruelty is no great asset to an adventurer. On the whole, the buccaneers were comparatively humane men. It was the riff-raff that followed, the scavenging pirates, who degraded the profession. Save for one or two like Howel Davis and Bartholomew Roberts, the pirates are of little interest. Petty thieves and assassins, most of them; or just reck-

less adventurers like Stede Bonnett, or play-actors like
Blackbeard who fixed lighted slow-matches under his
whiskers which "he was accustomed to twist" with
"Ribbon, in small Tails, and turned them about his
Ears." A noisy boaster, he once forced his crew to stay
with him under the hatches amidst stinking sulphur so
that they might start training for a future of hell-fire.
These are not the antics of true ruffians, they are the
deeds of small boys prancing in the shadows of men.

Morgan was the perfect ruffian, a leader with an indomitable will who never shifted aside from his brave
purpose no matter how insurmountable appeared the
hardships ahead. Without this core of faith, no man
can ever hope to become a ruffian. It is idle to speculate
about Morgan's cruelties, because they are of absolutely
no importance whatever in our estimate of him.
Brutality is by no means a necessary part of the ruffian's
make-up, otherwise our select Hall would be crowded
with a slinking collection of men too cowardly to face
their enemies, who have used the dirty trick of poison
or a knife in the back ; and of superstitious thieves
of medieval times who slit the bellies of pregnant
women so that they might get the little fingers of unborn
babes to melt to candles, the light of which would bind
all sleepers into sleep until the flames puffed out; and
of crazy beasts like Dr. Cream who, under the incognito
of Dr. Fred, wandered about presenting capsules to
prostitutes, then leaving them to die in the agonies of
strychnine poisoning. No, we will not allow such peculiar
pariahs into the Hall, nor the sadists whose orgasm
is reached in the gasps and twitches of the soul being
ripped or strangled from beloved flesh; nor Madame de
Brinvilliers, in the guise of a sister of mercy, experiment-
ing with her poisons on the inmates of hospitals; nor the

Marquis de Sade whom Napoleon locked into a mental asylum at the demand of his family and whose descriptions of intricate sexual cruelties thoroughly warranted the act. These creatures, animals of purposeless violence, have naught to do with the true ruffian, who is very often a noble figure, if occasionally a brute and a murderer; he can kill or he can lead mankind towards some blessed dream, rouse nations at his call or send them to their destruction. He can be found counting his booty in the gutter or seated in a palace with a crown upon his head—or even mightier than a crown, with a tiara.

Without any disrespect to the religion, we can count numerous ruffians in the Vatican, although I am afraid we can count far more of the lower breed unworthy of our Hall. Until the renascence brought enemies to watch Rome with critical eyes and had books printed, easily circulated, to spread truth, few sincere churchmen ever reached the papal throne; those against whom no misdeeds are recorded were usually of so great an age that, if they were capable of any passion at all, it was a passion for gold to be left to their children—politely called nephews and nieces. This is understandable enough, for the papacy had little to do with religion: it was a far greater temporal than a spiritual power, the seat of an emperor more than of a pope, a law court where money was amassed as Peter's pence. The Pope therefore had to be a politician rather than a churchman, and a clean moral record can scarcely be expected in politics. The tradition of the old Roman Emperors—of whom practically all, save those who were lunatics, were ruffians—was kept living by the Popes; and the Vatican was even sold on occasions, as the Praetorian Guard used to sell the ancient Empire.

But, apart from the great and famous Borgias, two men stand out as splendid ruffians in the Vatican: Popes Gregory VII and Innocent III. These men were sincere, yet in their determination to create a more powerful church they brought terrible destruction on humanity. That did not worry them so long as their ambitions were attained. True, these ambitions were what one would call unselfish; in other words, neither man desired only personal profit. That, however, is beside the point. The ruffian associates himself so completely with his phantasy that the two become almost indivisible. A man, for example, like St. Francis of Assisi we accept under the benediction of G. K. Chesterton as an unselfish, humble nature-worshipper, but it is surely an accepted fact that humility is often the mask of intense arrogance? Dickens has given us the supreme examples of this in Uriah Heep and Seth Pecksniff, and hypocrisy remember is by no means always conscious. St. Francis was tormented by his own arrogance. "You see," he said when young, "one day I shall be worshipped by the whole world." He first had his fling as a soldier, but a few days in armour quickly taught him that he would not find worship on that path, so he turned to the only other outlet possible in the Middle Ages, to the Church. His ideal was magnificent, but it was swiftly twisted out of shape; his dream of a penniless, propertyless army soon became quite a wealthy confederation—which, of course, does not detract from the dream itself. It is this point I have been striving to make: that the ruffian, spurred on by his huge egoism, can often achieve the noblest and most beautiful ambitions.

Both Gregory VII and Innocent III were sincere men; so was St. Francis, and St. Dominic who indirectly created the inquisition, and the friar Savonarola who destroyed manuscripts of incalculable value and paintings by men like Leonardo and Botticelli. That they were sincere neither heightens nor detracts from their achievement, for the ruffian is necessarily sincere; only by sincerity can you attain all that you desire; only in that fashion can you impress your will upon the people who are not so easily deceived by deliberate lies.

Hildebrand, later Gregory VII, came of peasant breed and as he grew up, trained at Clugny, he was aghast to see the decay of his church. There were three rival Popes brawling to steal the tiara: Benedict IX, a rascally small boy, a kind of baby Heliogabalus, who had been elected by the Tusculum Counts and then promptly ejected by the Romans who placed John of Sabina in his place as Silvester III. The Counts then threw down Silvester and put Benedict back, which pleased nobody but the Counts themselves, for the boy was apparently in love with his cousin and wanted to marry her. He was a vile creature, whose sins stank so badly that the chroniclers can but hint at most of them and it must be presumed that he was a pederast, which was common enough in the Church of those days—Hildebrand's friend, Peter Damiani, wrote a book on the subject called *The Book of Gomorrah*—his vices, writes one of his successors, Victor II, " were so horrible that I shudder to tell them." Anyhow, he was determined to marry, and he sold the throne to his uncle, John Gratian, for the year's Peter's Pence from England. Gratian was a sincere, pious man, and assumed the name of Victor III. The Tusculums refused to accept him, they dragged Benedict away from his bridal bed and pushed him back into the Vatican, with the result that there were three Popes in Rome: Silvester, Victor and Benedict. Then Henry III, Emperor of the Holy Roman Empire, entered to settle the dispute: he dismissed all three and elected a fourth, Clement II, a genuinely good choice, for there was nothing evil in Clement. But he died before he had scarcely settled into the throne, and Benedict grabbed it again, and held it for nine months until Damascus II got it, clung to it, and died within twenty-three days. This was the scandal that so appalled young Hildebrand and bred in him the great ambition to cleanse the temple of Peter, and his first thought was to sever that loose union, the Holy Roman Church from the Holy Roman Empire. He could not tolerate the thought that a temporal lord like Henry should elect the Vicar of Christ, and he swore to break that power when, on the death of Damascus, the Emperor offered the throne to Bruno, Bishop of Toul in Lorraine. Hildebrand was with Bruno when the offer came and he stood up bravely, calling the bishop a usurper if he dared accept. To him, the Church had supreme power and must not be interfered with; what did it matter if the Isidorian Decretals on which it based its claims were proved forgeries? That did not affect the basic truth that Christ had spoken to Peter in a vision and had said, according to Matthew, " Thou art Peter, and upon this rock I will build my church." Before the young man's vehemence, Bruno gave way, he refused the offer unless he were also chosen by the Ecclesiastical Courts. For two months he and Hildebrand walked barefoot, dressed as pilgrims, all the way to Rome; and in Rome Bruno was, of course, immediately elected as Leo IX. The first blow had been struck, weakening the power of the Emperor, and now Hildebrand turned his energies towards abuses in the Church itself. Fornication, incest, adultery, infanticide, sodomy, bestiality, every sin lived in the monasteries; clergy kept women in their kitchens and beds as " spiritual sisters," and even sometimes married them, so that their bastards inherited lands that should rightfully have descended to the Church; there was simony too on all sides, that gravest of ecclesiastical crimes: church offices were sold to the highest bidder, the ordination could be bought by the dirtiest rascal unmurdered, women-pilgrims were raped inside St. Peter's itself when they slept there at night. Hildebrand struck with all his force, but the blow was weakened by the cautious arm of Leo. A fierce squabble arose with the Normans of Aversa over the Duchy of Benevento which claimed papal protection; the Normans retorted by killing two priests the Pope sent as mediators; then the Pope hurried over with an army that was immediately slaughtered and himself taken prisoner. A mighty ransom was demanded for him, and paid; and Leo came back to Rome in a litter, exhausted, dying. He demanded to be carried to his tomb in St. Peter's, and there sorrowfully they laid him in the choir. The aged Pope dragged himself, weeping, on hands and knees, over the tiles until he reached the coffin and clutched it in his skinny hands. " Of all my honours, dignities," he cried, " only this little dwelling remains to me!" And after praying and wailing, rolling and lying on the floor, tearing at his garments and hitting fiercely at his own face, the miserable Pope died.

Again Hildebrand demanded free ecclesiastical election, and he was helped in the fight by quick-witted Peter Damiani; they chose the Emperor's right-hand man, Gebhard, as that would cripple Henry; but Gebhard quickly died to be followed by Stephen IX, who died almost as quickly as his predecessor. Hildebrand was not in Rome at the time, and the Tusculum Counts seized the opportunity to elect a Benedict X. There were riots in Rome, St. Peter's was looted by the hardy Counts, but when Hildebrand elected a Nicholas II, Benedict fled for his life. He fled to the Fortress of Galeria and was besieged by Hildebrand with an army of mercenary Normans. It took quite a time to cajole the terrified Benedict into the open, and he only unbarred the gates on a strict pledge of safety; but he was no sooner out than he bounded for sanctuary in the Church of St. Maria Maggiore, where Hildebrand allowed him to chew the cud of terror for the allotted thirty days, after which he dragged him to the Lateran before the new Pope Nicholas. They put the sacred robes upon him, then instantly wrenched them off again, and they made him sign a long list of his sins, some of which he had probably never even thought of. Satisfied with these humiliations, they banished him to the monastery of St. Agnes where he remained, never seeing the world again, for another lonely twenty years before he died.

Hildebrand's next move was the most dangerous he could attempt. He called a council and passed a decree insisting that church property in any part of the world was papal property and that Popes in future be elected only by an ecclesiastical council without interference from the laity. This law would have brought about half Europe under Roman control, depriving kings like Henry of Germany of huge sums. Then in the midst of the argument, Nicholas died, and Hildebrand had hurriedly to elect another complaisant Pope. He chose one of his closest friends as Alexander II. Things were not going quite so easily as he had hoped, for within the Church itself was being formed a strong anti-Hildebrand party, made up chiefly of men fond of luxuries and careless living who feared the holy fanaticism of this peasant monk. They could do nothing, however, for Hildebrand hired Norman soldiers to guard the streets when Alexander was carried through by a horde of monks with gourds rattling on their left sides and with filthy sacks on their right; the mob, foiled of an uproar, could but shout insults at the new Vicar of Christ, yelling, " Away, lepers and bagmen!"

Henry of Germany saw that the blow was aimed at him, and quietly, without ostentation, he gave the tiara to another Pope as Honorius II. Then it was bloody war until, in the midst of the conflict, Henry died, his young son was kidnapped and the regency taken from the Empress, who immediately became extremely pious and pro-Hildebrand. For twelve years, under the strong thumb of Hildebrand, Alexander kept the throne, then on his death, Hildebrand attained at last the miraculous fulfilment of his dreams—the Vicarship of Christ. He arranged his election in rather a crude manner, for even while Alexander's obsequies were being chanted, his friends started to shout, " Hildebrand is Pope! Hildebrand is Pope!" Hildebrand leaped on to an ambon, a reading-desk, and strove to still the clamour, but now all were taking up the cry, the dead Pope forgotten in homage to the new.

When we examine the extraordinary life of this poor Tuscan youth who attained the greatest power that the eleventh century world could offer, it is impossible not to respect the unflickering determination that kept him to the one path. " My Holy Satan," Peter Damiani is said to have called him, and it is an eminently suitable nickname; he had the strength and the stubborn pride of Milton's Lucifer, that consuming fury to achieve all his ambitions. Nothing could deter him, not love nor pity nor fear; we can see his type duplicated to-day, for the dictator system, the effort to hold the skeins of multiple powers in the hands of one, is little different from the early Roman tenets. But the very fire of such men, their refusal to compromise, eventually brings their own doom upon them. Hildebrand, now Pope Gregory VII, returned to the early battle against church corruption. Clergy, in those times, married quite openly, and the people saw no shame in it: we find even cases like that of Rainbaldo, Bishop of Fiesole, who, apart from innumerable mistresses, possessed a legal wife whose children formed a very powerful family, yet this Rainbaldo was honestly credited with the power to work miracles. To a fanatic like Hildebrand such a state of affairs was abominable, and his path had already been made plain to him by the gibing violent works of Peter Damiani. Hildebrand was right. Marriage must eventually split the power of the Church, creating a temporal aristocracy that might turn against the spiritual in a squabble over property; he was right morally, but we cannot condemn him for being unable to see the future laid bare to us in the pages of Lea's *History of Sacerdotal Celibacy*. In 1074, Hildebrand held his first synod and decreed that no man be admitted to orders without a vow of celibacy, reviving the law of Nicholas II, which forbade the faithful to attend the ministrations of sexually unclean priests. Such things had been decreed often before, but as with most unpopular legislation, like the United States' attempt at prohibition, they were universally ignored. Gregory was determined to see that this time they would not be ignored, and the riot he created was appalling and would have daunted any lesser man. Further riots were produced by his efforts to annex most of the wealth of Europe by making Roman all church lands. " If the Pope is supreme in spiritual things," he said, " he had all the greater right to inter-

vene in the smaller matters which are called temporal,"
and to prove these rights he was reduced to forging
credential after credential. Furiously he set to work,
hundreds of clergy were flogged from the temple of
Christ; in St. Peter's alone, over sixty priests had hoarded
up wives in the presbytery, and now they found themselves homeless, and starving clerks crowded clamouring
in the streets of Rome. There were even plots to kill
Gregory: soldiers strode into St. Maria Maggiore on
Christmas Eve, 1075, while the Pope celebrated the
beautiful Midnight Mass, and one struck at Gregory's
head with his sword, but slipped and fell, while a second
gashed him on the breast; then they ripped off his robes
and dragged him by the hair to a tower in the Parione.
All night he lay imprisoned while civil war bloodied the
Holy City until in the morning his rescuers carried him
back in triumph to St. Maria's where quietly he finished
the interrupted Mass. But these quarrels over celibacy
were of little account compared to Gregory's battle with
the Holy Roman Empire, now ruled by young King
Henry IV of Germany. Henry commanded Gregory to
surrender the papacy, and at the Council of Worms
forced the prelates to condemn him of innumerable sins,
of licentiousness, cruelty, witchcraft, and even simony,
all of which—save perhaps cruelty—were entirely false.
Gregory retorted by excommunicating Henry and laying
his country under an interdict: that is, forbidding any
church rites whatever to be celebrated, so that couples
could not marry nor could the dead be buried, nor could
the newly born be baptised or souls washed clean by
confession and the eucharist. Before this threat of inevitable hell, the people deserted their king, and Henry had
to give way. There is a legend which is most plausible
that while Gregory stayed within the Castle of Canosa

with his friend Mathilde, the boy knelt for three days
outside in the snow, imploring forgiveness. The story
comes from Lambert of Hersfeld's chronicle, upon which
many doubts have been cast, yet it seems possible and
certainly fits in with Gregory's character, although it is
difficult to imagine the proud Henry kneeling so humbly
before an enemy. True or not, the King was soon again
in arms, leading his troops on Rome. Gregory thereupon
deposed him and gave his kingdom to Rudolph of
Swabia; after which he suggested that both kings come
to him for arbitration. But Henry was not going to
accept his own crown at the hands of one whom he
considered a rebel, nor would Rudolph surrender his
new power, and for a time it seemed that the Pope would
be forced to crown Henry and excommunicate his own
claimant. To Gregory, the blindness of these kings was
appalling, for as the Viceroy of Christ, his alone was
the power to decide all earthly claims. Yet he was reduced
to feeble resources such as papal bulls with which to
fight his enemies. Henry and Rudolph battled together
while in the Vatican Gregory excommunicated some
Normans for grabbing church territory, and carried on
his quarrel with that grim ruffian William the Bastard,
now King of England, who merely smiled at Lanfranc's
arguments, while the archbishop strove to wheedle and
bully him into surrendering his lands to Rome. Henry
and Rudolph were growing bored by their war, attempts
that came to nothing were started for arbitration, then
Henry was defeated, and both kings rushed to Gregory
with their claims. At last, Gregory had humbled his
enemy, and he deposed him at once, proclaiming
Rudolph the King of Germany by right of Rome.
Henry retorted by deposing Gregory and started gathering another army. This time his troops were really

formidable, and Gregory was forced to implore Norman aid, after raising the excommunication ban. Then Henry killed Rudolph near Leipzig and marched on Rome, but in typical medieval fashion, instead of staking everything on one definite battle, he preferred to wander over the countryside enjoying the sweets of plunder—women and gold, wines and foods. Gregory now elected Hermann of Luxembourg in Rudolph's place, which turned Henry from his pleasure-tour of Tuscany into making a determined assault on Rome which he besieged for the good round Biblical sum of forty days and forty nights. Within the city, there was rebellion, the people tiring of this endless war, and Gregory's own bishops refused to let him take the church treasure with which to buy arms. Then Guiscard, the merry luxurious Norman, came to the Pope's rescue with chests of gold and swiftly purchased Roman loyalty, and also he came with six thousand men-at-arms and thirty thousand foot, many of them being Saracens. Henry promptly fled. In triumph, through streets pillaged by Norman and Moslem, Hildebrand was carried, and the Romans renewed their oath to him as Gregory VII. They quickly repented of it. The Normans and Saracens had not joined in the war for holy reasons, they came for loot, and they took it—flesh of Roman ladies, gold from Roman homes—until the Romans in fury drove them out and their Pope with them.

In exile, in Salerno, Gregory died. When the frightened bishops asked him to absolve his enemies from the ban of excommunication, he violently refused; all, he said, he would absolve save Henry and Guibert, the anti-Pope. "I put my trust only in this," he said upon his death-bed, "I have always loved righteousness and detested iniquity." But there were others who were not blinded by his magnificent dreams. Peter Damiani is reported to have once remarked to him, "Thy will has ever been for me a command, yet lawful. Would that I had served God and St. Peter as faithfully as I have striven to do your bidding." But that was a point of view which Gregory was incapable of appreciating; for to him, as with most ruffians, there is nothing relative in life: there is only right and wrong, his right and your wrong. He had served God and St. Peter, but so had many others in their different fashions. Except for an unsubstantiated accusation of immorality with Mathilde, there is no hint of any carnal weakness in him, and the Mathilde tale is undoubtedly a lie. Men of this type somehow store their sexual vitality as a kind of electric charge for the spirit, they sublimate it as the artist sublimates his into the act of creation. Undoubtedly it is from this impulse, the strongest in man, being the urge of life, that spiritual strength is derived. The magus when preparing himself for a dangerous experiment, fasts and avoids all carnality; not only sex but every sensual delight being weakening to the spirit. One cannot expect to do one's finest work after a heavy meal, and drink is probably the most pernicious of all to the will. These are the outlets of the soul, and the greater one's vitality, more often the more reckless is one's escape; therefore it is so common amongst artists to find them periodically flinging themselves into extreme debaucheries. During these times, of course, they are not creative; it is only by repressing the desires that art is created. Stekel, if I remember rightly, remarks that it is not unusual for artists to become temporarily impotent, the physical image being obscured by the mental, one powerful image obliterating another for a time. Except in the unimportant cases of casual lechery, one's desire

F

for a woman is not physical. The expression may and should be so, but surely not the impulse itself? The desire of a man for a woman or a woman for a man is as inexplicable as the ecstasy one derives from looking at certain paintings, hearing certain music, reading certain books. It may seem to hit you in the belly, but the reaction is more truly spiritual, and did not D. H. Lawrence insist that the psyche's centre was the solar plexus? I believe that it is even lower than that, secreted in the sexual glands themselves, wherever they may be. Therefore, the magi are right in testing the neophyte with alluring women before creating him an adept. Man must be able to metamorphose his sex into action, mental or physical, before he can achieve true greatness.

Again and again in the ruffian we find the unimportance of love. The conception of a cavalier roistering, drinking, leching, is the portrait not of a gallant soldier but of a will-less scamp who would be killed within a moment if faced by a real ruffian. He is the cheap fantasy that Dumas easily avoided: D'Artagnan has no interest in anything except the sword, his love for Constance is as romantically vague as the love of an errant-knight of the Middle Ages for his cold mistress, and even when he lusts after Milady the affair has little effect upon him; Athos, noblest of them all, has transmuted his love to strength within himself by hanging his beloved; Porthos sees naught in women but an easy way of obtaining ready cash; while Aramis, the only lover of the group, is also the only one swayed by varying purposes, by conflict between sword and cassock. No, love is dangerous to the ruffian. Against Cromwell's determined army the cavaliers could do nothing. He led his men from victory to victory with a hymn for a battle-cry. "I raised such men," said he, "as had the fear

THEY DWELL IN HIGH PLACES 83

of God before them, as made some conscience of what
they did; and from that day forward, I must say to you,
they were never beaten; and whenever they were engaged
against the enemy, they beat them continually." Of
course they beat them continually; who could stand
against such arrogant fighting-men " armed within by
the satisfaction of their own consciences, and without
by good iron arms, they would as one man charge firmly
and fight desperately?" So too in India with Havelock
and his Saints. Of them, Sir Archibald Forbes wrote,
"better soldiers have never trod this earth." They
marched to Cawnpore, singing hymns instead of the
usual *British Grenadiers* or any such tawdry martial
tune to whip the blood to a false and temporary courage.
Havelock himself was somewhat of a miniature Cromwell. "He was always," wrote one of his men, "as sour
as if he had swallowed a pint of vinegar, except when
he was being shot at, and then he was as blithe as a
schoolboy out for a holiday." You will find this stern
asceticism continually in many a true ruffian: for
example, Chinese Gordon with his Bible, weakened only
by his fondness for the bottle; but drink is a common
outlet for soldiers and sailors. General Grant in his early
days was dismissed the army for drunkenness, and
although we must ignore as the invention of a journalist
the story of Lincoln offering to send Grant's favourite
brand of whisky to all his other generals, he nevertheless
drank heavily indeed; it was the same with Alexander
the Great who despised all other sensual delights as
being worthy only of helots; Antony too was a
drunkard, and when he let his energies turn instead
towards a woman, Cleopatra, he was destroyed. Henry V
lived the life of a saint and his laws were strict against
the female camp-followers. Napoleon was one of the

few great ruffians capable of rising above the weakness
of sex; he was able to surrender to women and yet retain his power, but he was almost in every way an
exception to the laws that bind us common men.

We have wandered far from Gregory VII and have,
in fact, devoted so much space to him that little is left
for Innocent III. Innocent's life, however, is close enough
to Gregory's to be examined only briefly. He too strove
to drag the church's temporal possessions into the fist
of Rome, and in his desperate battle for property and
power was forced to resort to shyster tricks, wheedling
Sicily from the old widow of Henry VI under the pretence of looking after her son, and then encouraging
adventurers to steal the lad's heritage for Rome; he
wrung England from King John and denounced Magna
Carta as a " diabolical document "; he condoned the
fourth crusade for seizing Constantinople with appalling
butchery, and then denounced the knights for not hand-
ing the Greek Church over to him; but the terrible result
of his policy, one of the blackest episodes of the medieval
times, was his crusade against the Albigensian heresy.
Into the most cultured lands of Europe, into the gay and
beautiful world of Provençe, he sent an army of murderers. " Kill them all," cried his envoy, " God will
know his own! " And the soldiers needed little encouragement, the butchery that followed is sickening to
read. The papal legate boasted that he had massacred
forty thousand men, women and children in one town
alone; and for two years, he led an army of two hundred
thousand men through the most civilised parts of
medieval Europe. Even this horde was not enough, and
another hundred thousand had to be called on to wipe
out the remainder of the gallant singers of Provençe.

Like Gregory, Innocent was a strong-minded, chaste

and deeply pious man; and as with Gregory, his policy, the aggrandisement of Roman power, brought nothing but calamity on the world. Such is the way of the ruffian, such was the way of Napoleon, of Edward III and Henry V. They are obsessed by an idea the consummation of which is of greater importance than humanity itself, they are men driven by dæmons, by a fury that terrifies us, that few can withstand. They are tortured by their own frustration, by the blank stupidity of a world that does not acclaim them immediately as saviours. In such men we find the epitome of the ruffian, the logical result of arrogance transmuted into something holy, tremendous. Their will becomes the will of God, and all are heretics—therefore soulless and worthy only of death—who dare withstand them. The principle to-day is labelled fascism, but it is as ancient as the teaching of old prophets who built Jehovah in the image of their own hate and lust for power; older than that, it has existed as long as man has been. The Stuarts in England strove to force it upon the people, but there were gallant, unselfish men like John Hampden and the fiery Pym to stand against them until the determined Cromwell came to mould an army out of yeomen. England since then has never tolerated the fascist system, it died here at the heels of James II, and only feeble efforts like Lord George Gordon's no-popery riots have appeared to attempt a political or religious tyranny.

Fascism may represent the ultimate expression of the ruffian, but there are many different branches, offshoots from the main trunk of arrogance; and although royal tyranny left our shores with James, we have had other kinds of ruffians on our throne.

IV

The Prince Regent

EVEN as a child, George, Prince of Wales, showed that he had a vile temper. This was, in fact, about the only thing in all his life that he ever did show his friends, intellectually or emotionally. He knew his position, God damn, and his dignity. Despite his appearance, England had to accept him as her future king. And he made you realise it. The minute he opened his little mouth you knew that he was Prince of Wales and, during his father's periodic bouts of lunacy, the Regent of this land. He put everybody in his or her place, being of royal blood. Yet he was not easily ruffled, so he said. If women were but kind to him and he had enough gold to toss on the turn of a card, George always kept his temper. Women, undoubtedly, were kind to him, he being a Prince. He was fond of complacently counting up his bag of female flesh, and he spoke of them as a sportsman does of his catch, exaggerating just a little. Not that he had any need to exaggerate, but a man's mind gets confused after such countless acres of flesh, he is liable to believe that he's possessed so-and-so when perhaps, after all, he forgot all about her until it was too late or was too drunk to do aught but snore. What woman could ever resist a Prince, so charming a Prince, even a fat Prince, particularly when he is King in all but name?

Hold the candle up close to his red face. It is not beautiful any longer; yet so it had been once, quite beautiful. But a slothful life and the creamiest of foods had quilted the belly, unmuscled the jowls. He was growing old, yet still his lunatic father wandered about Windsor, calling parliaments, talking to angels and listening to the music of the spheres. The Prince clamoured for more power under the regency and, almost vindictively, bounced into the laps of ladies, innumerable ladies, from lady to lady he bounced, often weeping at his own sorry penniless state and the stupidity of that vulgar place called parliament. He possessed every woman he wanted and a great many whom he did not want. Fat and growing fatter, he bounced his way amongst the silks and laces of gracious femininity; he waddled superbly into drawing-rooms, blinding the world with his huge new buckles; he pulled up his belly with deep breaths and waited serenely for laughter at his condescending witticisms. There was that *bon mot* he had tossed off about Lady Parker and Lady Westmorland— he'd given himself a week's headache trying to phrase it properly. But it was worth it. Everybody still repeated it with his name attached. "There isn't an honest woman in London," he had said, then paused—a long pause during which he gazed waggishly from woman's face to woman's face—" excepting Lady Parker and Lady Westmorland "—again a pause—" and they are so stupid I can make nothing of them. They are scarcely fit to blow their own noses!" Now, that was wit! Brummell never said anything to equal that!

Brummell, indeed! What were his remarks, after all? Silly jests, schoolboy stupidities, such as his talk about his " favourite leg," and his excuse for being hoarse that it was the result of being put into a room with a damp stranger. Who the devil was Brummell, anyway? True, he had deceived George at first by the simple cut of his clothes, George had quite liked the fellow for a time, but eventually he just had to put him in his place. The

upstart upstarted too far indeed! To dare to ask a
companion of England's Prince of Wales, " Who's your
fat friend!" George could never forgive Brummell that.
After a pretended reconciliation, at dinner he had turned
to the Duke of York and remarked loudly, " I think we
had better order Mr. Brummell's carriage before he gets
drunk," and with a low insolent bow, the Beau went,
crushed. Anybody who stood in Prince Florizel's way
was crushed. George was quite complacent on that
point.

Yet he was a good friend—to some, some of the time—
and a prime joker. He still laughed whenever he recalled the trick he played on the Abbé de la Fai. The
abbé said that he could charm fish out of water, and
George scoffed at the idea. " I'll show you," said the
abbé and with his bastard brother, the Duc d'Orleans,
went over to the bridge—this was at Newmarket—to
whistle a fish out of water. " You musn't give me a
shove from behind," said the abbé playfully, and George
swore on his royal oath that he wouldn't. But he did.
Over went the abbé with a most unchurchmanlike comment, into the deepest part of the river. Orleans grabbed a
horsewhip and, purple with rage—not being able to
appreciate an English joke—made for George. George
fled. He rushed into his inn and bolted the door.

All London had laughed for weeks about that, and
about the trick he played on Mrs. Vaneek once at her
home. While she talked sprightlily to somebody, George
had crept up behind her and with his handkerchief
measured her beam, holding up the measurements afterwards for all the room to see.

Jests, clothes, cards, and love affairs—that was the outward husk of George, Prince Regent of England. Yet—
although he confessed it to no one but women, his

THE PRINCE REGENT

friends, himself and his valet—he had a bleeding heart. At night, when the starch-powdered wig was taken from his shaven skull and deposited upon its stand, when the expensive clothes were unwrapped from the flopping body—his clothing bill came to £10,000 a year—when the damask coat, the embroidered waistcoat, the under-waistcoat, the laced shirt, the breeches, stockings and shoes, all fell from him like marvellously coloured autumn leaves from some pulpy tree, and George stood naked, white and hairless as an egg, fat and naked before the fire, his grotesque belly lurched in thick wrinkles of creamy flesh when he sighed and his blurred eyes became opaque and troubled, like a fish's. A Prince has a tragic life, he moaned, nothing's his own, except his debts; how sweet to be a ploughman on the uplands, perspiring in old friendly clothes yet with the wife of his choice merrily heating supper in their humble cot! Ah, Mary Robinson, his sweet Perdita! it had cost that miserly old loon of a father of his £5000 to buy George's burning letters from her escritoire. She had been worth all his father's £5000, and more; aye, even the wigging his father gave him over what the old fool called " a shameful scrape " . . . Mary . . . Maria . . . The names pursued each other in his head . . . Maria Fitzherbert . . . Then he spat into the burning coals as he remembered that he had a wife, that Brunswick whore, the sallow Caroline.

George, Prince of Wales, hated his wife almost as much as he hated his father. He had hated her long before he met her and had hated her even more afterwards, he would never have married her if it hadn't been for his damned father tagging so much money to the bridal.

Maria Fitzherbert had been most beautiful, most beautiful of women. In gay defiance of silly fashion, her long soft hair was of a delicious pale gold, never greased and powdered, her large eyes were a hazel-brown, brows high and arched, mouth small yet full, the nose a trifle curved and long. In short, a damned fine woman. She was twenty-eight when George first met her—he was twenty-one—and she had twice been widowed, yet had kept her figure firm and luscious and had remained in every way a lady of the first fashion: George was the First Gentleman of Europe, so only a dolt like his father would have failed to realise that God had made them specially for each other.

He saw her on the banks of the Thames at Richmond, during a water-party. He was lolling on cushions in his punt with some charmer poling—he forgot her name: damme, a man can't remember all their names!—when suddenly he saw Maria walking on the tow-path. He caught but the merest flicker of her face, he caught but the swiftest blur of her gown, then she was gone, magically, before his startled eyes. But soon again he saw her, in Lady Sefton's box at the Opera. He was on the opposite side of the theatre, the play was dull, nobody interesting being present in the audience, and George was talking of leaving when suddenly he saw Maria. Her long curls were unpowdered and swung to her white shoulders, her cheeks were unrouged and as delicately tinted as any china. The Prince gaped boldly at her but she never once looked at him.

Now, this Prince—Prince Charming, as he was called —had a truly voluminous knowledge of women. Young as he was, he had bagged more than many a hunter four times his age, and he prided himself on knowing the sluts, inside and out—inside the bedroom and out.

But he failed when he tried his tricks on Maria Fitzherbert. He wrote to her until he got the cramp, he followed her coach, he bullied her, he pleaded with her, he chased her down streets, he shoved himself into her box at the Opera, he bribed her servants . . . everything failed. At last, desperate, he proposed marriage, but the Royal Marriage Act stumped him there, he couldn't marry without papa's permission, and she knew it; besides, Maria was a Roman Catholic, and a Roman Catholic Queen of England was a kind of treason and not allowed by that damned interfering parliament. To all his pleas she answered as Lady Waldegrave had answered the Duke of Gloucester— before she became his duchess—" Though I am too inconsiderable to become your wife, I am too considerable to become your mistress."

George had a wicked temper. Like a child deprived of a sucker, he set up a great howl when he realised that the fascinating Maria actually meant what she told him. He smashed the furniture, he kicked his servants, and insulted his friends. Then he sat down and wept. Awful, he moaned, is the penalty of a crown, lucky his poorest subject able to marry the wench he loves. Had he but been an ordinary gentleman instead of the first in Europe he might have won Maria and lived happily ever afterwards. As it was . . . He drank until he was sick, he refused to see any of his harem, and even the gaming-tables could not hold him for long. What was to be done? O, dear me, what was to be done? The poor big Prince in his mighty palace moaned in lonely despair, just like any common person subject to vulgar woes. Then one morning in November, 1784, when Maria, exhausted by these royal frenzies, was about to run to the Continent, a coach dashed up to her London home, and four men, dishevelled, excited, even perspiring a little, burst through her doors. They were all of the

Prince's household, Lord Onslow, Lord Southampton, Mr. Edward Bouverie, and Dr. Keate. "The Prince!" they cried and clutched their cravats. "The Prince?" repeated Maria, blanching a little. "Yes, the Prince! he's fallen on his sword and calls for you!" Maria was twenty-eight, twice-married, well-versed in man's duplicity, and even after Dr. Keate had sworn on his most professional oath that he had told the truth, she held back from entering the notorious gates of Carlton House. She insisted on a chaperon, and they agreed, suggesting the honey-hearted Georgiana, Duchess of Devonshire. So the duchess it was, and they all set out to see the dying Prince Charming.

He lay on a couch in his luxurious ground-floor apartment; behind him, the tall open windows showed dark trees, filled with autumn's last red leaves, against a dirty sky. His even in those days plumpish face was waxen, he breathed laboriously, spoke in a whisper, and clutched at his side that was drenched in his own royal blood. Poor Maria almost swooned at the sight. He had not lied, he loved her truly! In a feeble voice, George asked the duchess for a ring and she slipped one from her finger and gave it to him. Then upon that pledge, Maria and George solemnly swore to become man and wife. As immediate proof of his determination to keep to his part of the bargain, George there and then strove to drag Maria on to the couch; being a dying man, however, he feared to exert all his strength, and she escaped. Once outside, away from that pathetic tableau, Maria became sane and fled to Aix-la-Chapelle, while the Prince enjoyed champagne for the first time in months and congratulated that clever Dr. Keate at having bled him with such little loss of blood. He strolled off to the country, to Lord Southampton's, to luxuriate amorously in dreams of coming joys within the white arms of his gentle Maria. Then when he heard of Maria's treason he almost swooned; in his first apoplectic fit of rage he thought of pursuing her to the continent, but as he couldn't leave England without papa's permission, he was reduced to writing woefully to friends and creditors, for he was as heavily in debt as he was in love—in fact, even more heavily. When weary of writing, he called on friends to give an exhibition of frustrated love, bursting into tears, flinging himself on to the floor, rolling on the floor, hitting his own head, biting table-legs, stamping on his wig, falling suddenly into yelping hysterics, and swearing grandiloquently that he would renounce the crown of England, sell his jewels and plate, collect enough gelt to live on and fly with Maria to that land of the free, America. He sent out spies and quickly they ferreted out Maria's continental address, then he had her shadowed like a criminal. He wrote to her on enough sheets to make a dozen Bibles, swearing to die if she came not to him, to blow out his brains, to give himself up to his creditors, to murder his father. He was a cuning letter-writer and knew well how to chafe blood from a woman's heart with his pen. But against Maria's obstinacy it seemed that even he must fail—abominable destroying thought! His couriers passed each other on the road, they made a kind of race of it, and so mystified was the French government by all this activity that they tripped up three of them on suspicion of plotting against King Louis.

Then at last persistence triumphed. Exhausted by the chase, Maria distractedly promised George that she would marry nobody else, ever. It was but a step after that to promising to marry George himself. After over a year's exile, during the first week of December, 1785, she returned to England. Prince Charming met her at Dover and was all tenderness during the drive to her home in Park Street. The Prince was very happy in the days that followed, although his rage overmastered him now and again when complications arose, particularly the difficulty of finding a clergyman bold enough to do the deed, as under that accursed Act of 1772, a clergyman solemnising a marriage contrary to the King's wishes was exposed to the penalties of the mysterious premunire, which, although mysterious, were undoubtedly awful. The Prince's private secretary, Colonel Gardner, suggested trying the Rev. Philip Rosenhagen, a debauched military chaplain, but as no good round sum was offered, the Rev. Philip Rosenhagen virtuously spurned the treasonable idea. Gardner then fixed on the Rev. Johnes Knight, Rector of Welwyn in Hertfordshire, who also held a living in the city. Parson Johnes was a jolly rogue who loved fine foods, fine wines, fine hunting, and fine women. He was far too gentle-hearted to stand out against the Prince's blandishments—and the sight of the scar where Keate had bled him—and reluctantly he gave in; on reflection, however, away from George's charm and Maria's beauty, prudence returned and he refused; and again Prince Charming jumped on his expensive wig and rolled on the floor with rage. At last Gardner unearthed the perfect parson, a poor curate but recently ordained, the Rev. Robert Burt; Burt agreed to perform the ceremony for £500 on the nail and definite promises of future preferment.

December 15, 1785, was a gay night for Prince Charming. He had succeeded as he always must succeed; it was the first time in his life that anybody had ever refused him anything except money, and he had got it just the same. He got it on December 15 at Maria's home; Maria's uncle,

Henry Errington, gave her away, and he and her brother, Jack Smythe, acted as witnesses. It was all hurried through very secretly, then as darkness came over the flowerless squares of London, the lovers set out for Maria's Richmond villa and a night of long-dreamed-of superlative ecstasy. It was ghastly cold, but it was warm under the rug protecting their four legs, swathing them firmly together, knee to responsive knee, hiding exploring hands that fondled each other lovingly. The snow was mountainous, it shot up from the wheels and splashed to die against the heat of their faces; so warm and loving were these two that the flakes melted as if they fell on a lit candle. Lovers do not mind the cold, for there is fire in their blood, burning on their mouths. Once the carriage broke down and the impatient lovers had to fret in dreams, had to content their strong desires with merely gazing amorously on each other in a Hammersmith inn. Then on again, at last; and at last, Richmond. . . .

It was, of course, a glorious scandal; everybody talked about it, everybody wrote about it, but nothing happened. George blandly weathered the uproar by ignoring it, and parliament actually shouldered his debts. Times grew more placid for him then. He spent many of his days at Brighton with his adoring adorable wife, and once again he became London's Prince Florizel, the First Gentleman of Europe, the jester, the gambler, the drinker, the roisterer. Mrs. Fitzherbert was cut by a few laced dames, but not by many. It seemed that they would be happy for ever. It wasn't so bad being a Prince, after all. Then their cup of happiness seemed full indeed when the old King went mad. For a while, they even thought that the loon might die, and Maria rushed jubilantly to London from Brighton to be with her husband who was cracking bottles of champagne and dancing with excitement. Unfortunately, however, the King recovered his health if not his wits, and once again Prince Charming gave one of his unique exhibitions of titanic rages and abused his mother for trying to steal the regency from him.

He flung himself into debauch, and before very long discovered that he had flung himself in so heartily that he couldn't crawl out again. The Jews locked away their money-bags when he came knocking at their doors, at sight of him his friends dragged out their empty pockets, he was waylaid in the street by duns, and the workmen on Carlton House threatened to stop building if they weren't paid. He tried to raise money at a colossal interest on his father's life, but collected only a paltry £30,000; he offered an Irish peerage and £10,000 after the King's death for every £5,000 lent him; but nobody any longer believed his promises, even when they were written down. And at last he had again to visit his father who was sane at the time, unluckily for young George. The King agreed to liquidate all debts if the Prince married as he was told.

Then appeared the Lady Jersey, the once beautiful Miss Twysden. She sailed consolingly into his tormented life, and Prince Charming dropped on his knees to her. She was a grandmother, her family was larger than a hen's, but George always preferred women older than himself. He wrote instantly to Maria, saying that he never wanted to see her again; to his amazement she did not pursue him, she did not come rushing weeping to implore his mercy. Cut to the heart, George locked himself in with Lady Jersey to weep with her about the frail short-lived loves of women, and to agree to act the martyr and to marry whomever they liked to give him. And that was how he came to marry this damned mulatto-like bitch,

Caroline. The Prince spat into the fire when he thought of her. The little fool thought that she could be witty: she had said, the liar, that she had only committed adultery once, and that was with Mrs. Fitzherbert's husband; on another occasion she had made George wince with rage by crying, " O, mein Gott! let out dat poor old King and shut up mein husband!" And just because George happened to like the wench's brazen looks, Caroline had thrown poor Lady Douglas out of the house. She was a nasty-tempered bitch, this so-called wife of his. George hated her.

When she first came to England and arrived at Greenwich, he had deliberately delayed his carriage to be as insultingly late as possible. Lady Jersey, too, had helped to make the foreign wretch uncomfortable; she had abused Caroline's clothes, then dressed her most unbecomingly in a white gown which did everything but suit her, and she had even tried to shove an outrageous turban on the poor girl's head; but here Caroline had stood firm and kept to her own beaver. Yet Lady Jersey did manage to rouge Caroline's cheeks which, being already red, turned scarlet. Nobody received the new Princess when she reached St. James's Palace. Lord Malmesbury sent for George and at last he arrived, swollen with obese dignity. Caroline flopped on her knees to him, as she had been taught to do, and George picked her up and embraced her, as he had been taught to do. Then he dropped her, darted to the other end of the room, and shouted, " Harris! I'm not well, pray get me a glass of brandy!" Lord Malmesbury tried to intervene, pitying the girl who stood flushed and silent. " Sir," said he, " had you not better have a glass of water?" and the Prince yelled at him, " No, by God! I'll go straight to the Queen!" and did so, without another

G

glance at Caroline who had travelled many hundreds of miles to become his wife. That put her in her place, by God!

Ah, who would be a Prince? thought the Prince, warming his white silky nakedness before the fire; he has no happiness, he can't even marry the woman he wants to. Yet he gets them just the same. That, of course, was a little consolation. Yet who would be a Prince?

Who would be a Prince's wife? sighed Mrs. Fitzherbert in her home at Parson's Green, lonely, despairing, and very dignified.

Yes, indeed, thought poor Caroline, lonelier still in this outlandish country, in this strange big cold palace: who, who would be a Princess?

The Prince Regent rolled his huge quivering naked body into bed, tried to remember all his debts, groaned, tried to recall all the women who had said they loved him, and smiled. Then he wept. He was so lonely. Oh, so lonely, being a Prince. To-morrow would bring the same old round of dissipation, of gambling, wenching, riding, dressing, drinking, talking, jesting, and toying with politics, waiting for his idiotic father to die. If only he were King! Ah, then, my God . . . if he were King!

V

They Have But One God

In silks and satins we can find the ruffian. He need not wear the steel of a warrior or be driven by the powerful lust of spiritual conquest; he can appear a gentleman above gentlemen, a prince of the royal blood. George IV was no admirable ruffian, for we cannot resist a certain admiration for the murderer who risks his neck or the cheat who might lose his liberty. George risked nothing except the good opinion of his fellows, and that he despised.

> " A noble, nasty course he ran
> superbly filthy and fastidious;
> he was the world's first gentleman
> and made the appelation hideous."

Brummell also, in a small way, was a ruffian. It is said with possible truth that he was the son of a tailor, and certainly he did not come of a good family. Once when talking to a lady of a common acquaintance he remarked, " Who ever heard of his father? " " And who," she asked, " ever heard of George B.'s father? " " Ah, dear lady," he replied, " who indeed, ever heard of George B.'s father, and who would have heard of George B. himself if he had been anything but what he is? Do you know, my dear lady, it is my folly that is the making of me. If I did not impertinently stare duchesses out of countenance, and nod over my shoulder to a prince, I should be forgotten in a week; and if the world is so silly as to admire my absurdities, you and I know better; but what does that signify? " His insolence, draw attention though it might, eventually proved his ruin, not only by his insult to George, but by arousing the antagonism of Mrs. Fitzherbert when he ordered his servants to call the carriage for Mistress Fitzherbert and when he dubbed her " Benina " because she was growing so fat: the point of this second allusion rests in Brummell having already nicknamed George " Big Ben " because of his alleged likeness to an enormously fat porter at Carlton House. Arrogantly Brummell commanded the attention of dukes and duchesses, and when his brother William came to London was asked by friends at White's when he was going to introduce the man into society. " In a day or two," said Brummell, " but I have recommended him to walk the back streets till his new clothes come home." Being entirely disinterested in women, he was unable to resort to the beaux's most lucrative profession, marrying wealthily. He did make one or two feeble efforts but they came to nothing and at last he died, babbling, half-crazed, in a house of charity in Caen. Yet this inability to marry saved him at any rate from the ridiculous situation in which an earlier gaudy ruffian of society found himself involved. Robert Feilding was so handsome a fellow that when he walked the streets the feminine part of the traffic stopped to gape on him with adoration. " Let them look and die, look and die! " the Beau used to say gleefully, and the *Tatler* informs us that " he sometimes rode in an open tumbril of less size than ordinary, to show the largeness of his limbs and the grandeur of his personage to the greater advantage. At other seasons all his appointments had a magnificence, as if it were formed by the genius of Trimalchio of old, which showed itself in doing ordinary things with an air of pomp and grandeur. Orlando therefore called for tea by beat of drum; his valet got ready to shave him by a trumpet to horse; and water was brought for his teeth when the sound was changed to boot and saddle." But the doom of Narcissus came to him when he turned from his own reflection to contemplate the joys of a marriage-jointure. Twice already he had married well, spent his own and both his wives' fortunes, when, being about fifty and his good looks rapidly going, he considered the possibilities of wedding a wealthy widow, Mrs. Deleau. Feilding took great care over the case, first of all ferreting in doctors' commons to make quite certain that his intended was worth the £60,000 with which gossip credited her; finding that gossip had not lied, he enlisted a lady's hairdresser called Mrs. Villars as go-between. On discovering the widow's address, Feilding visited her home, and afterwards told Mrs. Villars " that he saw the lady through a casement; and that she might have the more perfect view of him he took divers turns in the garden, pulled out his watch, and set it by the sun-dial; and that he came round the country, and almost mur-dered his horses, to get a sight of her." The only mis-fortune here was that the lady Feilding saw was appar-antly not Mrs. Deleau, and when Mrs. Villars discovered the mistake it was too late for her to do anything except to push the marriage through with the wrong person so that she could grab her fee. This person was a Mrs. Wadsworth and, in Mrs. Villars' own words, when she took the lady to Feilding's lodgings he ran into the room " with a great deal of joy, and took Mrs. Wadsworth into his arms, and said nothing could ease his mind but a promise to make him happy, in marrying him pre-sently. He said he would fetch the priest; but Mrs. Wadsworth refused his proposals, and would have dis-suaded him from going then, and desired him to put it off till another time, and would have gone away. But he would not hear of it; and said she had disappointed him before, but now he was resolved to make her his own, before she went away. Mr. Feilding then went for the priest, and locked the chamber door after him, and took the key with him, for fear Mrs. Wadsworth should go away." For over six months the Beau remained in his contented dream until his wealthy wife asked him for money. Feilding, however, was a cautious man and, probably doubting the legality of his secret Roman Catholic marriage with the supposed Mrs. Deleau, had wedded the Duchess of Cleveland sixteen days after he had wedded Mrs. Wadsworth. Evidently he lived with them in turns, and beat them both, he beat the duchess so superbly in fact that she had him locked into Newgate for a time to cool his amorous choler. It is a pretty picture this, the ruffian beau wedded to one of the most notorious female ruffians of the realm, for in her young days when she had been Barbara Palmer, the Duchess of Cleveland had acted so outrageously as Charles II's mistress that Evelyn called her " the curse of our nation " and Burnet wrote that she was " enormously vicious and ravenous." At any rate, when Feilding discovered that he had been cheated over the wealthy Mrs. Deleau his rage was so tremendous that Mrs. Wadsworth fled and told the duchess of the bigamy. The only way that Feilding could think to wriggle out of the net was to make a forged entry in the Fleet marriage-register to say that Mrs. Wadsworth had been wedded previously to meeting him, but the forgery was easily exposed and Feilding was sentenced to being burnt in the hand. Even this, however, he avoided with a Queen's warrant to suspend execution.

They are not an attractive regiment of our ruffian army, these Beaux with their deliberately bad manners and pre-fashionable garments. They are the riff-raff ex-

ploiting society with frank cynicism, living only to satisfy
the lusts of their vanities, loving their own physical
appearance above all others. They are selfish and pettishly
arrogant. Said Beau Nash, Bath's tyrant of fashion,
when asked to settle a debt: " Doing that vulgar sort of
thing never procures you a friend; lending money does; "
and they could be disgustingly rude, these Beaux, rudeness
often being confused with wit then as in these modern
days, for once at Bath when a deformed lady told him
that she had come straight from London, " You have got
damnably warped by the way," sneered Nash; and they
knew all honeyed subtleties of amorous conversation:
" Richard," said a lady one day to Nash, " you have a
tongue that would debauch a nunnery." But for all their
arrogant tricks and their insolence, we cannot place them
on the dais of Ruffians' Hall. Their circle was too cir-
cumscribed, their ambitions and conquests too petty, to
give them eminence. Rather would I promote some murderer defying the laws of man, even such a bloodthirsty
cockscomb as Lacenaire whom Hugo considered worthy
of the immortal shrine of *Les Miserables*. Before his
beheading, he was asked why he had not written some of
the masterpieces of which he talked so grandly: " I had
to choose," shrugged Lacenaire, " between writing a play
and murder, and I chose murder because it was easier."
In Lacenaire's case, this was true enough, yet he was no
abler a murderer than he was a poet, he was an amateur
in both: in real amateurish fashion he staged the killing
of an old man called Chardon, without taking the
trouble, as would any professional, to make certain that
the man actually was the miser that people believed.
He stabbed Chardon on the back of the neck with an
awl while his confederate, Avril, choked him and
then finished him off with a hatchet; Lacenaire for no

apparent reason, save perhaps a growing fondness for the sport, went into the next room and, in his own words, " found Madame Chardon in bed, and killed her with the awl. Avril took no part in this second murder, as he did not enter the room till I was pressing the mattress upon the body." For all their trouble they collected a paltry five hundred francs and an ivory Virgin worth three francs which they threw into the river. Lacenaire's second exploit was even more clumsily mismanaged, for when with another comrade, a rascal called François who boasted that he would murder any man for twenty francs, he attempted to kill a bank-messenger and the bank-messenger naturally yelled at the first blow, François ran for his life " and I after him. François, believing that if I was taken he might escape, pulled the door after him, but I succeeded in opening it, and ran out, crying, ' Stop the murderer! ' " A dirty pair of rascals, unworthy of our refined observation were it not for Lacenaire's behaviour after arrest, his proud insolence towards the judges, and his passion to finish writing his memoirs before the guillotine finished him. " It is a document," he said pompously, " that the world will prize." He wished with true ruffian vanity to die in a flare of publicity as a kind of satanic genius, as some ferocious inhuman menace to life. When the judge probed into his early apprenticeship days of petty crimes he blushed and fidgetted like a modest girl caught in some undignified posture. " Your questions," he said, " remind me of a surgeon amusing himself with paring a man's corns when about to cut off his leg."

These are the gestures of arrogance that qualify a ruffian, that lift men like Lacenaire from the cheap ranks of the butchers into the vainglorious sphere of ruffianly genius. Deacon Brodie, for example, amuses us by his cleverness in apeing the good citizen so well that he could commit robbery in front of an old woman and yet get away with it because she refused to believe her own eyes; but our interest is more fully aroused by his passion to make the most of his appearance in the dock, and by his fury at reading a not too flattering description of his five feet four inches of superior dignity. " I make no doubt," he wrote from hiding, " but that designing villain Brown [the informer] is now in high favour with Mr. Cockburn [the sheriff], for I can see some strokes of his pencil in my portrait. May God forgive him for all his crimes and falsehoods." These letters of Brodie's unchink some little light into the darkness of inside the ruffian's skull, for even while he is scurrying for his life, Brodie can yet ask questions about a cockfight, " Write me how the Main went; how you came on in it; if my black cock fought and gained." These are the qualities that arrest us at once in the ruffian-character, so peculiar they are, almost frightening in their inhumanity, in their refusal to recognise the inevitability of death and the powers of an enemy-society. So certain is he of the omnipotence of his personal guardian angel that the ruffian will take the most incredible risks and see no danger in them, often hanging himself by his apparent carelessness. It should have been a simple matter for Captain John Donellan, let us say, in 1780, to give the laurel water to his brother-in-law when the lad was alone, and nobody would have inquired into his death, he was so rotten with syphilis; but no, he must pass the lethal draught to his mother-in-law to administer and thereby get himself hanged. And Birchall with his businesslike scheme to kill would-be immigrants to Canada, a fool-proof scheme almost, destroys all hopes of success in 1890 by his greediness in taking two victims with him instead of one; Burke and Hare must knock on the head one of the most popular whores in Edinburgh, a girl whose lovely body had been explored inch by inch by half the medical students who saw it on the table; Dr. Cream betrayed himself by complaining to the police that he was suspected of murdering a girl who, in fact, had spat out his strychnine pill and yet lived to accuse him; Dick Turpin, when he might have bluffed his way to freedom under the alias of Palmer, must needs write a letter and have his hand recognised. Too often in this fashion, his own arrogance belittling the cleverness of others, is the ruffian undone. "To the Greeks FOOLISHNESS," said the Newgate ordinary in Fielding's *Jonathan Wild*, that ruffian's bible, and it is an excellent ruffian text, for all is foolishness that is outside their world; honesty is foolishness if it interferes with their ambitions, while the rest of mankind is beyond contempt beside their greatness. Therefore commonly the ruffian, feeling secure on his own pinnacle of supremacy, commits the most stupid careless acts, thinking himself as safe as any prince in a fairy tale, under the protection of some kind of invisible godmother. I have mentioned this divine belief of the ruffian before, but it is a point we must not forget. "Here the inhuman provincials," writes Captain John Smith, founder of Virginia and beloved of Pocohontas, modestly referring to himself in the third person singular, "with a rabble of pilgrims of divers nations going to Rome, hourly cursed him [Captain Smith] not only for a Huguenot, but his nation they swore were all pirates, and so vilely railed on his dread sovereign Queen Elizabeth, and that they never should have fair weather so long as he was aboard them; their disputations grew to that passion that they threw him overboard; yet God brought him to that little isle, where was no inhabitants but a few kine and goats."

God does practically everything for the ruffian, God drives the sword in his hand, God, who stops the sparrow falling, deflects the shells of enemies. If they are proclaimed atheists, to satisfy their ego they must create a god in the astrological stars or, like Beau Brummell, blame a toy like a missing sixpenny-bit with a hole in it for their ruin. If he is in danger, the ruffian relies on God to extricate him; if he is attacked, God, he knows, will see that he is revenged. Thus, Hans Staden, a sixteenth century captive amongst cannibals in Brazil, relates with pious satisfaction the death of a native who had once abused him: the man became ill and was brought to Staden for a medical opinion. "Now the savages," writes Staden, in Malcolm Letts' Broadway translation, "are accustomed to use for several purposes the teeth of a wild beast called Backe, which they sharpen, and when the blood is sluggish they cut the skin with one of these teeth so that the blood flows freely. This is equivalent with us to letting blood. I took one of these teeth, intending to open the median vein, but I could not cut it as the tooth was too blunt, and the savages stood round about. . . . Then they said, 'He will surely die. Let us kill him before he is dead.' I answered: 'No, do not kill him, for possibly he may recover,' but I could not restrain them . . . Then the man came up, to whom the Cario had been given, and beat out his brains, after which they left him lying before the huts ready to be eaten. But I warned them that he was a sick man, and that they might also fall sick if they ate him, and they knew not what to do. Nevertheless, one came from the huts where I was and called the women-folk to make a fire beside the body. Then he cut off the head, for the man had lost an eye from the disease and his appearance was horrible, and throwing away the head, he singed the body at the fire . . . I told the savages that this Cario whom they were roasting and eating had always spoken ill of me, saying that while I was among the Portuguese I had shot several of their friends, and that he lied, for he had never seen me before. ' Now see,' said I, ' he had been several years with you and had never been sick, but on account of his lying stories about me, my God was angry with him and smote him with sickness and put it into your minds to kill and eat him. So will my God do to all evil persons who seek or have sought to injure me.' And they were greatly terrified at my words, but I thanked God that he had in this wise shown his might and power through me. Note reader, and mark well my writing, for I do this not in order to tell you strange things, but only to make known the wonderful works of God."

This strange and watchful God of the ruffian is built in his own image, for it is himself he worships, a potent and remorseless God, a God in Whom you can fully trust and Who will not betray you. Take the miraculous tale of " John Foxe, an Englishman, in delivering 266 Christians out of the captivitie of the Turkes at Alexandria, the 3 Januarie 1577 " as an excellent example of the strength and cunning of this terrible God. Fox was captured in 1563, despite the courage of captain and crew, and of the owner who, fearful of losing ship, cargo and liberty, " manfully encouraged his company, exhorting them valiantly to shew their manhood, shewing them that God was their God, and not their enemies," and Fox was imprisoned. For thirteen or fourteen years he worked in the Alexandrian bagnios, plotting to escape. With seven comrades at last the venture was made. They

had supplied themselves with whatever weapons they
could steal or make, John Fox having " an olde rustie
sword blade, without either hilt or pomell, which he
made to serve his turne, in bending the hand ende of the
sword, in steed of the pomell "—the pommel of a sword,
by the way, being the knob on top of the grip, not the
guard or the quillons or cross-bar, and Fox is apparently
using it in two senses as both guard and pommel. They
were unfortunately discovered in their confabulations by
a keeper, and there was nothing to be done, of course,
except kill him, which John Fox promptly did, despite
the man's entreaties. Fox lifted up " his bright shining
sword of tenne yeeres rust, and stroke him so maine a
blow, as therewithall his head clave a sunder, so that he
fell starke dead to the ground." Then they crept softly
towards the road and met six warders whom they
slaughtered. In the jailor's lodge they found the keys to
fortress and prison, and also a great chest of " duckats,
which this Peter Unticaro, & two more, opening, stuffed
themselves so full as they could, betweene their shirts
and their skinne: which John Fox would not once touch,
and sayde, that it was his and their libertie which he
sought for, to the honour his God, & not to make a
marte of the wicked treasure of the Infidels." This was
more than just pious nobility, it was wisdom, for when
they had to fight they way out, " John Fox was thrise
shot through his apparell, and not hurt," but " Peter
Unticaro, and the other two, that had armed them with
the duckats, were slaine; as not able to weild themselves,
being so pestered with the weight and uneasie carrying
of the wicked and prophane treasure." At last they
managed to find a boat, and then does John Fox
(or Foxe) burst out in triumph to his God. From
both sides, the garrisons fired frenziedly at them as they

tried to trim their galley to the wind. "Here did God," writes Fox jubilantly, "hold foorth his buckler, he shieldeth now this gally, and hath tried their faith to the uttermost. Now commeth his speciall helpe: yea, even when man thinks them past all helpe, then commeth he himselfe down from heaven with his mightie power, then is his present remedie most readie prest . . . And verely I thinke their [the Moors'] God was amased thereat: it could not be but he must blush for shame, he can speake never a word for dulnes, much lesse can he helpe them in such an extremitie. Well, howsoever it is, he is very much to blame, to suffer them to receive such a gibe" as letting Fox's gang escape so easily, for in their fury the garrisons missed the tiny galley with every shot. "But howsoever their God behaved himselfe," continues Fox in triumph, "our God shewed himselfe a God indeed, and that he was the onely living God: for the seas were swift under his faithfull, which made the enemies agast to behold them, a skilfuller Pilot leades them, and their mariners bestirre them lustily: but the Turkes had neither mariners, Pilot, nor any skilfull Master, that was in a readiness at this pinch."

I am not absolutely certain whether the pilot referred to with a capital P towards the end of this ecstatic panegyric refers to God or to Fox; but it does not matter as it is the habit of a great ruffian often to confuse the two, God and himself. He feels genuinely, without the least hypocrisy, that God is behind him, cheering him on, slapping him genially on the back. For God, remember, is always his God and never his enemy's, an inspired state of mind which with certain religious people can produce a condition similar to lunacy. There were the early Quakers, for example, who thought as missionaries to convert the Pope; there was John Robinson of the seventeenth cen-

tury who called himself God Almighty, and his contemporary John Tannaye who took the odd assortment of
titles of Priest of the Tribe of Reuben, Earl of Essex
and King of France. But most particularly there was the
tragic James Nayler, backsliding Quaker and soldier of
Cromwell's army, who suffered terribly for this confusion of God and himself, being put in the pillory and
whipped from Palace Yard to the Royal Exchange with
a knotted cat-o'-seven-tails until " there was not a Space
bigger than the Breadth of a Man's Nail free from Stripes
and Blood from his Shoulders [to] near his Waste," and
later had hot iron " near the bigness of a tobacco pipe "
pressed on his tongue as a blasphemer to imprint the
letter B: " He did not move nor shrinke," we are told,
" all the time while they did these things to him." And
these savageries were inflicted on him because, inspired
by the fanatic adoration of hysterical women, he had permitted them to lead him into Bristol, seated solemnly
on a horse, with the maenads around him shouting,
" Holy, holy, holy, Lord God of Israel! " and throwing
their wet cloaks into the mud for his horse to trample.
Nayler's own defence of this parody of Christ's entry
into Jerusalem is not very convincing: " I do abhor that
any honour due to God," he said to his accusers, " should
be given to me as I am a creature. But it pleased the Lord
to set me up as a sign of the coming of the Righteous
One. And what has been done as I passed through the
towns, I was commanded by the Lord to suffer such
things to be done by me, as to the outward, as a sign, not
as I am a creature." A rare piece of quibbling, for there
is not such vast difference between being God Himself and
so intimate a confidant of His that you know exactly
what He wishes you to do; from this the transition is
simple to pure megalomania, the belief that every act of

yours is at God's command. And whatever Nayler might say in his own vindication, he nevertheless permitted his disciple, Hannah Stringer, to address him as "The Fairest of Ten Thousand" and "The Only Begotten Son of God," and her husband wrote to him, "Thy Name shall be no more James Nayler, but Jesus;" while at his branding his followers stood about him and one of them, Robert Rich, a merchant, held a placard over Nayler's head with the words *This is the King of the Jews* inscribed upon it. No, we cannot absolve him of all blame for his disciples' frenzied adoration. After the bloody battle of Dunbar, an officer who heard him preach on September 3, 1650, wrote that "he had been inspired with greater fear by Nayler's sermon than he had felt in the battle."

These fanatics are, however, beyond real ruffianism, they are an exaggeration of the qualities that constitute a ruffian; men, too, like lean John Brown, dragging with him to their death his reluctant sons, taking them from home and families to deliberate heroic suicide to arouse the States against slavery, are ruffians beyond ruffianism, the God-complex carried to its most dangerous extremity. More delightfully is this complex expressed in a half-gibe such as used by Ethan Allen in the American War of Independence when he knocked on the gates of Ticonderoga, demanding entrance. "On whose authority?" asked the British captain. "In the name of the Great Jehovah," shouted back Allen, "and the Continental Congress."

One of the major problems we must solve in discussing the ruffian is to disassociate him from the lunatic. In what category are we to put a creature like Lope de Aguirre, for his ruffianism trespasses surely into the Hyrcynian Wood of madness, out of which we shall

never find our way? He is about fifty years of age when
we meet him; a short and lean man with small face,
black beard and gaze as piercing as a hawk's. He always
looked you sternly in the eye—I advise you to note that,
it is a common trick of the ruffian and, strangely enough,
often convinces the sucker of his innocent intentions—
and was a rowdy talker. He never unbuckled his armour
in defiance of lice and assassins, and for precaution's sake,
slept only during daylight. He set out on an expedition
to explore the Amazon under Pedro de Ursua in 1560,
but eventually mutinied and murdered Pedro, giving the
leadership to one Guzman, and then murdered Guzman.
With Pedro had sailed his mistress, the beautiful Dona
Inez de Altienza, and after killing her lover, Aguirre
decided that her mattress was too large for the boat and
killed her too. These murders, which any lout could have
committed, do not entitle Aguirre to enter Ruffians' Hall,
but his arrogance carried him to such astounding lengths
as to write an insulting epistle to the King of Spain,
stating that " I firmly believe that thou, O Christian
King and lord, hast been very cruel and ungrateful to
me and my companions for such good service, and that
all those who write to thee from this land deceive thee
much, because thou seest things from far off . . . Hear
me! O hear me! thou King of Spain. Be not cruel to
thy vassals . . . I take it for certain that few Kings go
to hell, only because they are few in number; if they
were many, none of them would go to heaven. For I
believe that you are all worse than Lucifer, and that you
hunger and thirst after human blood; and further, I
think little of you and despise you all; nor do I look
upon your government as more than a bubble of air."
When at last he found himself trapped without hope of
escape, he murdered his small daughter, shouting, " Die!

H

because I must die." He then surrendered and was immediately shot.

What is one to do with this animal—class him as insane and put him into some asylum under the patronage of the noble Hall? I confess myself uncertain, and find the neat treatise I had mapped out becoming a little unwieldy, all sorts of rogues are creeping in who apparently have no right to be there. If we exclude Aguirre, there are many others also who must be excluded with him, for the edge is so fine between ruffianism and lunacy, as between lunacy and genius, that it is often difficult to decipher it. What of men like Pierce and Cox, convicts in the early days of Australia, who used to do a bolt, taking comrades with them for commissariat to be eaten on the way, an episode handled so vividly by Marcus Clarke in *For the Term of His Natural Life*? They ate because they had to eat, not for love of killing; but if cannibalism be passport enough for Ruffians' Hall, we must also usher in that eminently respectable couple, Captain Viaud and Madame La Couture, who being shipwrecked with a negro slave off the Isle of Pines, out of sheer hunger were forced to kill and eat the unfortunate wretch. "When I looked at Madame la Couture," writes Viaud, "she turned her eyes upon the Negro; and, pointing to him, cast a look at me so full of horror, as spoke her wishes stronger than Speech could. I seemed to have waited for this encouragement. I hesitated no longer: but seizing my knotty Staff, ran at my sleeping Victim, and struck him on the head with all my force. He awoke! but so stunned, that he could not rise. My uplifted hand trembled, and refused to repeat the stroke. My heart shook within me. The unhappy Wretch was on his Knees! and with joined hands, and a terrified look, cried out, *My dear Master!*

*have I offended you? Have mercy on me! O spare my
Life!* Compassion succeeded Cruelty; my Tears fell
faster than his, and for some moments I stood motion-
less: but at length, Despair and Hunger returned; a
second groan from *Madame la Couture* completed my
Phrenzy, and I became a Monster. I fell upon my miserable Slave, pressed him to the ground; and roaring
aloud, to smother his Cries, tied his hands behind, and
called to my Accomplice to assist me in this barbarous
action. She readily obeyed my summons; and keeping
down his head, whilst I remained on his body, I drew
my knife, and buried it in his Throat; then I placed the
Carcase across a large tree, that the Blood might flow
more freely; and she assisted in this work also." Reading that isolated passage one would be inclined to push
M. Viaud neck and crop into Ruffians' Hall, yet he and
Madame la Couture were a most decorous couple: one
can imagine them half-naked in the wilds, their faces
swollen to puddings with mosquito-bites, deferentially
bowing and speaking the most perfect French and
still modestly disappearing alone under the flimsiest of
pretences to perform what are rightly called the natural
functions.

Between the brutality of M. Viaud and the barbarism
of Aguirre is a middle course that we must keep, but it is
difficult to find and is rather slippery with many an
alluring bypath to tempt one aside. The definition of
ruffian to which I set so bold a face seems now to me
as difficult as it must have looked to the makers of the
N.E.D. at whom, with the crass superiority of ignorance,
I jeered eternities ago, at the beginning of this book.
We must be so careful with each ruffian's credentials,
seeking always the motive and never being dazzled by
some splendid unique act of personal gratification or by

a murder more terrific than the average; and we must try to forget the idiotic importance that frightened man, so small beneath the stars, has placed upon his own insignificant existence: death is often a very minor thing.   In those terrible early Australian days of the convict system on Norfolk Island, it was a more or less common trick for prisoners to draw lots: he who drew the longest straw—the winner—was murdered, he drawing the next longest became executioner; while the others would be given a trip to Sydney as witnesses at the trial.   Often when told that they were condemned to death these wretched convicts, " as their names were pronounced, dropped on their knees and thanked God that they were to be delivered from that horrible place, whilst the others remained mute, weeping.   It was the most horrible scene I have ever witnessed," writes one who watched.   Men have killed from boredom.   In eighteenth-century India, British soldiers, weary of the tedium of duty in a tropic land, occasionally murdered somebody just for something to do.   One, William Beck, deposed in a trial for murder that the prisoner had said to him that " he was tired of the regiment, and would rob some men or kill some black fellow to be rid of it."   He then went out and shoved his bayonet into a passing Hindoo's stomach. Another soldier remarked that he would shoot himself or somebody else when he came off guard: he shot two palanquin boys.

Assuredly we take this nonsense about the sanctity of human life with far too much solemnity, and its destruction can be no passport for the ruffian, otherwise our Hall would be invaded by a gang of drug-crazed American gangsters, the riff-raff of Italy and Ireland, which is not to say that quite a few modern gangsters are not eligible.   At least they have taught us the real

importance of life and death. Men like the great Monk
Eastman of New York must be admitted, he and his
rival, the handsome, gentlemanly Paul Kelly of the Five
Pointers. Eastman, by the by, brings strong substantia-
tion of Dickens's comment that he was constantly perplexed by the bad company that birds keep: this trait
can be found continually when studying the lives of
criminals who quite often set up as bird-fanciers. Can
it be the symbolism of the caged pretty creature? or is
it the cold, cruel, unflickering eye of the bird, remorseless and evil, that attracts them? " I like de kits and
boids," Eastman would say. " I'll beat up any guy dat
gets gay wit a kit or a boid in my neck of de woods."
Yet he was a brutal ruffian, thief and murderer, whose
one act of refinement apparently was to slip off his
knuckle-dusters before punching a woman. Yes, these
gangsters do make death seem an infinitesimal matter,
an everyday and casual occurrence, which of course it
is. One of the most astounding revelations I have ever
come across is a book entitled *The Confessions of a
Gunman*, by Danny Ahearn. Anyone interested in
criminal psychology must read this truly appalling book
which could have been produced nowhere but in the
United States of America where you can evidently confess to a crime without anything being done about it.
Mr. Ahearn blandly tells us how he murdered a man
who had punched him in the face. " I was so mad and
scared," writes—or rather dictates—Ahearn, " I didn't
care what I did. I hit him in the mouth. I knocked
him down. When he fell over, a gun fell out of his
pocket. I picked it up and shot him three times, and
he said: ' Please, for my mother's sake.' ' Screw, kid,' I
said to my Jew friend. He screwed." Mr. Ahearn then
set to burying the body in an empty allotment nearby,

and tells how he and his friends intimidated all the witnesses until he was able to avoid execution with a faked
alibi. Truly, this is the most fascinatingly horrible book
I have ever read, and I have read a great many in my
time, sublimating my more dangerous criminal desires in
the common manner of transferring them to somebody
else in print. Whatever art of the underworld you wish
to be taught, Mr. Ahearn will give you expert advice
on the subject; even on the intricacies of how to commit
a murder with safety. "The best way to kill a man,"
he informs us, "is not to confide in anybody. Keep it
between yourself—you can't trust everybody. He might
have somebody in my own gang giving him information
that I'm looking to clip him. I would look to see where
he lives, or if he had an automobile I would put a piece
of dynamite in his starter and blow him up in his car;
or try to blow up his house. I would scene another way,
how to get a girl. I would get a broad to make him
and give him a steer for me. I would take him that
way, or else scheme him through her to give him a
walk, and when he walks with her pick him up and
throw him into a car. Take him and torture him. Find
out who is steaming him up on me. When he gives
that information, kill him. If I had trouble with a man,
wherever I would see him I would kill him. I'd take
a chance. Don't care if I burn in the chair or not.
Wouldn't care if it was in the Palace Theatre or any-
where else. The real point how to commit a murder
is always use your head and scheme a man out.
Have a little patience, and you can get him in a right
spot . . ."

It's all so delightfully simple the way that Mr. Ahearn
puts it, throwing off advice to the busy stenographer
who made shorthand notes of these confidences in a

publisher's office. Very simple indeed! I feel that Mr.
Ahearn can have his passport into Ruffians' Hall immediately, not merely for his contempt of human life,
but for the ruffianly wisdom he gives us here and there,
such profound axioms as: "Always keep your bowels
open and your mouth shut"; "Don't never trust a
cop"; "What's the use of fighting for a woman when
you can fight for money"? "Any guy with sense who
comes to you and says: 'Listen, I'll kill that guy for
you,' and he goes and kills him, you got to watch him,
because he might kill you, too." . . . Yes, you really must
read this book, for odd quotations will give no conception of the savour of the full work, a classic in its way.
Would you like to murder a woman? So many husbands have the desire, but how few have the knowledge
and the dispassionate courage of Mr. Ahearn. He says
that he " was once offered $20,000 off a man for to kill
his wife. His wife was going for every Tom, Dick and
Harry, and she was double-crossing him. I didn't want
to do that because I knew he would get a pickup, and
not knowing how he would stand with the cops. The
best way I know to do such a thing would be to drive
past with a car, pick her up, and be nice with her. Get
her to a cabaret, let her gain your confidence. Try to
induce her into an apartment. If lucky in doing so, such
women know what's the consequence. You do not have
to rape them. Be nice to her and then tell her you are
going to take her on a vacation. Take her to the moun-
tains, the two of you together. Get yourself a room in
a hotel, and every day go out to some part of the woods
and dig yourself a big, big ditch. Then every day dig
and dig until you know it is deep enough—about six
feet—and take her and tell her you will take her for a
walk through the woods, and when you reach this spot,

take her and hit her on the head and knock her on the head and kick her into the hole, which is known as a grave, and throw dirt on her and bury her alive. Before the murder, have her write a letter to her folks that she is running away, that she can't stand her husband and is going to run away . . ." But enough of Mr. Ahearn. You had best read the entire book yourself and rise afterwards at least a wiser if a slightly more frightened man, as I did when first I shut the appropriately black covers. But there is one more quotation that should be used here, an important point that I have already mentioned in the ruffian's credo and stated now authentically by one who knows what he's talking about. " I hate a woman," says Mr. Ahearn. ". . . Anybody that trusts a woman is out of his head, because they are with you to-day and when you are broke they are with someone else to-morrow. And then they fall in love—what I mean is passionate love not true, true love. I know in my own case I would never trust a woman. There's not a woman living who can say she ever heard anything from my lips. The best they can say for me is what they think. Any man that kills a woman is out of his mind. Why should he go to jail for a lousy bum, when he can go outside and pick up another one? "

This is an axiom to which most ruffians have kept very strictly, except when their world of ruffianism, as with Casanova and a few others, revolves almost entirely on sex. It is an axiom that Charles Peace might well have remembered when he hugged his pistol in the dark passageway of Banner Cross Terrace that night of November 29, 1876. Peace is an example we must not pass too briefly. In his coarse manner he exemplifies many of the ruffian qualities we are trying to disentangle; his very crudity, in truth, makes him a valuable

subject for trepanning, for it reveals in the strongest of
colours his different reactions, the peculiar mental reflexes that are called psychology.

Like so many perfect ruffians, Peace was physically
very short, being only above five feet four or five inches
tall; usually clean-shaven, with prematurely grey hair,
he had a projecting monkeyish jaw which he could twist
into the most extraordinary shapes, disguising himself so
thoroughly that he quite used to enjoy chatting with
detectives on the lookout for him, and he once actually
visited Scotland Yard and stood complacently reading
the notice offering a reward for his arrest. As a youth he
was injured in, it is said, a tinsmithy, with the result that
he became permanently a little lame and lost one or two
fingers of his left hand: these peculiarities, one might
think, would exclude him for ever from success as a
criminal, making it impossible for him to conceal his
identity. But Peace never thought so, he had a justifiable
contempt for the policeman of those days. " A policeman," he would say, " always goes by your face. He
never thinks of looking at people's hands." To cover
the missing fingers, Peace made a sheath of cloth and
wood with an iron hook attached, and this he put completely over the hand as if he had lost it to the wrist.
Instead of deterring him from crime, this accident in
1846—he was born in Sheffield on May 14, 1832—resolved him definitely on his career. " I never cared to
work after that," he said, accepting the first rule of the
ruffian, the detestation of all authority. He also soon
learned another ruffian axiom: " I believe in God," was
his credo, " and I believe in the Devil, but I don't fear
either." And a man inspired by such a faith is a very
dangerous person indeed, it is the breeding of the
old God-complex, the demanding of an equality with

heaven. Armed with such sentiments, with courage, with a slight education and ability with a revolver, with treacherous cunning and with utter contempt for all mankind, Charles Peace settled down to the lucrative profession of burglary. If he could have concentrated purely on his work, he might never have been caught, but like the true artist, he was too often deflected by emotional needs, and this weakness flawed his genius as a great ruffian. He had what is colloquially called " a dirty mind "; he was the kind of man who sniggeringly shows an innocent girl a set of pornographic postcards, or who would take pleasure in horrifying modest women by sudden gutter-phrases. A by no means congenial type of person, you will find many of his breed even to-day in the front row of a music hall training opera-glasses on pink pneumatic nudery. One of his mistresses, the most famous, his betrayer, Mrs. Thompson, tells us in her not too trustworthy *History of Peace* that " his tastes were depraved and disgusting. But there, I cannot tell you of it; it is too bad. There is one thing I will say which will give you an idea of his character at that age [his youth, although there is no reason to suppose that he altered in later life]. There was a fête at Sheffield, and for the purpose of plunder he attended it and concealed himself in the ladies' lavatory. There he had to remain the whole day, for, the place being constantly occupied, he was unable to escape without being discovered. He used to gloat over this when telling it to me." An unpleasant mind, the sort of mind that relishes not physical beauties of flesh but the physical functions of that flesh, chuckling gleefully over that natural act of Cælia's which so appalled Dean Swift. And that Peace did not lose this zest for smut in later years is shown by the statement of Mrs. Dyson to

the *Sheffield Independant* after her husband's murder,
that the quarrel between Peace and Dyson started because " Peace was plausible enough but his language was
not good; in fact, he very soon began to show that he
was anything but a gentleman.   Mr. Dyson could not
stand that, and Peace showed him some obscene pictures,
and my husband said he didn't like a man of that kind,
and wouldn't have anything more to do with him.   Besides, another thing greatly repelled Mr. Dyson.   It was
this.   Peace wanted to take him to Sheffield to show
him what he called ' the sights of the town.'   Mr. Dyson
knew what that meant, and being, as I have said, a
gentleman, he became much disgusted at Peace."   Discreet Mrs. Dyson forgot to mention to the reporter that
one of the main reasons why her husband kicked Peace
out of the house was because those very qualities which
revolted him apparently attracted her.   Despite her rather
shifty denials in the box, I feel that Peace conclusively
proved that irrelevant part of his defence: unquestionably
Mrs. Dyson was his mistress in the garret of the empty
house and received money and gifts from him.   There
are many women who are attracted by obscenity, as one
is attracted against one's will by some repulsive reptile at
the zoo, turning again and again for a second shuddering
glance, or as one longs to risk pain by putting one's
fingers too near a parrot's beak. Most normal sex reactions, after all, are vaguely ambivalent, swinging
between love and hate, desire and repulsion; that was
the deepest secret of the magus, to keep the equipoise
of the spirit between light and dark, good and evil.   In
many, the balance is lost and dips too far one way, too
far towards repulsion or desire, towards hate or love,
disgust or attraction.   Women, such as Mrs. Dyson
appears to have been, can find a masochistic delight in

surrendering to a man of the most degraded type, to a man like Peace, obscene both in conversation and appearance.

This story is no romantic one of great love, and is only worth retelling here to show how the straight line, or rather the parabolic curve, of the ruffian's life can be shifted from its course by outside emotions, and how those emotions can also merge into that life and be coloured by it. Peace should have remained content with his more or less respectable *ménage* housing a wife, children and a mistress in peculiar amity, together with innumerable musical instruments—for he loved music—and dogs, cats, rabbits, canaries, parrots and cockatoos—you will note that Peace again bears out Dickens's observation on the habits of birds. But Peace's lewd eye lighted on Mrs. Dyson, an Irish-American, living with her husband in the house next-door-but-one to his in Victoria Place, Britannia Road, Darnall, a suburb of Sheffield. While Dyson was a tall, lean, weakly man, his wife, Katherine, " though, perhaps, not what might be termed a handsome woman," was " an exceedingly fine-looking woman—tall, well-built, and robust," of about twenty-five years of age. The couple were happy enough except for the usual marital squabbles during which the husband threw things expertly at the wife and the wife showed great skill with the poker, and only on one or two occasions was it found necessary to call in the police to help settle family differences. Noting the buxom Katherine, Peace wormed his way into her home; first he " used generally to speak to Mr. Dyson on going in and out," said Mrs. Dyson. " Mr. Dyson was a gentleman, and, of course, when Peace spoke to him he used to reply." Finding that he did not succeed by this neighbourly method, Peace next put " his parrots and his other birds upon a wall. He could then call our attention to them, and to what they could do, and thus got us into conversation with him." At first, Dyson tolerated the queer little man, but then, probably suspecting an intrigue with his wife, threw a curt post-card over Peace's wall, telling him not to call again. This, however, couldn't keep the pertinacious seducer out, and he " became awfully impudent. He would, for instance, stand on the doorstep and listen through the keyhole to what we were talking about, or look through the window at us . . . He would come and stand outside the window at night and look in, leering all the while; and he would come across you at all turns and leer in your face in a manner which was really frightful . . . He had a way of creeping and crawling about, and of coming upon you suddenly unawares; and I cannot de-scribe to you how he seemed to wriggle himself inside the door, or the terrible expression on his face. He seemed more like an evil spirit than a man . . . He once said, ' I am never beaten when I have made up my mind. If I make up my mind to a thing I am bound to have it, even if it cost me my life.' " Reading these statements of Mrs. Dyson it must not be forgotten that at the time she was putting up a brave battle to defend her " honour " against the malice of Peace. When he was arrested for the murder of Dyson, he seemed more eager to prove that he had seduced Mrs. Dyson than that he was innocent of the crime, and his defence's explanation that this line was taken to discredit Mrs. Dyson's evi-dence as being untrustworthy seems very puerile; as the prosecution put it: " Even if the defence had succeeded in that direction [of proving the affair with Mrs. Dyson], would it not have suggested that there might have been jealousy on the part of the prisoner, and was not jealousy the passion that more than any other prompted men to the commission of desperate deeds?" No, Peace's vindictive hatred of Mrs. Dyson was based on some strange twist of his character and had nothing to do with the legal planning of his defence; nor can this hatred have been purely rage at her giving evidence against him, although that must partly account for it. He was blaming her, his lust for her, for his predicament. His finger had pressed the trigger of the gun, but she had been the impulse behind it; she was to blame for putting Charles Peace in this idiotic position of being badgered in a box. He had eluded the police for years, he had actually sat in court and seen two men sentenced for murder which he had committed, and now he was to be hanged because of her. She was to blame, she was the murderer, the murderer of godlike Charles Peace.

His vanity was huge. "I have been," he once said to one of his mistresses, "and my father before me, a tamer of wild animals, and I think I shall tame you, my lady." Mrs. Dyson, however, he never really did tame, she may have surrendered her body to him, but she wisely preferred the security of a lifetime with her genteel husband—to whom, Peace insisted in his rage, she was not married—to the ups-and-downs of an existence in the tyrannical Peace seraglio of women, children, musical instruments and birds. It is idiotic to pretend that Peace was in love with Mrs. Dyson, he was in love with the image of himself in her eyes; he wanted her surrender as incense to his egoism, as proof of his irresistible fascination. It was here that sex impinged on ruffianism, the point already noticed in Charles Gibbs who became temporarily a drunkard when his mistress cuckolded him; and in Casanova whose whole later life became a series of failures because of the unattained Charpillon.

It would not surprise me to know that Peace was drunk on the night he shot Dyson. Everything is very confused, and Peace himself cannot explain the motives that made him follow the fleeing Dysons from Victoria Place to Banner Cross Terrace. Already Dyson had taken out a peace summons against his persecutor who had been flourishing Mrs. Dyson's love-letters about Sheffield, and a warrant was issued for his arrest; Dyson had seen these letters, he said, and they were " most impudent forgeries," but from various details—the use of an Americanism, the irrelevancy of various remarks, likeness to Mrs. Dyson's hand—they seem genuine enough to me: that is, if these are the same letters that were produced at Peace's trial. The murder is really inexplicable. Peace said that he visited the new Dyson home to get the warrant withdrawn, but why did he take with him a loaded revolver, and why did he choose the night time? According to Mrs. Dyson's evidence, he turned up at Banner Cross on the day of their moving, conducted secretly while they thought he was in Hull; to their horror, she and her husband were accosted by the very man from whom they had fled, for he had kept a spy watching them; Peace merely remarked, " You see, I am here to annoy you wherever you go," and left them alone for about a month, when on the night of the murder he suddenly appeared at about ten minutes past eight in the evening. A passageway ran down the side of Banner Cross Terrace, at right angles to the street, Ecclesall Road, and in this passageway stood the communal closet. Mrs. Dyson was in the closet with a lantern, and on coming out, said she saw Peace standing in the darkness with a revolver in his hand. " Speak, or

I'll fire," he cried, and Mrs. Dyson promptly screamed and darted back into the closet, locking the door behind her. Then she heard her husband walking down the passageway and cautiously peeped out to see Peace fire. She heard the bullet strike the wall, then Peace fired again, and she saw her husband collapse. Peace then darted away and stood in the middle of the road, according to Mrs. Dyson, "thinking whether to fire again or not," until hearing people coming, he leaped over the wall and disappeared. Peace's defence was that he was attacked by Dyson and fired in self-defence, an argument borne out by the fact that the dead man fell on his back, which is most unnatural with a man shot from the front. Peace said that he saw Mrs. Dyson through the window putting her children to bed and gave her the familiar signals, whistling and cracking his finger-joints. " She knew the signal," he said, " and in response to it she came out and passed into the closet," which seems a very peculiar way of keeping an assignation. " If I had got that warrant withdrawn," he continued, " I should have gone away again. Mrs. Dyson became very noisy, and used fearful language and threats against me, and I got angry. I pulled out my revolver, and held it in her face, and said, ' Now, you be careful what you are saying to me. You know me of old, and know what I can do. I am not a man to be talked to in that way.' She did not heed what I said, but continued her abuse and threats, and while this was going on Mr. Dyson hastily made his appearance. As soon as I saw him I immediately started down the passage which leads to the main road. Before I could do so, Mr. Dyson seized me. I struggled to get past him. I said, ' Stand back, and let me go,' but he did not, and I then fired one barrel of my revolver wide at him to frighten him. I assure you

I purposely fired wide. I could have shot him dead at the first shot had I cared to do so, I was so near to him," which certainly seems plausible. "I made a desperate effort, wrenched the arm from him, and fired again. It was a life-and-death struggle, sir; but even then I did not intend to shoot Mr. Dyson. . . . If I had meant to murder Mr. and Mrs. Dyson, or either of them, I knew the place well enough. All I had got to do was to go to the door, walk in, and shoot them both as they were sitting."

The whole affair is so involved in lies, it is difficult to know the truth, but Peace's last argument that had he wished to kill Dyson he could have killed him in far simpler fashion has no significance. This was no business-like murder such as Mr. Ahearn would map out; Peace's vanity was badly hurt and he needed melodrama to assuage it. Always he liked to strut. "You know what I can do!" he cries, or at least says he cries—which is the same thing—to Mrs. Dyson. That he went deliberately to kill, I do not believe, but I think it possible that he went with the vague intention of creating a scene, of perhaps again seducing Mrs. Dyson and thus recovering his power over her—his pride being rehabilitated by the act—and if necessary of killing her or Dyson. He had already got clean away with one murder, and the ruffian's arrogance is such that he takes little heed of consequences, having complete faith in God or luck, which are often synonymous terms. Whatever Peace's real intentions may have been, the episode gives us an excellent glimpse of the lower-grade ruffian in amorous mood and shows the distinction between this kind of lover and the pure ruffian-lover such as Casanova. To Casanova, every fresh woman was an adventure, an uncharted body, a mysterious spirit for his

I

curious and excited explorations; those who jeer at him
as a petty philanderer should remember that he loved
each of these women passionately and was prepared for
the moment to sacrifice everything for their sakes, and
often did sacrifice his whole rich future. He did not
only take, he gave, and he gave magnificently with all
his being; to any woman with normal passion, a week
with Casanova would compensate for any sorrow, would
equal the lifetime lovemaking of an ordinary man. But
Peace was the more common ruffian to whom sex was
but a pastime—to Casanova, the opposite was truth: the
other aspects of ruffianism, cheating and swindling, and
such, being to him the pastimes beside his all-consuming
interest in women—and therefore when the pastime
began to get out of proportion Peace strove crudely to
put it in its proper place with the aid of the only weapon
he knew, a gun. Somehow he managed to keep order
in his house with a placid wife and a mysterious mistress,
Mrs. Thompson. When resident at Peckham, his wife
was known as Mrs. Ward and lived in the basement,
while Mrs. Thompson and himself lived upstairs in
state as Mr. and Mrs. Peace, an astounding arrangement,
which would have made poor Shelley envious, he was
so puzzled when his wife Harriet threw herself into the
river because he wrote suggesting that she stay with him
as his sister while Mary Godwin lived with him as wife.
How Peace controlled such an establishment is, to me,
little short of miraculous, but he must have had his
wife completely terrified, while Mrs. Thompson, a pretty
woman with masses of fair hair and light brown eyes,
probably didn't care a damn so long as Peace gave
her enough shillings to keep her acquiescently drunk.
Having handled these two women, and probably many
others, with such ease, suddenly Peace found himself

faced with the hard determination of the Irish-American, Mrs. Dyson. She took money and jewellery from him, had drinks at his expense in public houses, chalking them up in his name, and more than likely permitted him in return to share her body with her husband, but she never gave to him that surrender of the spirit which his consuming vanity would demand. He had to prove to her his power, and he showed it in the weak man's manner, with a gun, like some cheap modern gangster. Peace stands as a warning to all ruffians to remember Mr. Ahearn's advice that any man who murders a woman is "out of his mind." Peace was temporarily out of his mind, his ruffian-vanity being hurt.

In other ways, he was the perfect ruffian, keeping to the end his vast ego unsoiled. Even the fact that he confessed to the previous murder of a policeman and thereby freed the man condemned for the crime, fits in with his character: [1] this was not an act of generosity, it was the same mood that would inspire an artist to claim his work if he saw it attributed to a rival painter. His attempt at suicide, too, was brave—or was it an effort to escape?—wishing to avoid the sordid futility of a trial that was a foregone conclusion. On the way from London to Sheffield, he very cunningly exasperated the detectives by disappearing into a public lavatory at every station; at Peterborough, for example, they had had so much trouble with him that they had practically to

---

[1] There was nothing miraculous in Peace getting away with this murder: the wrongfully condemned man, William Habron, would have been convicted by any court to-day. Habron had publicly sworn to murder the policeman, his boots fitted into prints beside the corpse, he possessed cartridges similar to the one extracted from the body, and he used two different alibis in court. Peace's confession released Habron after eight years in jail and brought him £800 compensation. It was a most damning case against him and makes one further plea for the abolition of the barbaric revengeful death sentence, for the man was indeed lucky not to have been hanged, as many an innocent person has suffered beyond question.

throw him back into the train. To escape this incon-
venience of dodging in and out of lavatories, the detectives bought a pile of paper bags and grimly told their
prisoner that he'd have to use them in future, which
gave Peace the opportunity he wanted of getting the
window open. When near to Darnall, he threw out a
bag, and threw himself after it; but one detective grabbed
at his foot, and Peace hung suspended until the boot
came off and flung him to the ground rushing past.
Surprisingly, he was not killed, although he made a
great deal of fuss about his injuries so as to postpone
the trial. During his two trials, he behaved with majestic
truculence. "I have seen a great deal of injustice done
in different Courts," he growled at one stage, "but I am
not going to have injustice done here," exactly as if he
were master of ceremonies and not merely the creature
whom they were determined to hang. On another
occasion he made a mighty fuss, damaging his own case,
because a witness said that she had recognised him when
in fact he had been disguised during the time she saw
him. They tried to stop him from speaking, but he was
most indignant at such an insult. "I beg your pardon,
sir," he cried pompously, "but my life is at stake, and I
am going to vindicate my character as well as I can.
If you don't want me to speak, put a gag in my mouth.
When I hear a person perjuring herself I will speak. I
wish to say it openly and in Court that up to the time
when this woman saw me in Newgate I had disfigured
my face so as not to be known. I was not then known
as Charles Peace, and I had disfigured my face, so that
I had deceived all the detectives in London. My face was
disfigured when this woman saw me." "It was merely
for your own sake," said the stipendiary, "I told you not
to speak." "I am bound to speak when I hear wrong

statements," snarled Peace. Aye! even if they hanged
him for it, he was not going to have it said that a fool
of a woman had seen through his disguise after it had
deceived all the detectives in London! There speaks the
authentic ruffian who will die to keep his professional
reputation intact, his genius unsmirched. He made a
good end, like a true ruffian assured of his own salvation, God being the God of ruffians. Just before he was
to be hanged, Peace heard hammering in the prison.
" That's a noise that would make some men fall on the
floor," he remarked complacently; " they are working
at my scaffold," and he became quite indignant and refused to believe them when they told him that he was
mistaken. After writing a collection of pious letters, he
ate a good breakfast on his final morning and complained
about the quality of the bacon, then he said to a warder,
" I wonder if Marwood [the hangman] would cure this
cough of mine? " In his usual fashion, he over-stayed
his time in the lavatory, and when they started banging
at the door, growled irritably, " You're in a hell of a
hurry; are you going to be hanged or am I? " After
which he contentedly smoked his clay pipe for the last
time, asked Marwood not to " punish " him, and said,
" I hope to meet you all in heaven. I am thankful to
say my sins are all forgiven." Without protest, he allowed
the executioner to fix around his waist the usual leather
belt to which his arms would be strapped, and calmly he
walked the eighty yards to the scaffold in the prison-yard—
a six-foot high platform with a pit beneath. Marwood was
about to slip the white cap over the murderer's head when
Peace stopped him, for he wished to hear the chaplain
finish the service. " Stop a minute! " he cried; " I must
hear this." A moment later, Marwood again came forward with the cap. " No, no! " shouted Peace, " I want to

speak, and thereupon delivered a noble homily to the press, rich with the most Christian ethics. Marwood had waited patiently until Peace had finished, then once more he approached with the white cap, and for the first time we glimpse fear in Peace, realisation of his imminent death. "Almighty God," he groaned, "have mercy upon me;" then he added in a louder voice, "I should like to have a drink." None answered, only the chaplain's voice snuffled on: "In the midst of life we are in death . . ." "Can't I have a drink?" whined Peace, trembling a little, then feeling the rope about his neck, he cried, "Oh, it's too tight, it's too tight!" "Keep still," said Marwood gently, "I won't hurt you a bit." The chaplain was droning, "I am the resurrection and the life," when Peace cried, "God bless you . . . good-bye!" as Marwood pulled the string which released the bolt, and the trapdoor sprang open. He died without a struggle on February 25, 1879, at the age of forty-seven.

We have devoted quite a large space to Charles Peace, but he thoroughly deserves it; we will find few more complete examples of the simple ruffian, so secure in his own cunning, so able at his profession, so calm before a violent death because he is convinced that he is one of God's chosen, and so quick to defend his honour, to prove himself a master at disguise and an irresistible seducer, in all ways the superior of others. What would have been his reactions had he known that boozy, pretty Mrs. Thompson had put in her claim for the £100 reward because of information about him which she had given the police? He probably would have refused to believe it, for the ruffian wears protective armour to shield his easily bruised vanity. Only against the indomitable heart of Mrs. Dyson did Peace fail, but he could have consoled himself with the thought that many

greater ruffians than he have been destroyed by women
—although undoubtedly he would have rejected with
imperious indignation the bare suggestion that there ever
had been a greater ruffian since Cain, that child of Eve
and some dark incubus.

Yet others, too, men remorseless in their ambitions,
have found themselves suddenly open to weakness because of a woman's smile, because of an unexpected
tenderness chafing their cold hearts: Benedict Arnold,
for example . . .

VI

Benedict Arnold

"The Dark Eagle comes to claim the wilderness. The wilderness will yield to the Dark Eagle, but the Rock will defy him. The Dark Eagle will soar aloft to the sun. Nations will behold him and sound his praises. Yet when he soars highest his fall is most certain. When his wings brush the sky then the arrow will pierce his heart." Those had been the words of Natanis, the Indian chief who had secretly helped to guide the Americans through the New England wilderness from Cambridge to Quebec on their heroic senseless invasion of Canada in 1775. He had watched the little army struggle forward, and had been amazed by the courage and calm endurance of these mad white men, and when he realised that their scouts had become confused, he left a birch-bark map in a stake to show the route. At first they had distrusted Natanis, but their courage won his friendship. In buckskin breeches, wearing leggings and moccasins, in loose jackets fringed at skirt, cuff and collar, with fur caps on their dirty heads or with felt hats pinned up at one side by a cockade, with axes, swords, knives and tomahawks in their belts, and lugging guns and accoutrement, barrels of flour and pork, tents, oars, poles and many tools, the Continental army of less than two thousand men strode as casually into the wilderness as if they walked the streets of their home-towns. Well might Natanis wonder at such superb insanity and at last find courage enough to steal to the white leader and read his future in that dark face with the bright blue eyes and firm prominent jaw. This Dark

Eagle's true name was Benedict Arnold, as yet an unknown Connecticut soldier who at various times had been
a West Indian trader, a chemist, a dealer in cattle and
horses with Canada, and only once before had essayed this
profession of the sword. He had been but a lad then,
fifteen, when he had fled from home to join the troops
at Norwich in the Old French War; sent back, he
scuttled off again immediately and followed the soldiers
on their long march to Albany and the Lakes. But he
was considered too young as yet to kill the French and
they gave him a bag of parched corn and a flintlock and
sent him off to a likely death in the wilderness. But
the wilderness could not kill young Arnold. Alone he
tramped from Lake George to Connecticut, a braver exploit than any battle with the French could have been.

He had always longed to become a soldier, hating his
stuffy shop of drugs and books under the motto painted
on his sign, *Sibi Totique*—For himself, for all. His
fingers crooked more readily around a sword-grip or a
flintlock-trigger than around the marble pestle or the
bleeding-irons. Only by duelling could he consummate
this desire to kill in proof of honour. There had been
that British merchant captain, Croskie, in the Bay of
Honduras who had asked Arnold aboard his ship for a
drinking-night, but Arnold was too busy smuggling to
attend and too troubled by risks of capture to remember
to send Croskie an apologetic note, with the result that
next day Croskie damned him as a " Yankee, destitute
of good manners or those of a gentleman." In the
morning, on an island in the bay, the two met, Britisher
and Yankee; and firing first, the Britisher missed; but
Arnold did not miss. His ball slightly wounded Croskie,
and he calmly said that he was still prepared to take his
turn and face the pistol again. Croskie quickly apologised

. . . Being a stout family man, as alert to defend his sister's honour as he was his own, Arnold noted a gay young Frenchman who had the amorous presumption to call twice. Such impudence demanded honourable reparation, so the two fought in the dark but, because they were in the dark, the Frenchman cleared off unhurt and Arnold remained secure in the comforting knowledge of his sister's essential chastity. And she loved him for it, always Hannah loved Benedict through the difficult years that were to come, tending his three sons after his first wife died in 1775.

His long struggle for recognition, battling against envy and his own military insignificance, never once daunted Arnold, he was so certain of his genius. When Britain forced America to fight, he was as eager to take down sword and gun for his country as once he had been to use them on the French in Canada.

In scarlet coats faced with buff, in white breeches and leggings, with cockaded caps, a trim little army of about sixty men swore to follow him to Boston where help was needed. But the select men of the town would not give them powder. Colonel Wooster strove to soften Arnold's rage, suggesting that he wait like a soldier for regular orders. "Regular orders be damned," cried Arnold; "none but the Almighty God will prevent me marching!" and he gave the select men exactly five minutes in which to produce powder enough. It was given him well within time, for there was that about this dark young man with the fierce blue eyes and powerful jaw that warned you that to disobey was not only useless but dangerous. Then with his little troop Arnold set out to save America.

He was never quite certain how the idea developed. Looking back, it would seem that he had always been possessed by it, that it had been his spur from the very beginning of the war. That others, Allen's Green Mountain Boys, for example, were inspired by the same ambition was, of course, merely a coincidence. Arnold always remained absolutely certain that the plan was entirely his, this plan of invading Canada. It appeared an absurd adventure to many Continentals unable to understand the necessity of fighting the British on their own ground; let the British strike south, it was said, let them be met here, and defeated here on American soil. But Arnold and many others would have none of that craven wait-and-be-killed talk. Destroy the British power in the north, they insisted, take Ticonderoga, even Quebec—then Canada, they believed, would automatically join its southern comrades in this war for Independence. Besides, there was that Quebec Act of 1774 which gave liberty for Catholic worship. To the average Colonial, bred on crabbed Puritan text books, this Act seemed diabolic, something that all instinctively must loathe, failing in their Protestant enthusiasm to remember that Canada was mainly French. No! they felt quite certain that at the first approach of the Continental army, saviours of religious as well as political liberty, the Canadians, itching beneath this insulting Roman Catholic act, would pull their guns from the rack and slaughter all priests and tyrannical British.

But Arnold had to chafe under a muddled administration before he could have his way and travel north. He managed at last to bluff a commission and a little money from the Massachusetts Committee of Safety and was then sent on the tiresome work of recruiting. This work however was necessary, for in this vast disorganised country it was impossible to recognise embryo military merit in tradesmen and farmers; commissions were therefore offered mainly to those who could gather enough men under their command in medieval fashion. Then before the unknown Arnold could get his troops together he heard the appalling news that he had been forestalled; although he was a colonel with official orders to take Ticonderoga, he yet discovered that Ethan Allen with his Green Mountain Boys had set out on that very adventure. Arnold bothered no longer about recruiting, he left two lieutenants to carry on the work, while he spurred after Allen, indignantly clutching his commission, and arrogant with his three days' old colonelcy. Allen, a giant of a man, merely grinned at Arnold's scrap of paper when he ordered him to surrender his command; he told him to take his servant and show the commission to Ticonderoga; "See if they'll lay down their arms for you!" he jeered. This was Arnold's first rebuff and in his huge pride he writhed beneath it. Damn it, he had been given the command; and the fact that Allen had gathered the men was, in Arnold's eyes, of no importance beside his own official and divine rights. Alone of these stupid Colonials, he knew that he was bred for immortal deeds, for the salvation of his country; if they would only give him the chance to prove it! . . . But Allen, a man who could crumple twopenny nails between his teeth, just hunched his brows and grinned at the impetuous Arnold striving to pluck his men away from him. And Arnold, rather than lose all prospect of glory, stifled his rage at last and begged to join the Cambridge army at least as volunteer. Allen could not refuse and reluctantly he let the young upstart enter the ranks, permitting him to keep his title but not allowing him to give orders. Ticonderoga, defended by a small force, fell with little bloodshed, and although Arnold had been in the front of the fight, he remained

BRIGADIER GEN.ᴸ ARNOLD.

still obscure, unhonoured, and he knew if he was given
the opportunity, he would prove to all the world that,
not only brutes like Allen, but even Washington himself
was his inferior. So he waited, watching Allen; ready to
grab the first chance to topple the giant aside and steal
his troops. He scowled to himself, having no consolation
but the pen with which he recorded all the damned
impertinences of Allen who, ignoring that magnificent
colonelcy, had for four days not bothered even to discuss
plans with Arnold, leaving him to sulk alone as " a
private person, often insulted by him and his officers,
often threatened with my life and twice shot at by his
men with their fusees." His situation became intolerable
and with abrupt anger he posted his resignation to the
Provincial Congress. This was only a threat, he never
intended to desert so mighty a stage as war, but his sense
of his own frustrated genius had in some way to find
an outlet, had at least to threaten if it could not act.
Then Arnold's luck suddenly changed. Lieutenant
Oswald, whom he had left recruiting in Massachusetts,
arrived with fifty men, having captured on the way a
schooner owned by a British Agent. Arnold instantly
wrote to the Committee of Safety, extolling his own
commendable zeal in seizing the ship, boasting that he
would now capture a sloop of which he'd heard, and
doubling the number of his men to a hundred. " I have
done everything in my power," he wrote, " and put up
with many insults to preserve the peace and serve the
public. I hope soon to be released from this troublesome
business." Already, that resignation was forgotten; he
had men of his own now to lead, and he was a colonel;
even when he set out for Crown Point and found that
Allen had already captured it, his self-importance did
not lessen, but he was cunning enough to smile genially

at Allen while he suggested a combined attack on St.
Johns farther up the lake and close to Montreal. In his
ship, *Liberty*, he set out on the adventure, Allen sailing
and rowing with him in hastily built bateaux. The garrison at St. Johns was easily taken, and Allen, thrilled
by his continual success, swore now to capture St. Johns
settlement as well. The impetuous Arnold for once
restrained his own impetuosity, for he realized that this
task was beyond even their united means. Nevertheless,
he made no attempt to dissuade Allen, he even lent him
supplies and, smirking, saw the reckless giant sail and
row towards inevitable failure. Then he sat down and
wrote to the Committee of Safety, explaining how he
had tried futilely to stop Allen; but he did not send the
letter immediately, he put it aside lest fate should betray
him by some monstrous freak and let Allen succeed.
Fate being obedient to its servant, Arnold, Allen was
fittingly punished by having his force almost blown to
pieces, and the letter was quickly on its way and Arnold
became temporarily his own master. He tackled the
situation at Ticonderoga with frenzied energy, gathering
stores and ammunition and whatever else he could lay
his hand on. Then hearing that the defeated Allen was
in conference with two other officers, Elmore and
Easton, at Crown Point, he hurried there, organised a
council of his own and commanded the three to attend,
which naturally they did not bother to do. Their contempt Arnold denounced as mutiny, and when that evening Allen tried to sail by the recently captured sloop
Enterprise, passes were demanded, and on their not
being produced, he was marched to Arnold's quarters.
Colonel Easton, maddened by all this senseless battling
for position, suddenly rushed into Arnold's room with
drawn sword and was instantly hit on the head and

kicked out when he refused to fight according to gentlemanly rules. Yet, no matter how many letters he wrote,
how determined he was to be made commander-in-chief,
Arnold was again ignored, Connecticut appointing Allen
captain of Ticonderoga; then in Allen's place it appointed
a Colonel Hinman whom Arnold insulted on sight of
his credentials, still refusing to bow to any authority but
his own. Finding that conspiracies, threats of resignation and brawlings about precedence did not seem .to
advance him very far, Arnold decided on action and
worked out a plan for capturing St. John and Montreal.
But Congress took not the slightest notice, it gave the job
of conquering Canada to General Philip Schuyler who
was so impressed by Arnold's suggestions that he wanted
him made Deputy-Adjutant-General of the New York
forces. Again Congress did not listen: apparently it
rather suspected Arnold. Then Allen, all on his own
buccaneering judgment, assaulted Montreal and was
promptly captured and shipped to England. Fate again
had come to Arnold's rescue, taking from the game the
most violent of his enemies, but at the same time it dealt
him a dirty card. Whispers had reached Congress about
his rule at Ticonderoga, there was talk of stores
gathered that had mysteriously disappeared, and a commission was sent to investigate, and it had the powers to
arrest Arnold should his alleged peculations be proved.
Such distrust knocked Arnold into terrific furies. He
disbanded his troops and resigned his command, and
when the investigating committee tried to entice his men
back to the colours, they were fired on. And in the midst
of all these uproars, Arnold had news of his wife's
death ... He was fighting immaterial opponents, struggling with inexplicable enmities that he could not drag
into the open. A bullet in a vacuum, he could but rage

and seek a non-existent target. Fully aware of his own predestined greatness, he was continually maddened by the indifference of a Congress that merely asked with treacherous politeness for details of his accounting at Ticonderoga. The country's base ingratitude sent Arnold in impotent rage upon his horse and galloping for Cambridge where Washington was biting his nails over plans to invade Canada. On paper such a venture looked feasible enough, but Washington fully realised all the dangers, the battle with the wilderness to be waged before the battle of armies could be fought; he knew little of his officers, his men were untrained, Congress had no definite mind, being but a confusion of politicians running in circles of terror, and almost in despair he wondered whom of all those around him he could trust. Arnold was as yet but the name of an insolent untried soldier, suspected of peculation and known only as an arrogant, swaggering rogue defying authority. At that moment, while Washington and Schuyler puzzled over the Canadian idea, Arnold was arguing for his honour amongst zigzagging figures on reams of paper. He did not convince Congress, nor did he convict himself, and reluctantly the charges were dropped and he was granted a miserly sum, less than a thousand dollars, when he had demanded and expected at least two thousand. And on top of all this, fate twisted him into bed with a swingeing attack of gout; and lying in pain and despair he learned that he was to have no part in the Canadian invasion, his treasured dream, the plan that he practically considered his personal property, his as if by some divine right. He dragged himself to his tortured feet and sought out Washington. Schuyler had already sailed for Canada but he would need reinforcements: Arnold offered to follow by way of the Maine wilder-

ness to the very heights of Quebec. Now that he was
dealing with a soldier and not with a pack of suspicious
politicians who could not soar beyond material matters
like irregular figures on pieces of paper, Arnold's magic
worked for the first time. Washington listened, he was
impressed by the determined spirit of this dark man,
by the fury in his blue eyes, by the strength of the jaw,
and the quickness of his mind. Arnold got the job.

Fate threw this chance into his hands, for fate will
always offer to her favourites one opportunity that must
be seized; she is a woman and is insulted when her
favours are ignored, who gives when she is assaulted and
defied, spurning those who whine for her caresses, surrendering always to the ravisher. Men like Benedict
Arnold, men who demand all and who give all to attain
their purpose, such are the darlings of capricious destiny;
yet when their spirit weakens, when they falter and
doubt their august purpose, she withdraws coldly and
leaves them to miserable failure or to death. Arnold
never questioned his greatness, he considered life as booty
that must surrender everything to his superb braggadacio,
and now that he had attained his ambition, this invasion
of Canada, he was quite gay again, reckless and assured
of victory. Yet it was an adventure that few would have
dared risk, a march through unexplored forests, over
lands that even Indians might avoid, so fever-stricken
the mushy earth, so confused the paths, so rare the pro-
vender. One thousand one hundred and seventy men
were to carry food and armaments through unknown
wilderness and even when reaching the end of their
journey, they were to fight to win a city so impregnable
that it had appalled even Wolfe with his disciplined
men and the strength of Britain at his command. These
Continentals, massing before Cambridge, knew what

K

they had to face yet did not flinch before its terror; there were woodsmen amongst them, Indian fighters, frontiersmen; Dan Morgan's company of sharpshooters who, it was claimed, could hit a seven-inch mark at three hundred yards at the run, knew fully all the malevolence of nature untamed—perils from animals at night and the menace of the silent Indian. Morgan was a giant, a hero; he had served with the British and, having once received, it was said, the incredible amount of five hundred lashes for knocking down an impudent officer who had hit him with the flat of the sword, he was now eager for revenge. Amongst the other leaders were men who would be remembered by their country, some like Aaron Burr and Charles Lee for dubious but arguable reasons; and there was also General Wooster with whom Arnold had quarrelled about the powder in Connecticut. That quarrel was now revived, for from Wooster came the news of Arnold's ship. A dirty rumour, raged Arnold, even though it be true; it was obviously only coincidence that a ship of his should be on her way to Quebec and liable to be impounded by the British if the Continentals could not get there in time to rescue her. A dirty rumour indeed, such as were to chase Arnold all his life, despite his frenzied denials, his furies of outraged innocence and appeals to honour.

On September 11, 1775, the army set out for Newburyport, north of Boston, where eleven schooners waited to sail the men over the first easy lap of their adventure; on the 15th, Arnold followed with instructions from Washington and with a ponderous proclamation to be delivered to the Canadians, calling on them to fight the British who " oppress them, and make them pay a great price for their rum." Fort Western was the real starting point, and from there Arnold sent ahead nine picked woodsmen to blaze a trail, with two guides. After the trail-blazers, went Morgan to build a road; then Colonel Green with three companies of sharpshooters, followed by Colonel Enos taking provisions and accoutrement. Arnold worked gaily, unhampered by authority, at last entirely his own master. That vanity of his, suppressed so long by acts of Congress, made of him now a little hero in Fort Western, organising, inspiring. Others found delight in more simple pleasures: handsome, amorous Aaron Burr, gay fondler of wenches, for example, discovered a Pocohontas in an Indian lass called Jacatequa, and with her help he conjured a glorious feast for the men. Jacatequa was to prove useful later, for she travelled with the soldiers, helping them, guiding them with her Indian intelligence, half-animal in the woods.

At last, into the silent forest marched the full army, into an unknown world, cheerily, assured because of their courage of ultimate success. And they found that the earth squelched under boots and moccasins, that it was not always solid but could turn to a vicious muck dragging at their heels; they had to use their swords, not on enemy-flesh, but against the tenacious grip of creepers, to mow down rushes and keen-edged grass; suddenly land would go as if sliced away by some tremendous axe and they would crawl to the jagged edges of a precipice to see before them an unbroken undulating expanse of trees like innumerable dark puff-balls swaying through the valleys; they found that rivers were shallow and choked with muck, that nature seemed set upon frustrating them, laying uprooted trees in their path, suddenly tumbling a placid river over sharp rocks into a rapid. And the boats, those hastily built bateaux, had been constructed of green wood through which the water soaked every second so that they had continually to be re-caulked. The men cursed those boats, they damned as murderers the rogues who had fashioned them; panting, the tired rowers dropped their oars and leaped out to kick against the current, to tumble over hidden weeds or catch their toes in crevices, while the boats gently seeped and seeped as if they were of sponge. Again and again, boats were lifted from the water, heavy cargoes unroped and dried, while the caulkers set once more to work. Yet Arnold rarely lost his smile, he was prepared always for a jest, and never once did a flicker of discouragement show in those bright eyes or slacken the firm mouth. The bustling arrogant little colonel without a company had become a gallant cheerful woodsman, working shoulder to shoulder with his men, making a mockery of despair and all difficulties. Shivering with the cold, massaging bellies swollen with naught but wind and little food, at night the men lay down to be struck instantly into heavy slumber, but always dawn and the smile of the leader brought laughter back to their lips, and courage to their hearts. Each mile had to be fought as if against a stubborn enemy, and it seemed indeed to these exhausted men that nature of deliberate malice strove to hold them back; with that maddening persistence of inanimate things, branches struck at their faces, leaves switched their eyes, while roots and fallen trees waylaid them. Week after week, through seemingly endless forest, struggled the Continental army until men swore they could not walk another step yet staggered on.

The nine scouts sent ahead to blaze a trail would have been lost and probably none would have reached Canada had not the watchful Indian Natanis placed the birch-bark map for them to find. They knew the route now, but they were starving, and were so tired that it was agony for them to put one foot before the other, yet never once did they dream of surrendering to this silent forest. At last, on October 7, they reached a mighty pine towering without a branch for forty feet. Around its foot they sat, wondering if they could ever summon strength enough to scale its unbroken surface, for they realized that from such a height they would be able to see for miles. One of them, tall Robert Cunningham, offered to attempt the climb if they would give him extra food, and his eight famished comrades doled out their rations. Somehow, bravely, he managed the feat while, with held breath, the others from the ground watched his gradual ascent, the long-limbed figure clinging like a monkey to the wood, swaying and rising in slow jerks. From that height Cunningham could dimly make out the river flowing for fifteen miles into the vast Lake Chaudiere that emptied eventually into the St. Lawrence, near Quebec. The goal was close, and excitedly the nine struggled back only to be caught in a violent storm: they sprawled in puddles, thrashed by the rain, they were nearly frozen under drifting sleet. Yet slumber came to them, so exhausted were they that even hunger and cold could not keep minds and bodies alert. Eventually they stumbled back to where Morgan and his gang toiled to build a makeshift road. Arnold had paddled up in an Indian canoe and was working with Morgan who was dark with his own blood after fighting thorns and tearing his hands on wood.

Rains fell and turned the earth to mush, and snow and sleet followed the rains, flecking with white the dark trees, bleeding colourlessly upon the unwashed faces and torn clothes of these indomitable invaders of Canada. Then hurricanes whirled down, widdershining over the skyline, upflinging trees like splinters, shrieking as if they were huge clouds of wasps. Arnold was forced to build a hospital, so many were the sick; two hundred and fifty already had died, mostly from exhaustion, just falling, unable to rise against the drowsy bonds of weariness and hunger that tied them to the ground. A gigantic storm swirled on them, it lifted the river ten feet in a night; scarred, foaming, with snapped trees and driftwood, the water tossed the clumsy bateaux like toys, spilling men with their precious cargoes, dragging them to death by drowning or smashing them against the ragged spines of submerged rocks. Arnold sent messages to friends in Quebec—his one stupid act, for the notes were intercepted by the British who thereby for the first time discovered that the enemy was close. He also posted some men to the rear to get provisions from Lieutenant-Colonel Enos's troop. And here his luck did not hold, for Enos had deserted, taking with him not only his men but more than his share of food. They courtmartialled him for it when he reached Cambridge; as all witnesses, however, were for the moment in Canada, he was acquitted, but ruined, as Washington never forgave him or trusted him again. Unaware of this disaster, Arnold built a house to contain Enos's expected supplies, then dashed forward to lead his army. Starved, almost frozen, fighting their way through trackless woods, through continual storms, it seemed that the soldiers were doomed, yet never once did anxiety show in Arnold, always he was gay, confident, and the men watched him with loving admiration, relying on him as one would upon a god. Such is true leadership, that quickening inspiration which can lift dying men to their feet, which can inflame a dozen to charge an army; this fervid concentration of hope riveted in one man, in the leader, Benedict Arnold. To see him there, the dark face flushed with pride and determination none would have recognised the petulant colonel of a few months back. Even his despatches to Washington showed continual courage, no hint of despair, never a complaint, not even justified rage when he learned of Enos's retreat. He merely apologised for the time he had taken on the march, explaining it with airy references to the hardships endured, but with no arrogance, no self-pity. Now stood Arnold in all his greatness, a truly noble, a magnificent figure.

Even when Canada was reached, starvation was not ended. They settled down to finish their scanty supplies in a fierce snowstorm, each man being given five pints of flour from which could be baked five cakes under hot ash. Then they slept only to wake up buried beneath inches of snow that crumbled squeaking off them when they threw aside their blankets and thawed their gluey eyelids. Roots were dug up whenever found and were eaten raw, men fighting for a bite as if for some dainty; the two dogs that had accompanied the expedition now sustained a few of the men as soup; leather breeches were broiled, anything that even looked edible was wolfed, only afterwards to torment an empty belly. Starvation pinched at the men so that while they marched they slid continually from the ranks and tumbled into the snow to freeze to death; and Arnold, masking whatever fears he might have felt, yet smiled and strove to bring spirit to the exhausted. But food was necessary, and in desperation, with ten men, he set out in canoes along the tricky rushing Chaudiere with its hidden rocks and unexpected rapids. The water flung them along, jerking them forward at a pace of about ten miles an hour; so furious was the going that three canoes were splintered against the rocks and six men just managed to swim to safety through the villainous current. Yet this accident was their salvation, destiny once again put forth a hand to aid her master, brushing his canoes towards the rocks, for just ahead of them rushed a great uncharted water-fall that would have flung them inevitably to death. With four men, on land, Arnold continued his explorations until he reached an encampment eighty miles from the lake. At sight of these unshaven emaciated men coming so suddenly from the wilderness, the Canadians fled in terror, unable to believe that anything human could have marched so far from the south. Slowly, however, they returned, slowly they realised that these were actually starving men and not devils, and in the morning driving cattle and carrying flour, Arnold hurried back to his army. With food at last to quicken their limbs, the Continental troops marched into Canada, a half-blind drummer-boy rat-tatting before them.

The worst was over, there was only fighting ahead, and that was the task these men had set out to perform, one for which they longed. And soon the army was on its way to Point Levi on the St. Lawrence opposite its objective, the city of Quebec upon its rock; at this point, on December 13, Arnold reviewed his tattered troops. That night he sailed and rowed with them over the river, adroitly avoiding British patrols. It was not until the men had landed that the enemy discovered what had taken place, for a fire was built at which to dry wet clothes and warm life into half-frozen limbs. A patrol-boat saw the glare, came close, and was fired upon. No longer was there cause for concealment, as the moon cut its way through the clouds, outlining all in brilliant violet, the Continentals raised their ladders to the cliff and scaled the sharp defiles until they stood upon the Heights of Abraham where Wolfe had died.

Arnold had no spies and therefore he knew nothing of the city's. defences, otherwise he could have taken it easily, for the commander, Colonel McLean, was a skimpy-hearted wretch quaking at sight of the desperate Colonials lined up before the walls of his Quebec. But Arnold waited, distrusting the inviting gates, the silence from within; he dared not attack without reinforcements from Montgomery who had superseded Schuyler. He contented himself therefore with staying quietly outside the walls while his quick-eyed men potted at any Britisher incautious enough to let even an inch of himself be seen. Besides, his ammunition was running dangerously low, it. was down to five rounds a man, and at last, with reluctance, he withdrew to a point twenty miles above Quebec for he had had news that Sir Guy Carleton, Governor of Canada, was approaching with reinforcements. He had acted wisely, scarcely was he encamped at Point Aux Trembles than the guns told him of Carleton's arrival; had he stayed, without question his gallant army would have been destroyed at a blow. It was not in Arnold's nature to turn from a fight, his was the spirit that prefers death to the faintest whisper of cowardice, but he stilled the urge for battle in his heart, even when his demands for the city's surrender were met by an insult unforgivable in war. His envoy with the white flag was twice fired upon. But Arnold's supplies were frighteningly low, and a British attack would have brought disaster, for his men could have put up only a puny defence. Growing impatient at Montgomery's delay, Arnold sent young handsome Aaron Burr to him with a dispatch. Burr managed the dangerous mission, and soon Montgomery with three hundred men was at Arnold's side on Point Aux Trembles. But the lack of men was well compensated for by supplies of food and powder, besides, Indians and a few Canadians had now joined the Continentals, so that altogether Arnold could muster roughly a thousand men. He dared not delay the attack, for the heavy winter was coming swiftly, snow was thickening, and, at two o'clock in the morning of the last day of 1775, in a heavy storm the long awaited assault began on those strong walls guarded by two hundred cannon and a great disciplined British force.

It was a magnificent but hopeless attempt. Montgomery was shot down at the very start, and his men retreated; Arnold was tumbled over with a musket-ball in his left leg and carried off the field; Morgan, the one remaining officer, was trapped in narrow streets. Defiant, weeping, his back to the wall, he stood at bay, alone. He would not surrender his sword; he would not surrender it to these detested British who once had flogged him near to death, although his own officers and men implored his surrender. "Shoot!" he yelled when a squad of British lined up before him, muskets at the shoulder, "Shoot!" Then, noticing a priest, he offered him the sword, saying, "No scoundrel or coward will take it from me. I'll give it to you." He was not the only American to show such splendid foolish courage on that day. Lying in hospital, Arnold cursed when his men begged him to retreat, to let himself be carried to some hiding-place. Maddened by failure and the damned accident of a splintered leg, he loaded both his pistols and laid his sword beside him on the bed, swearing to kill as many British as dared enter. But his defiance was never tested, the British did not follow. Carleton, realising that his Canadians had been stirred by the Americans' courage and fearing lest they rebel, thought best to remain snugly inside Quebec, taking no vengeance on the defeated.

When Congress heard of Arnold's heroism and of his gallant fight, it made him a Brigadier-General, but as if to balance the honour, it put his enemy Wooster in charge of Montreal in place of the dead Montgomery. And Wooster hated Arnold, he sent him no reinforcements, no supplies, no money, while Arnold carried on through the icy winter a futile blockade of Quebec. Then Wooster himself turned up, and inevitably there was quarrelling between the officers until Arnold, loathing his inactivity in bed, got prematurely on his horse to review the troops and was badly thrown. With Wooster's delighted permission, he retired raging to Montreal.

The Canadian venture was finished, but Arnold could not bring himself to face the truth. He clung to his dream that could have succeeded only had he surprised the British, but continual defeats and the continual arrival of British reinforcements, made him at last reluctantly put aside the ambition that until now had driven him since the outbreak of the war. He wrote, " Let us quit and secure our own country before it is too late. The junction of Canada and the colonies is now at an end . . . These arguments are not urged by fear of my personal safety. I am content to be the last man who quits the country, and fall, so that my country may rise." No idle boast. Until the end, he clung to Montreal, and when he did eventually retreat it was to blow up bridges and destroy roads, fighting to the last. " I am making every possible preparation to secure our retreat," he wrote. " I have secured six tons of lead, ball shot and merchandise. The inhabitants I have not yet taken hold of; I intend to begin to-morrow. Everything is in the greatest confusion. Not one contractor, commissary or quartermaster. I am obliged to do the duty of all."

There was to be quite a deal of fuss about that merchandise, enquiries why unmilitary supplies like silk and such, should have been collected so zealously only mysteriously to disappear. As after his administration at Ticonderoga, Arnold now had to face investigations about Montreal. With outraged innocence, he glared at the court martial and strove to double aside by accusing a fellow-officer, a most upright man with an honourable reputation, one Colonel Hazen, of the very crimes of which himself was charged. He cursed the court, and the court demanded an apology which he would not give. Instead, he swore to meet anyone present on the field of honour: his inevitable reply to all unanswerable accusations. The court demanded his arrest, but General Gates refused to obey, he had Arnold released, for, as he wrote to Congress, "The United States must not be deprived of that excellent officer's services at this important moment." For a short time Arnold was free, but then a Lieutenant-Colonel Brown produced thirteen charges against him and demanded that he be re-arrested. Gates, however, would not listen: Arnold was needed, the Colonials had few swords they could trust, few leaders with his courage, his genius at war. A mere matter of embezzlement—what was that?

Defiant of his accusers, Arnold strode from court and set about the amazing task of building a navy. Nothing ever daunted him, he could not comprehend a difficulty which he was unable to brush aside. His country wanted ships, so he would give them ships. And he did. He built a navy of flat-bottomed boats that he called galleys. Most of these were about forty-five feet long and could either carry sails or be rowed. In support were made gondolas, of roughly the same construction but only about half the size of the galleys. It was an almost in-

credible achievement, this building of a fleet on the edges
of the lake to defend Ticonderoga: when the trees by
the shore were exhausted, others had to be chopped down
further inland and dragged through unpathed woods.
Arnold, always superb in action, organised and strove to
shape his woodsmen into sailors and marines. Altogether, he gathered about eight hundred men, and with
these and a collection of eighteen tubs prepared to face
the great British fleet. His task was only to oppose this
fleet, for even he realised that it would be impossible to
win an actual fight: so he spread his ships over the nar-
rowest part of the lake and calmly waited to be blown
sky-high. As he waited, news came to him of rumours
being whispered in the streets of towns and cities about
his behaviour in Montreal; frenzied, he wrote to Gates
denying the accusations: they called him " a robber and
a thief," he had been told! Yes! " at a time, too, when I
have it not in my power to be heard in my own
defence! " But these infuriating distractions had to be
brushed aside when the British fleet came sailing down
the lake. One advantage Arnold had, he was to the
windward, and Carleton stared anxiously at these strange
vessels defying the power of England: when one of his
officers jeered, saying, " These rascals won't give us a
chance to burn powder," he answered quietly, " I
wouldn't be sure of that." He had faced Arnold and his
men before.

Arnold opened fire the instant the first of the enemy
came within range, but the crew of landlubbers promptly
ran his flagship ashore and he had to go aboard another
galley. This battle is one of the most idiotically heroic
in the history of the sea. While half Arnold's crew
sweated at the guns, the other half were gasping at the
pumps; galley after galley was smashed by the accurate

British fire, yet still others remained, defiant, pounding on until the overworked cannon burned unwary fingers. Night came at last, night split with jagged flames, with the yellow rush of fire in rigging, and the British contemptuously withdrew, sailing ahead to take in their turn the blockade of the lake. Somehow, Arnold had to run that blockade with his sieve-like vessels, and night helped him, for it was moonless and very dark when at twelve o'clock the remaining hulks of the American navy hoisted their anchors. Only a small lamp on the stern of each ship, burning to avoid collisions, shone like a glow-worm against the night; all other lights were out, and before a gentle breeze, Arnold gave the command to hoist sail, himself remaining in the *Congress*, last of the galleys, for always he claimed the most dangerous post, jealous of his honour, greedy for fight, determined to take to himself all possible glory. So battered were the ships that they had to stop and waste precious hours repairing them before they could continue, and then the damned wind changed and blew in Arnold's teeth. Oars were shipped but, being careful to make little noise, it was slow going and they feared that dawn would catch them before they had slipped far beyond the enemy. And their fears were realised, for soon the sun lit up the lake, coiling in quicksilver-flashes on the water and tinselling the singed ropes of the American navy, flaking the dirty sails with silver, gleaming along the broken timbers of the hulks: it didn't take the British long to catch them up, and Arnold in his *Congress*, with the *Washington* and four gondolas, turned to cover the remainder of the fleet. Two battered galleys with four small vessels stood at bay against the towering ships of England. Arnold was unafraid, prepared to fire the guns with his own hands, for never did he disdain to work beside his men,

soldier and sailor as well as commander. Broadsides
quickly smashed the *Washington* to such a state that her
captain hauled down his colours, but all the pounding
they liked to give could not make Benedict Arnold surrender. With the four gondolas, he kept the mighty
enemy off, firing ceaselessly, until after hours of battle
he realised that to remain was madness, for the *Congress*
was sinking under him. He ran her up a creek, and
there, in true romantic fashion, set fire to the worthless
skeleton, and trekked for Ticonderoga.

Arnold had been magnificently defeated, yet he had
succeeded in his task: the British were held off and, as
autumn was threatening, Carleton abandoned his intentions of assaulting Ticonderoga and turned back to
Canada. Then with the calm knowledge of work
gloriously done, Arnold waited for his reward—for at
least a major-generalship. But those rumours were still
being whispered, the question of Montreal had not been
settled, and Arnold found to his amazement that Congress ignored him. He was given nothing. Aghast, he
demanded " a court of inquiry into my conduct " to
refute the rumours, and threatened once again to resign.
It was Washington who dissuaded him from this, and
nobly then he promised to continue fighting " for the
safety and happiness of my country, in whose cause I
have repeatedly fought and bled, and am ready at all
times to risk my life." His country might not have
wanted to reward him, but it certainly needed his sword.
He struck bravely at the British near Ridgefield with a
half-disciplined army of but a hundred men. No longer
now could he be passed over. Congress at last made him
a Major-General and presented him with a horse; all
those disturbing charges about his peculations they
shuffled on to the Board of War, which gave the hero

a most noble character; nevertheless, those accounts of his were very disturbing, items extremely difficult to explain cropped up in almost every line, and whatever the Board of War might say, a committee had to be appointed to investigate. Lost, however, in the cunning mazes of Arnold's arithmetic and perhaps fearful of impeaching so popular and necessary a man, the committee abandoned the investigation, while Arnold truculently called for further honours. As Congress ignored him, Washington, who admired Arnold to the end, suggested that he command the Hudson. This was an important post, but in Arnold's eyes by no means important enough for a man of his dignity, he was obsessed by the thought that he was not superior to the five major-generals appointed after he had built and fought with the first American navy. These five were his superiors, he was considered their junior, and the insult was such that he could think of nothing else; even the prospect of fighting, even Washington's splendid honour of the Hudson, could not wipe from him the shame of his inferiority. No soldier in the Continent had fought so magnificently as he, and just because there was a small confusion in his accounting, he was ignored. Damn it, he was a soldier, not a clerk, and as a soldier he demanded justice. He could think and talk of nothing else, so Washington gave him a letter to the President of Congress, and in triumph, dressed in buff-faced blue with a scarlet sash around his waist, he rode to Philadelphia. But Congress would not listen, even his gorgeous uniform dripping with epaulettes did not blind them to those unexplained accounts; and Arnold fumed and argued and cursed without success. Meanwhile he had another, lesser worry—he was in love. The lady he called " the heavenly Miss de Bois," a beautiful sixteen-year-old Bostonian with, needless to say, quite a fortune attached to her beauty. Arnold impressed her no more than he impressed Congress. The "tall, straight, elegant" Miss de Bois was already in love with somebody else and was preparing to elope with that somebody, a certain Mr. Brimmer. The elopement failed because the lady's courage dissolved at the last moment. Mr. Brimmer was to drive a wagon of hay under her window, and she was to leap the three feet and be carried quietly off, unbruised. Perhaps it was maiden modesty that held Miss de Bois from essaying that three feet jump; anyhow, when at midnight, Mr. Brimmer faithfully passed with his wagon, the hay remained undisturbed, never to become a bridal-couch, while Miss de Bois stayed virginal—at least, to all knowledge— until her death many years later.

With the thought of the heavenly one in his mind, Arnold faced Congress, and lost both the wench and his hopes of promotion. He resigned his commission at once, but the country could not lose him. General Burgoyne, that excellent orator if rather casual soldier, was marching from Canada with eight thousand British. Even when faced by this danger, Congress hesitated before giving Arnold a command, although Washington wrote most strongly, urging it; but Arnold, proud of Washington's commendation, asked that his resignation be temporarily waived, and for the last time he rode to defend his country.

He stopped at General Schuyler's at Fort Edward only to discover that Congress, more intent on the problem of those missing supplies than on the salvation of its country, had curtly refused all applications for the restoration of his rank. Immediately, Arnold resigned again, and this time he meant it, so terrific was his natural indignation; but as Washington had calmed him in the

L

past, now Schuyler strove to dissuade him from this desperate act. Perhaps the knowledge that Schuyler himself was deeply troubled at the time, threatened with proceedings on more or less the same charges that still menaced Arnold, caused Arnold at the last moment to revoke his resignation. He wrote to Gates in proud style that " no public or private injury or insult shall prevail on me to forsake the cause of my injured and oppressed country, until I see peace and liberty restored to her or nobly die in the attempt." His first task was to relieve Fort Stanwix which, with a small garrison and failing powder, was preparing to defend itself against the whole British army. When Schuyler called for volunteers, not a man stepped from the ranks, but when he mentioned that Arnold was to lead them, eight hundred came at once, so magical had grown the name of this young soldier. But there was no need to fight, after all. On the way to Fort Stanwix, Arnold captured a half-crazy Dutchman called Hon Yost Cuyler whom he sent to the British with faked reports of the approach of huge Continental armies. Like many early Christians, the Indians reverenced lunacy as a sign of God's favour, believing that through an idiot's babble the Almighty sent cryptic messages; therefore, when Hon Yost told of the huge enemy, the Indian allies slipped from the British camp and, in panic, the British regulars followed their allies, leaving huge supplies of ammunition and food for Arnold's weary troops. In triumph, Arnold returned to Fort Edward only to discover that Gates had superseded Schuyler, and this Gates was a weak selfish creature dominated by only one ambition, to usurp Washington as commander-in-chief; with him now as adjutant-general was one of the most treacherous cowards in America, James Wilkinson. Gates had defended Arnold against the charges of peculation,

but this magnanimity had obviously been dictated by the
desire to draw as many soldiers as possible into his cabal
against Washington. Inevitably, he and Arnold soon
loathed each other.

Slowly the British came close, destroying the bridges
on their way so that there could be no possible retreat to
Canada. Burgoyne's intention was to reach General
Howe in New York, who, amusing himself with that
"illustrious courtesan," Mrs. Loring, for he "liked his
glass, his lass, and his game of cards, as indeed did all
British officers," was keeping a wary eye on Washington
and made no attempt to help his gallant poetical comrade in the north. Made commander of the left wing,
Arnold was fortifying Bemis Heights with the help of
the "timidly modest" Polish engineer, Kosciusko, and
here all the Continental army gathered to withstand the
oncoming British. Gates was in every way the opposite to
Arnold: as the enemy came near, he insisted on lurking
in trenches and behind breastworks while Arnold urged
him to attack, and it was only with extreme reluctance
that he at last permitted a small body to assault the out-
posts. They assaulted with such vigour that they swept
right into the main army and had to retreat, were surrounded, almost cut down, when Arnold ordered reinforcements to their help. He saw the field clearly, having
the quick mind, that almost bird's-eye mind, of all great
soldiers: he saw that Burgoyne's men were struggling to
join Fraser's, and determined to stop the meeting, to
force back both flanks of the arm apart he charged, and
Gates almost screamed with rage. Arnold swept down
on the British and struck them from their guns, but as
his men carried no linstock the cannon could not be
fired; he shouted for reinforcements, seeing how easily
and swiftly the battle might be his at that moment, but

Gates behind his breastworks cursed him when Arnold galloped up to tell him what a damned poltroon he was. Nevertheless, on his own initiative, Arnold called on a division to follow, and follow him it did, no matter what the raging Gates might say. Perhaps Arnold realised that he had gone too far, that he was mutinous and could be court-martialled, for when Gates sent Wilkinson to call him back, he sullenly sheathed his sword and obeyed. Without his inspiration to lead them, the Continentals were quickly driven off.

Now began the real quarrel between Gates and Arnold. The fact that Arnold's charge had halted Burgoyne's advance, that but for it the British by now might have reached New York, was not mentioned in despatches to Congress, and Arnold, always jealous for laurels he deserved, cursed his superior. In retort, Gates demanded to see Arnold's commission, asking if he had not resigned, and threatening that as General Lincoln was soon due, Arnold's services would be no longer required. Once more Arnold resigned, but every officer in the army implored him to remain for " they had lost confidence in Gates and had the highest opinion of Arnold." Again Arnold tore up his resignation after writing a letter imploring himself to remain, which he had signed by all the general officers, except the newly arrived Lincoln. Gates got his revenge by giving Arnold no command and himself took charge of the left wing, presenting the right to Lincoln. To all this, Arnold had no reply except to mutter darkly that in the coming fight, it would be " death to any officer " who interfered with the leadership of his division of the left. Yet when on October 7, 1777, the battle started, Arnold remained in his tent, fuming, sucking at his knuckles, while his comrades fought without him in the field. It was hell for him, his

body straining at the sound of conflict, at the thudding
of hoofs and crash of cannon, the battle-cries and high-
pitched screaming of the wounded; he was like a
starved man twitching at the smell of food, just to listen,
to remain in safety within the placid shade of this quiet
tent, sword undisturbed in its polished sheath, and to
take no part in battle, win for himself no glory, no
honour. He could not bear it, and at last called for his
horse, and galloped to the fray. He saw General Fraser
in gaudy uniform riding an iron-grey gelding to every
point of danger, to wherever the fight was thickest, and he
turned to Dan Morgan by his side. "That officer on
the grey horse," he said, "is of himself a host and must
be disposed of. Direct the attention of your sharpshooters
to him." Then lifting his sword, he called on his men
to follow, and charged, while Fraser, refusing to retire
before this sudden accurate hail of balls, stumbled and
fell, dying. Gates's aide, Major Armstrong, shouted to
Arnold to come back, but he dared not follow him to
battle; glumly he returned to Gates who, with superb
contempt for the result of the fight, was fuming in his
tent, quarrelling with a captured British officer about
the rights and wrongs of the war. He yelled at Armstrong to bring Arnold somehow off the field, then he
continued his fascinating political argument.

Immediately that Arnold charged, the army followed,
at once acclaiming him its leader. The enemy ran,
but Arnold fell, his horse shot dead and himself with a
ball in that left leg of his which once before had toppled
him in a fight. Armstrong rode up while Arnold was
trying to drag himself from under the weight of the
horse and while the British were fleeing before the
triumphant Continentals; he delivered Gates's message,
but Arnold was too engrossed with the surgeon to worry

about Gates. The surgeon diagnosed a compound fracture and insisted on amputation. "That's a lot of damned nonsense!" cried Arnold. "If you have nothing more to say, my men will lift me on a horse and I'll see this action through." Even his men, however, would not obey him in his rage, and he was carried from the field at the very moment of victory. An aide ran to tell Gates that the enemy were in retreat, and all that Gates had to say, turning from his quarrel with the dying Britisher, was, "Did you ever hear a more impudent son of a bitch!" After thus sweeping aside all pro-British argument, he condescended to hear how the battle progressed and immediately claimed all honour for his own, while he prepared to meet the surrendered Burgoyne.

Until the spring of the next year, that accursed leg of Arnold's kept him in his bed in Albany, then when he could mount a horse again, he rode in triumph to Connecticut. Washington sent him epaulettes and swordknots, and through every town he passed the people fought to gaze upon their hero. Now was his hour of glory, and he drank it in ecstatically, now for a brief time old suspicions were shuffled aside and even Congress pigeonholed those peculiar accounts of the exodus from Montreal. Who would dare suggest even the most minute blemish in the man who had defeated Burgoyne? Only Gates and Wilkinson and that crew, but they were soon trapped in their own net, the garrulous Wilkinson boasting of their plot against Washington and thereby exposing all. It seemed that Arnold's enemies were gradually being defeated, that before him stretched naught but mounting honours and revered old age, for this crippled leg of his threatened to keep him out of further wars. From Washington he begged work, he asked for the military governorship of Philadelphia, and

it was given him. This was a most important post, for
the Quaker city was one of the richest and most aristocratic on the Continent; here the wealthy citizens had
fêted British General Howe quite recently, in their Tory
enthusiasm even smothering horror at the sight of the
lovely Mrs. Loring with the amenable husband who
lurked in her dainty shadow to pocket whatever scraps
the gay Howe might toss to him in his post of com-
missioner of prisoners. Into this City of Brotherly Love
now rode General Benedict Arnold at the head of a
regiment of Massachusetts troops, and on June 19, 1778,
he took over the most luxurious house in all Philadelphia,
a house built by Penn's grandson in which Howe with
Mistress Loring had junketed during their brief visit.
While there was work to be done, Arnold acted with
his usual energy, and an evacuating army leaves behind,
not only broken hearts and seedling sons and daughters,
but muck of all description. Arnold thoroughly cleaned
the city, and then, when all was fresh again, turned to
his favourite and most congenial task of investigating
merchandise, prohibiting sales of any kind until owner-
ship could be proved, which threw the whole city's trade
into his hands. Secretly he signed agreements with the
clothier-general of the army and a friendly merchant to
sell at their own profit whatever military goods might
not be needed; then a ship, *The Charming Nancy*, was
restrained from sailing because the owners were suspected
of Tory sympathies: Arnold examined the affair, and,
assuring himself " of the upright intentions of the
owners," let *The Charming Nancy* sail where she willed
on condition of being made a partner in the company.
But there were those watching him who were eager to
betray: Colonel Melcher nabbed Arnold when he was
about to retail about a thousand pounds worth of public

goods, and Arnold damned him for his officiousness, swearing to " shake the pillars of their liberty temple about their ears "; then a merchant who had trusted Arnold with fifty thousand dollars to pay for certain produce, squealed because he got in return neither produce nor dollars. To such intolerable suspicions, to such ungentlemanly accusations, Arnold would never listen. He might have to hobble because of this leg, but his eyes were undimmed and his hand remained firm: let any who doubted his honour meet him on the field and prove which was the better man. He rode about like a lord, sprawling in gorgeous coaches, surrounded by footmen in livery. At last, he had attained the ultimate satisfaction—power. Even the thrill of leading armies could not equal the subtle joy of seeing men's eyes narrow with hatred when he strode near or of listening to the slow silence that fluttered through a company at his approach. All the glory of his fighting had been won for this—to act the petty tyrant, snapping up gold, stealing the government's goods, plundering citizens, a miniature god strutting through the Quaker city. None dared accuse him, he was too brave, too quick with sword or trigger. Two duels he fought and each of them he won. If the people might hate him, there were many doors, and those the most splendid, the most exclusive in Philadelphia, that were flung open gladly at his knock. The champion of liberty became the intimate of Tories, of those reactionary merchants and men of money who dreaded the thought of an equality that might dip into their coffers. And thus it was that he met Peggy Shippen, the beautiful, foolish Peggy with large grey eyes and tumble of golden curls; petulant Peggy, quick to throw herself into fashionable vapours at an unkind word, so very feminine was she that within

a second tears could trickle down her cheeks, subduing the most bearish of masculine brutes. Arnold loved
her at once, yet that did not restrain him from writing
to her a letter almost word for word identical with
a note he had once written to a certain heavenly Miss de
Bois.

The Shippen family was rather Tory and intensely
aristocratic. Peggy's father, Edward, was a lawyer
destined to become Chief Justice of Pennsylvania, and
he looked with suspicion if not with dislike upon the
crippled suitor about whose dark head circled the most
sinister rumours of extortion and peculation. But his disapproval was but brittle against his daughter's romantic
passion for the thirty-six-year-old hero. She fainted, wept
and kicked her heels at the thought of separation from
dark Benedict. So outrageous indeed became her vapours
that a nerve specialist was summoned to attend her and,
rather crudely, Mr. Edward was informed that " when
a delicate-minded, sensitive and well-bred woman falls in
love with a strong, coarse, passionate man, there was
nothing to be said but: ' Take her! ' "   Therefore, reluctantly, Mr. Shippen let Arnold take her.

On Mount Pleasant, surrounded by a huge park,
Arnold bought for thirty thousand dollars a house for
his new bride; and on April 8, 1779, he and the lovely
Peggy were married at the Shippen home. Those that
followed were most beautiful days for Arnold; he who
had found all sensuality in the slaying of others, all
magic in the bugle's cry and the heart-quickening rub-
a-dub of the drum, now knew the sweet delight of
woman's cooling flesh on his, her hands' slow, gentle
fondling and the musky odour of unbound hair rustling
shadowed about his face. With the enthusiasm that he
imparted to all he did, he threw himself most joyously

into love. He had been married before, but Margaret Mansfield had never been to him other than fallow flesh in which to breed; he had desired Elizabeth de Bois, that had been distraction, a cheat: the image of this Peggy now forever his had been fitfully glimpsed in the cold eyes of the de Bois, deceiving him but for a moment. He, the man of action, man of schemes and ambitions, was now soothed by the silly prattle of this childish thing, his vanity pampered by her physical weakness, by her petulance and ability to weep. He loved her, he bought her everything she asked, showed her off proudly at dinners and balls, surrounded her with all luxuries, all pomp; he liked to buy her things, to prove her impotence before his strength; yet it was her strength that sapped his, her neurotic will that twisted him, her slave. More and ever more, was her demand, more loving, for her body seemed to absorb love endlessly, languid limbs that were insatiable for kissings; more and yet more of all the riches of earth, of jewels and the ostentatious delight of clashing through the streets in a mighty carriage. Even Arnold's extortions could not glut her lusts or satisfy his own deep need to bed her on golden sheets and flash her like some bedizened Indian before the envious world. Money must be found some way; it must. This city could produce him nothing further, always his country had slighted him, cheated him of honours; he had given all and had received in return naught but slander and enmity. It did not deserve his love; and his wife despised the Colonials, although a Colonial herself. But she was an aristocrat, distrustful of rebels, of farmers who had dared lift weapons against the godlike King of England. And if her love was towards England, love of one so delicate, so fine, so gently nurtured, why should he struggle against her with vague words such as patriotism and loyalty because this ungrateful country had been honoured as the land of his birth? Why?

The rumours were still being muttered about him. The damned governor, Joseph Reed, dared ask thrusting questions about Arnold's income and Arnold threatened to murder him for it. The British strove to bribe Reed, who rejected the money indignantly, but Arnold swore that he had taken it. . . . And if Reed did not take it, why should gold be left to rust? England after all was the mother country, perhaps the Colonies were in the wrong, committing a kind of matricide. And if he should join with England he would be helping both countries, for quickly he would end the war, very quickly; and yet . . . Uncertain what course to take, he held his soft, beloved wife in his arms, a child in his arms that was hungry always for petting, mouth for ever puckered for his kiss . . . Hoping to still the rumours, Arnold decided definitely to resign from the army and become a land-holder, living at ease on his estate. He wrote to General Schuyler, suggesting this, then set out for New York State to choose some land, but on the way he heard that the moment his back was turned, enemies in Pennsyl-vania had risen to denounce him. Aghast, Arnold scribbled a letter to his wife, a horrified denunciation of his accusers, stating that he was heartily weary of human nature for every day he discovered " so much baseness and ingratitude among mankind that I almost blush at being of the same species." This time the accusations he had to face were clearly drawn up, but with such obvious malice that they defeated their own intention. There were eight charges brought against him: Firstly, he had permitted a ship owned by people of " disaffected character, to come into a port of the United States "; Secondly, he had shut the shops in Philadelphia while

" he privately made considerable purchases "; Thirdly, he had given menial offices to " the sons of freemen of this State "; Fourthly, when there was a dispute about a captured ship, he had " interposed, by an illegal and unworthy purchase of the suit, at a low and inadequate price "; Fifthly, he had appropriated wagons for " the transportation of private property "; Sixthly, he had given passes to men to go through enemy lines without the sanction of the executive powers of the State. Seventhly, he had answered enquiries about the appropriation of the wagons with " an indecent and disrespectful refusal of any satisfaction whatsoever "; Eighthly, he had discouraged and neglected loyal men, " with an entirely different conduct towards those of another character." These charges were examined by a committee of Congress who passed the Third and Fifth on to Washington, while the Sixth, Seventh and Eighth, were said to be offences " subject to no other punishment than the displeasure of Congress." All was so vague that Congress dismissed the matter, but the First, Second, Third and Fifth charges were referred to a court-martial to be appointed by Washington. Dressed in full regimentals, Arnold faced his trial on December 19, 1779, and acted the part of a misjudged hero really splendidly, limping with pathetic realism, and without troubling to give specific explanations of his conduct, made a rousing speech, offering to fight his accusers in soldier-fashion, extolling his own bravery, reminding his judges of his exploits, and concluding by reading aloud every letter of recommendation he had ever received as if he were being charged with cowardice and not with misgovernment and peculation. But this was the right course to take, for his judges were soldiers like himself and were easily stirred by prattling about honour. " I have looked

forward," cried Arnold, "with pleasing anxiety to the
present day when by the judgment of my fellow officers,
I shall, I doubt not, stand honourably acquitted of all
the charges brought against me, and again share with
them the glory and danger of this just war." He then
modestly withdrew and waited with complacence for the
court-martial's vindication. To his astonishment and
horror, he was reprimanded for having commandeered the
wagons. The injustice of this drove him almost into a
fit. By God, now he was glad that he had started cor-
responding with the British! He'd soon show those fools
who had dared reprimand him that Benedict Arnold was
no man to be thus insulted!

Already he was writing to General Sir Henry Clinton
in New York, offering his sword. At first he used the
nom de plume of Gustavus—for had not Gustavus
Adolphus, that Lion of the North, been as great a soldier
as he?—but later he altered Adolphus to Moore, then he
shifted to Fox—for was he not becoming a politician, and
a crafty one at that?—but eventually he returned to
Gustavus as the most noble of pseudonyms. It did not take
the British long to guess the real name of their correspond-
ent and they bargained about the price until finally it was
resolved to give Arnold ten thousand gold dollars and the
rank of brigadier-general. Meanwhile, he was becoming
desperate, every day his debts mounted; he fitted out
privateers to attack British shipping and only lost on the
deal; he tried all kinds of dodges, but luck seemed continually against him, driving him remorselessly into the
arms of the British. He even called on the French and
begged money, but they told him politely that they only
bought their enemies, for there was no need for them
to purchase their allies' loyalty. He had no alternative
but to fight for England; and by God, he owed his

country nothing! Again and again he had been insulted, and that wretched court-martial had dared to reprimand him! Besides, he would be a kind of saviour, ending this seemingly endless war, bringing peace. The very mention of his name would split the Colonial army, he felt certain; as he wrote to Clinton, at from ten to fifteen guineas a man he could buy thirty-five thousand Continental soldiers for the British. Clinton, however, wanted something more definite in return for his gold, what could Gustavus promise? What? He was no longer a soldier, he was but a private gentleman with a crippled leg, what could he offer Clinton? He rode to General Washington to see if he could grab something really valuable as security for British money, and Washington suggested that he take command of the right wing of the army. That was no use to Arnold, he pointed at his leg as an excuse for not fighting, and asked to be given the command of West Point, a most vital position, something that Clinton would surely grab? Proudly Gustavus wrote to the British general of the prize he offered and asked to meet some intelligent officer who could finalise the agreement, Arnold demanded " twenty thousand pounds sterling," adding, " I think it a cheap price for an object of so much importance." Clinton did not quite agree, and he whittled down the sum to ten thousand dollars, agreeing to send the officer; the man chosen to meet Arnold was one of the most popular in the British army, beloved by both countries, young Adjutant-General John André, the English-born son of French parents. Wherever he went, men and women adored André, he was so gay, so witty, singing impromptu songs; yet thwarted love had driven him into the army, the loss of his adored Honora Sneyd.

On the night of September 20, 1780, Arnold and

André talked by lantern-light two miles below Stony Point. A careful plan of West Point was pushed by André under his left foot, beneath his stocking, but as he prepared to go, there came to them the sound of firing. Both men held their breath, listening, afraid. The British ship *Vulture* was waiting in midsteam to take André aboard, and now it had been sighted and chased off: André was trapped with a red coat under his greatcoat, far behind the Continental lines. In desperation, Arnold rode with him to the house of a wealthy friend, Joshua Hett Smith. Hurriedly telling a muddle of lies to Smith, Arnold made out a passport for André, and then galloped off, for he was expecting Washington for breakfast. The Britisher rode safely for a few miles until he came upon three foragers at about nine o'clock in the morning. These three were out for plunder; they were playing cards and waiting for passers-by to rob when they heard André coming. They darted out and stopped him, noting with lustful eyes the strong boots that he wore. One of the gang had on a British red coat which he had probably stolen or taken from a corpse, and at sight of it André immediately explained that he was a British officer. In reply they informed him that they were Americans, and, nervously saying, "My God, you know I must do something to get along," André showed them Arnold's pass. But they were suspicious, and besides, they wanted those boots; and when they had pulled off the boots they discovered the plans of West Point. As André could bribe them with nothing but promises, they marched him to North Castle, to Captain Jameson who was so astounded by the tale that he wrote to Arnold asking how this pass with his signature came to be in a Britisher's pocket.

Arnold was at breakfast when Jameson's note arrived,

and he discovered that all was known, that the in-
criminating papers were on their way to Washington
who was already in West Point inspecting the redoubts
before breakfasting here, in this house, at this very table;
he might be coming now, his hand might at this
moment be lifted to knock upon the door . . . It was as
if strong fingers caught Arnold by the throat, the
realisation that all was lost, that Washington knew of
his treachery, Washington with gay La Fayette and mad
romantic Anthony Wayne, they were here, in West Point
. . . Somehow he stilled the panic of his heart and
quietly excused himself from the table; his guests saw
only that his face was pale but glimpsed no terrors in
his eyes as, leaning on his stick, he walked slowly out
and up the stairs to Peggy's room. And there, with
sudden frenzy, he prepared for flight, despatching a
servant to bring Peggy from the table. Swiftly he told
her everything while she stood appalled, clutching the
table with both hands, numbed with horror, all blood
dying in her face, only the eyes seeming gigantic, dark
and bright. Then suddenly life rushed in her again and,
weeping she caught her husband to her, sobbing and
clinging to him, unable to realise the enormity of the
situation, unable to believe that God could be so cruel to
them. Kissing her hurriedly, Arnold ran from the room
and from that house, pausing however at the breakfast-
room door to explain that he must make arrangements
for Washington's reception. . . .

No longer an American, even the British not really
wanting him now that his plot had failed and the
beloved André would be hanged as a spy, Arnold, at the
point of the pistol, forced a crew to row him to the
Vulture. Countryless, a traitor for no purpose, leaving
even his wife behind, he tried to prove his mettle in the

new part, but he was not trusted fully, the Britishers, outwardly polite, did not like him, they moved away when he came close. Alone, depressed by the cruelty of a fate that had driven him to such an end, Arnold fought under his new flag until Lord Cornwallis surrendered to General Washington. Then in December, 1782, with his family, Peggy beside him, he sailed for England. The land of his birth dissolved into the sky and, his fingers tightened around the slim shoulders of his wife, Arnold felt deep pity for himself, the misunderstood, the man damned as a traitor when he had striven to act only for the best. He had no future save the pension England gave him; but he had this woman whom he loved—and for her, surely even a country was well worth the losing?

M

VII

Love is Often the Betrayer

From being one of the most famous and courageous men of his time, Benedict Arnold faded from history to become the notorious pensioner of England. In his adopted country he was so distrusted that when he offered his sword to fight against France, the offer was refused. Detesting idleness—even with his lovely Peggy to console him—he attempted to return to the West Indian trade and took his family with him to St. Johns, New Brunswick; but destiny had now turned from a failure. He had had his cards, never again was he given a chance, no matter how the powerful spirit might fret within his body, clamouring for action. Only once did adventure come to him. When in Guadeloupe, he discovered that the French had captured the place, and temporarily reassumed his American nationality while he built a boat to carry him through the enemy lines; in this boat, he rowed beyond the French fleet to give valuable information to the British. That was his one opportunity, save for a duel. It must have been the most bitter hell for the proud Arnold, being thus exiled in a country that rather grudgingly accepted him, and when he felt death chilling his blood he cried, " Let me die in my old uniform. God forgive me for ever putting on any other!" and the old blue and buff Continental uniform with its scarlet sash was taken from the lavender, with the sword-knots and epaulettes that General Washington had given him . . . A pathetic glimpse of the old warrior, and we may be sure that when he cried for God's forgiveness he was not thinking

of his treachery but of the loss of glory, of days when
he had dazzled his country and by sheer brilliance forced
it to acknowledge his greatness. He considered himself a deeply wronged man, in true ruffian fashion
hurriedly transferring his own guilt to others. After the
miscarriage of his plot, he wrote from H.M.S. *Vulture*
to Washington: " The heart which is conscious of its
own rectitude, cannot attempt to palliate a step which
the world may censure as wrong. I have ever acted from
a principle of love to my country since the commence-
ment of the present unhappy contest between Great
Britain and the Colonies. The same principle of love to
my country actuates my present conduct, however it may
appear inconsistent to the world, who very seldom judge
right of any man's actions. I have no favour to ask for
myself. I have too often experienced the ingratitude of
my country to attempt it; but, from the known humanity
of your Excellency, I am induced to ask your protection
for Mrs. Arnold . . ." It is wholly to misunderstand the
man to toss such an epistle aside as an example of
hypocrisy. Arnold was no hypocrite, and he sweated
under a wholly justifiable sense of being ill-treated; he
certainly had been ill-treated, although he had undoubtedly brought it on himself by his cupidity and
perhaps by too heavy drinking, for he liked his bottle.
All through his military life he was dogged by what he
considered a malignant fate; yet, in truth, fate was kind
to him as she inevitably is to all adventurers, to those
who claim her favours as their right. Only did she
forsake Arnold at the very end when to surrender to
him would have been to betray thousands of other
heroes; yet she relented enough to make that fool of
a Jameson send warning to the fatal breakfast-table.
Arnold reveals to us one of the deepest failures of many

ruffians—greed. He was never satisfied, continually demanding honours and gold, and considering himself insulted when either was refused. The ruffian never knows
when to stop; the darling of fate, like a too furious
lover he eventually exhausts the woman, flogs her into
rebellion. His giant arrogance is too powerful a belittling glass, and even Gulliver can be tied down by the
multitudinous threads of Lilliputians. The ruffian to
himself is Gulliver in Lilliput, never by any means in
Brobdingnag or the land of the Houyhnhnms; and his
opinion of humankind is best expressed by Gulliver's
method of extinguishing the fire in the Queen's apartments: thus does the ruffian feel that he can treat all his
fellowmen while he straddles the world.

There is something magnificent about Arnold, something one must respect; he is of heroic stature; whatever
he did he did on the grand scale without thought of
consequences, with wholehearted faith in his destiny.
Few ruffians have lived so complete a life, and few
ruffians have known love as, without doubt, Arnold
knew it. And it is, at first glance, strange that this
turbulent man of action should choose for his beloved a
spoiled, pettish girl subject, we are told by Major Franks
who knew her intimately, " to occasional paroxysms of
physical indisposition, attended by nervous debility,
during which she would give utterance to anything or
everything on her mind. This was a fact well known
amongst us of the General's family; so much so as to
cause us to be scrupulous of what we told her, or said in
her hearing." In other words, she was a neurasthenic;
the kind of wife who would drive any normal husband
to lunacy, felo-de-se or justifiable homicide. But Arnold
loved her, without question he loved her; she gave to
him that equipoise of the spirit on which the magi are

so insistent. Simon Magus married a harlot to balance
the influences of his horoscope, and there is some such
unconscious urge in all men and women that drives them
to their choice of lover: a mental, I believe, far more
than a biological choice, for which reason the idea of
breeding a nation of supermen from supermen and
women would result most likely in a race of idiots.
Peggy balanced Arnold, her ultra-femininity balanced
his ultra-masculinity.

Historians still argue whether or not Peggy knew of
Arnold's treachery. Aaron Burr told his biographer that
Mrs. Prevost, whom he eventually married, had told
him that Peggy had told her that she had turned Arnold
into a traitor. According to this tale, after being escorted
from West Point, Peggy cried to Mrs. Prevost, " I have
been playing the hypocrite long enough, and I am tired
of it." On the other hand, Peggy's defenders produce
Major Franks already quoted above, who earnestly insisted that she was too great a babbler to be trusted with
a secret. But anybody acquainted with the illogical and
bewildering habits of neurotics will not regard this
seriously: they may chatter stupidly for hours while re-
taining, with conscious, smirking cunning, some tremendous secret. Personally, I have no doubt that Peggy
was privy to the plot if not its entire inspiration,
although Washington must have believed in her
innocence, he was so kind and sympathetic to her after
Arnold's flight. But she was an untrustworthy animal,
noble only in her enduring love for her husband. She
had been born and bred a Tory, and although her de-
fender, Major Franks, speaks of " her warm patriotic
feelings," we may well have a sneaking suspicion that
the sentimental major, like La Fayette and the gay
André—hanged for her husband's treachery—was per-

haps fascinated by her coquetry and undoubted loveliness. She had the petty ambitions of such a woman, social power and masculine admiration, and these could be more easily attained during an aristocratic than a democratic rule. Under the control of this dæmon, this feminine part of himself, Arnold's desires and arrogance became so lunatic that they affected his mind until towards his end he lived over again his great exploits, climbing once more the heights of Quebec, and charging at Saratoga. His death, we are informed, was the result of "a severe nervous disease," which might mean anything, but he was probably so racked with regrets, so torn by unfulfillable desires, that the weary spirit murdered the useless flesh.

He was heroic, he could have been one of the truly great figures of the War of Independence, ranking with Washington, Greene and Wayne; but he disdained posthumous applause; like a true ruffian, living was his theatre. But while dazzled by his splendour in battle, by his large-handed graft in Philadelphia, and the grandiose dream of treachery, we must not forget that he was capable of cheap little acts. Romantic Anthony Wayne, whose bravery earned him the noble title of the "Mad", wrote of Arnold after his exposure: "What think you of his employing sutlers to retail the public liquors for his private emolument, and furnishing his quarters with beds and other furniture by paying for them with pork, salt, flour, etc., drawn from the magazines? He has not stopped here—he has descended much lower—and defrauded the old veteran soldiers who have bled for their country in many a well fought field, for more than five campaigns. Among others an old serg't of mine had felt his rapacity—by the industry of this man's wife they had accumulated something handsome to support them in their advanced age—which coming to the knowledge of this cruel spoiler—he borrowed 4,500 dollars from the poor credulous woman and left her in the lurch. The dirty—dirty—arts which he has been capable of committing beggar all description —and are of such a nature as would cause the *infernals* to blush—were they accused with the invention, or execution of them." At the same time, we may discountenance a little of Wayne's natural fury, for he also in the same letter accuses Arnold of never possessing "either fortitude or personal bravery. He was naturally a coward, and never went in the way of danger except when stimulated by liquor even to intoxication, consequently incapacitated from conducting any command committed to his charge." Such insults, even when written under the most justifiable fury, are puerile: Arnold was no coward, and it is idiotic to suggest that he was never sober: the man who marched to Quebec could not have been perpetually drunk, how could he have carried kegs and bottles enough through the wilderness to keep him in that condition?

Arnold is by no means the only ruffian who comes under our inspection when studying the fascinating American War of Independence and we really cannot pass without at least a brief examination of General James Wilkinson, a born traitor, which Arnold certainly was not: he was a traitor by accident, Wilkinson by sheer inability to be anything else. He was not even a good soldier although, being a bully who threatened to run any helpless insubordinate through with his sword, he made an excellent drill-master. We have seen him chasing Arnold at Saratoga with Granny Gates's command to leave the field, and he was at first a great friend of Gates, becoming involved with him in the conspiracy to oust Washington. This conspiracy was exposed by Wilkinson himself who talked too much; to prove that he had been maligned when evidence of his garrulity was produced, Wilkinson sent the wretched Gates a challenge, but on the morning of the duel Gates "burst into tears" and apologised most pathetically, saying that, far from injuring his friend's honour, he would "as soon think of injuring my own child." After this estimable picture of two scoundrels humbugging each other, it is not long before we find them in exactly the same situation, only on this occasion pistols were exploded harmlessly before Gates—Face of Clay, Arnold called him, while Burgoyne nicknamed him the Mid-wife—burst into tears and protestations of love for the second time. Wilkinson, true ruffian, was very tender about that "jewel of his soul," his honour, but he did not have the courage of Arnold in defending it save against a weak-gutted fool like Gates. He turned his genius of intrigue, having learned that first lesson of keeping his mouth shut, to bigger game than military cabals. The war over, he began trading in tobacco with Louisiana, and soon discovered that he had more valu-able commodities to trade than tobacco—his loyalty. So constant became the supplies of pieces-of-eight turning up at his home that rumour grew most insistent, and Wilkinson's talk of "tobacco money" by no means killed the suspicion that "tobacco money" was a synonym for "Spanish gold." Washington, whose worst failing was a disinclination to believe harm of his men, advanced the schemer to commander of the army on the death of Wayne in 1796; Wayne's death helped Wilkin-son not only by lifting him to this honour but by ridding him of a pest who was making strict inquiries into the source of that perpetual tobacco money. As a matter of fact, Wilkinson was getting so involved in treachery that he actually declared his allegiance to the King of Spain —for a good sum down, of course. He satisfied his conscience glibly enough, not denying that all men owed something to their land of birth, but refusing to believe "that an intelligent being, able to do as he sees fit, should plant himself like a vegetable that perchance was a witness to his birth, would be setting at naught the wisdom of Providence and condemning the universal practice of the human race," for "self-interest," he wrote, "regulates the passions" of mankind, a statement sadly true but not one to which many would have the courage to confess with the calm smugness of the general. After this confession, however, he is quick to produce noble sentiments to explain his treachery. Realising, he states, that "his resolution will wound the self-love of those he abandons," he was nevertheless unflinchingly determined to reason according to "truth and conscience." Truth and conscience obligingly informed him that he broke no "law of nature or of nations" by selling himself to one country while serving another, for he had already done enough for America, he had fought in the Revolution "for her welfare," and was therefore now justified in looking after his own; besides, his treachery was to "the real advantage to the country in which he dwells, as well as the interest and aggrandisement of the Spanish monarchy." Wilkinson's sentiments here are so similar to Arnold's, only more boldly put, that we may more or less accept them as the psychic juggling whereby most traitors justify their treachery: it is always for the betterment of others, as well as for his own good, that the ruffian insists he acts, and unquestionably he convinces himself that he is telling the truth. Even when alone, in silence of the night, he is not haunted by ghosts of his own stupidities and wicked tricks such as too often keep fellows like you and me awake, staring at a darkness peopled with horrible shames. He is safe in his arrogance, assured of his own integrity—fortunate man, undoubtedly the blessed of all gods.

Our interest in this slimy rogue of a Wilkinson, however, is centred on the Burr conspiracy. This is a very strange affair, not yet fully understood, the truth being hidden under so many lies, mainly spun by Wilkinson. We do not know Burr's real intentions, we can only guess at them: Wilkinson insisted that Burr meant to break the Union by staging a revolt in the West, but the defence was that he intended only to invade and seize Mexico, and of the two I prefer the latter, not only because you can't trust a word of Wilkinson's but because it was a logical and possible scheme. Whatever the conspiracy was about, Wilkinson inevitably got involved with it, then at the last moment exposed it to Congress. His motives appear inexplicable, but after all, he was a boaster and an opportunist. He must have doubted if Burr would succeed, he must have known that he himself was under suspicion because of the Spanish negotiations, and in him strongly was that true ruffian-trait, the desire to swagger on a mighty stage. He only destroyed himself, made himself an object of contempt. The stage was important enough, but far from posturing as the hero, as the saviour of his country, Wilkinson to his own horror and amazement found himself taking on more the rôle of the villain. When he strutted into court followed by an aide bent over a huge portfolio—" a wonderous cargo of words "—he tells us in a letter to Jefferson that he had " little dreamed of the importance attached to my person here," which is a childish exposure of fake humility, for he was the accuser, the star-witness. Then, after saluting the bench, "in spite of myself," he writes, "my eyes darted a flash of indignation at the little traitor," Burr, who strove with haggard eyes to meet the bold informer's glare, only "his audacity failed him. He averted his face, grew pale, and affected passion to conceal his perturbation." Washington Irving, then a young lawyer in the court, gives of this scene a version entirely different from Wilkinson's. According to Irving, a keen observer, Burr looked Wilkinson "full in the face with one of his piercing regards; swept his eye over his whole person from head to foot," then without a further gesture continued talking with his counsel: "no study or constraint; no affection of disdain or defiance; a slight expression of contempt." If ever there was the spectacle of a poor devil writhing on his hook, it was Wilkinson during this trial. He blustered into court, expecting to be cheered as a saviour, and found himself strangled in his own lies, while faced with papers he had tampered with in trying vainly to obliterate his own part in the conspiracy. Burr shows up nobly beside him, refusing as an honest man to produce letters which would have proved Wilkinson's guilt beyond doubt, disdaining to turn informer even for his own skin. Aghast, Wilkinson heard Burr acquitted, and cried in horror at the injustice —" to my astonishment I find the traitor vindicated and myself condemned . . . integrity and truth perverted and trampled underfoot by turpitude and guilt, patriotism appalled and usurpation triumphant." Only by great good fortune did he escape having the jury indict him for misprision of treason, and he was forced to keep his door bolted lest the mob tar and feather him.

Wilkinson's main interest to us is as a pendant to Arnold: in treachery, he was to Arnold what the footpad is to Capone, a very dirty imitation. Arnold's treachery was monumental, there was nothing sneaking about it, nor did he intend to turn spy, selling his sword to both sides at the same time; he reminds one of some character in a baroque novel, almost too colourful, too perfect. But there are many sneaks of the Wilkinson type in this world and he becomes of importance only during that confusing Burr trial. Looking back at that scene, knowing the records of both men, it is incredible almost that Wilkinson could have had the effrontery to impeach his friend and fellow-conspirator; the risks were great, had Burr been fired with even normal resentment at such betrayal, he could have had Wilkinson in the dock beside him, but contemptuously he refrained, letting the virtuous informer parade before the court until he tumbled into his own pit. Only a ruffian, secure in his destiny, assured of his own genius and self-righteousness, would have dared do what Wilkinson attempted; any ordinary man with ordinary imagination would have blown his brains out at the very thought. The comparison with Arnold is very slight, save in the adroitness with which both justified their treachery, almost sanctifying it. Everything Arnold did was in the grand manner, even the fury with which he threw himself into love; Wilkinson also drank heavily—that was one of the charges brought against him at the last of his numerous courts martial—but he obviously did not care particularly for women: his wife takes such prominence in his memoirs that he doesn't even bother to mention her name. It was different with Arnold, Peggy dominates all his last years, and the only point that makes us doubt the sincerity of his passion is that peculiar letter he wrote during courtship which is practically word for word what he had previously written Miss de Bois. But letters, after all, are little proof of love, valued far more by women than by men, for women have a curious and rather pathetic faith in the written or spoken word; but a trained seducer could undoubtedly inscribe more convincing a valentine than could some moonstruck lad solemnly prepared to surrender his life for his beloved. Arnold had not known Peggy long when he copied his note from Miss de Bois's, and as is very often the case, his real love might have grown with intimacy. On this question of sex, Arnold is one of the exceptions in Ruffians' Hall; few others, unless they have used women as a means of ruffianism, have permitted their souls to be exposed by this all-grasping passion, for in love nothing must be hidden, all must be given, all must be taken.

The mention of sex brings us to a portion of Ruffians' Hall which we have as yet not explored, the woman's side. We must not admit the lesbians, for they are an intrusion into masculinity, nevertheless there have been women ruffians who have yet retained their sex, and there have been woman ruffians in the true sense, those who have used their femininity for ruffianly purposes. Broadly speaking, ruffianism is more a female than a male trait, for the average woman is more self-centred, more ruthless and determined than the average man. Man has so many distractions, so many outlets for his energy that often it becomes dissipated, but a woman is concentrated within her own world. Economic pressure may be blamed for this, but not economic pressure alone; a woman, after all, is necessarily self-centred, her task in life is the creation of children and of courage in the man, while man's genius is based on both more material and more abstract rôles—in needs for money, trade, politics, fighting, art. Within her own world of the family, the woman is supreme and to maintain that world inviolate she will lie, cheat, or even kill. To her, metaphysical dreams mean nothing; abstractions such as honour, faith, loyalty—words to which man attaches so preposterous a value—are quite meaningless the instant her or her loved ones' happiness is threatened. A great deal of the mystery that has centred around women, so puzzling to the young, is undoubtedly this apparent confusion in their character, extreme sentiment with extreme brutality, generosity with meanness, but it is in truth no confusion whatever, for each is a counterpart of the other, the balance of spirit—the Yea and the Nay, the I and the Me—of which we have already spoken. What man has not been astounded by the magnanimity of a woman? and what man has not been terrified by her rapacious cruelty? Should a woman love you, it does not matter a farthing if you be penniless: she will flout a millionaire to buy fish and chips for the man she desires, she will drink ale with him in a public bar when champagne is offered around the corner, she will starve—even beg for him, if necessary. Noblest and basest of creatures, woman will always be beyond man's comprehension because she disdains to enter his stupid world of abstractions, being more intent, and rightly so, upon the necessities of living, necessities both for body and for soul. She who to you is so unutterably kind and loving that you feel despicable in comparison could be a cold-blooded devil to some other man. That is woman's world, a splendid concentration upon worthy objects, herself and those dear to her: a ruffianly world indeed only to those outside the circle. When we talk generalities in this fashion it is naturally concluded that reference is made to the average; there have been women without this balance, swinging too far into sentiment or too far into cruelty; and the latter we must choose for our examples of the inmates of this luxurious annexe of Ruffians' Hall.

Women, however, like the bawd and fence Moll Cutpurse who strode through Stuart London in breeches and was locked in the stocks because of it, place us in rather a quandary, for she was unquestionably homosexual, therefore spiritually masculine, being very strict about the purity of the girls in her house, no matter how she might act bawd for the heterosexuality of women outside. And there was Hannah Snell, the eighteenth century soldier who shouldered a musket at Pondicherry; Hannah is a doubtful case, she was such an obvious liar, and apart from those tales proved mendacious, I rather doubt her boast of having been twice flogged. Her biographer explains that her bosom was exceptionally small and that she tied a long handkerchief around her neck, and he makes the boatswain exclaim that her breasts were " most like a woman's he ever saw." Nevertheless, flogging was an unbelievably brutal punishment, and even the most powerful man inevitably jerked some cry from between his clenched teeth at the first swing of the knotted cat; Hannah must have been amazingly tough to have withstood this, with her wounds—some known to be false—and the effects of innumerable hurricanes. But many of the stories about her were the creation of a press-agent, for she acted at the Royalty Theatre " in her favourite character of a sailor," Bill Bobstay, in which " she cut a most genteel figure." Afterwards she bought a public house near Wapping and apparently did very well for herself, exchanging mighty lies with the sailors. There is nothing really exceptional about Hannah, save her presentation on the stage and that delightful ballad, *The Female Soldier*:

Hannah in *briggs* behaved so well
that none her *softer sex* could tell;
nor was her *policy* confounded
when near the *mark of nature* wounded;
which proves what *man* will scarce admit,
that women are for *secrets* fit.
That *healthful blood* could *keep* so long
amidst *young fellows* hale and strong
demonstrates, though a seeming wonder,
that *love* to *courage* truckles under.
Oh, how her *bedmate* bit his lips,
and marked the *spreading* of her *hips*,
and cursed the *blindness* of his youth,
when she confessed the *naked truth*!

Hannah has numerous rivals. There was Rebecca
Anne Johnson who was apprenticed by her father to a
Whitby collier, and served seven years before, in 1808,
her sex was discovered, while her mother had been killed
at Copenhagen when working in a gun-crew; and Mary
Anne Talbot, who was badly wounded at the Glorious
First of June under Black Dick Howe, and died in
poverty, a confirmed drunkard and beggar; and there
is this charming news item relating that " at St. Dun-
stane's in the East, in May, 1802, David Jones was
married to Anne Robinson. They had been old ship-
mates aboard *La Seine,* a frigate on the West Indian
station, where the lady bore a most conspicuous part in
the different actions in which the frigate was engaged ";
nor must we forget Mrs. Kit Davies, known as Mother
Ross, born in Dublin, 1667, who followed her husband
when he enlisted and fought in his regiment, but there
is a touch of inversion in Mrs. Davies when we read the
tale of how she became " so irritated " when a comrade
ravished a girl who was in love with her that she was
seized with a " tremor all over my body, often changed
colour," and could have killed him on the spot. Instead,

she fought him in a duel and won. There is also something rather peculiar in her behaviour when she surprised her husband hugging a wench, whereupon she swore that she was no longer his wife but had become his brother and presented him with a mug of beer and a piece of gold; nevertheless, after Lord John Hayes had discovered her sex and forced her to re-marry her husband, relegating her to the degrading position of cook, and she had produced a baby that soon died, she caught her husband with the same wench and cut off the girl's nose which was later miraculously stitched on again. Altogether, Mrs. Davies's sexual vagaries are most perplexing, but apparently heterosexuality was dominant, for she was to have two further husbands before she eventually died in Chelsea Hospital at the age of one hundred and eight, which is quite in keeping with all the other astounding events of her career.

When glancing at women-of-action, the pirate-lasses, Anne Bonny and Mary Read, naturally spring to mind, but they are too well known for us to spend time with, except to note their truculence beside the more cowardly noises of their lovers at the prospect of a choking death —"If you had fought like a man," jeered Mary to her Calico Jack Rackham, "you need not have been hanged like a dog!" All the same, we must not forget that, being women, Mary and Anne knew that they had a way to cheat the hangman, by hurriedly becoming enceinte, which in fact, they did. Their glory rather overshadows an equally splendid petticoat-pirate, Maria Cobham, who strode her quarter-deck garbed becomingly in full naval uniform, with cutlass and pistol in her sash. Her husband was also a pirate, having encountered Maria in some Plymouth den and carried her off to sea, to the great discontent of his crew who wanted to know

N

why they also couldn't have their doxies with them, for " where a man is married the case is altered, no man envies him his happiness; but where he only keeps a girl every man says, 'I have as much right to one as he has!'" Maria soon overcame the crew's jealousies and moral scruples at having a whore aboard by her dexterity with a pistol and her kindness of heart in rescuing many a handsome young sprig from punishment. Cobham was a particularly bloodthirsty pirate, entirely without finesse: on one occasion he sewed up his prisoners in bags and tossed them into the sea like kittens, sport that must have appealed strongly to Maria who once stabbed to the heart the captain of a Liverpool brig, the *Lion*, with her own little pearl-handled dagger; and on another occasion, a captain and his two mates were roped to the windlass whilst Maria took pot-shots at them with her pistol. Her last recorded act under the black flag was to poison the entire crew of a captured West Indiaman who were prisoners in irons aboard her ship. Being now prosperous, Cobham and Maria settled down at Havre on an estate bought from the Duc de Chartres, but out fishing one afternoon they sighted a becalmed West Indian brig, and Cobham and crew went aboard to visit the captain. Old habits cling fast, and before very long Cobham just had to shoot the captain, whereupon Maria and crew butchered everybody else on board. Carrying the prize to Bordeaux, they sold her for a fair sum. Cobham was shortly afterwards appointed magistrate and lived to a respectable age, but Maria, whether from remorse or by accident we do not know, swallowed a bottle of laudanum and died as violently as she had lived.

A curious thing about practically all these women-of-action is that they blame an early seduction or a disappearing husband for their adventures: plump Hannah

Snell, daughter of a soldier, married at the Fleet—where no questions were asked and no records kept that could not be faked—a Dutchman who quickly disappeared, leaving her pregnant: she joined the army to follow him. Mother Ross's tale is almost identical, except that her husband swore that he had been pressed into service; Mary Anne Talbot followed her soldier-lover in the disguise of a foot-boy; Anne Bonny donned breeches because her father threw her out-of-doors for marrying a worthless sailor; the exception is Mary Read whose mother dressed her as a boy to dupe her relations-by-marriage and who of her own will enlisted as a powder-monkey. It is difficult to know what truth can be accepted in such stories, myth has been woven so strongly about these Amazons by chapbook-Homers, yet there seems no reason to doubt that frustrated love drove many of them to adventure. Others who showed courage were camp-followers, wives and whores straggling in the wake of an army; of such was Mollie Picher who went a-soldiering with her husband in the American War of Independence and who became known as Captain Mollie after working a gun against the British at the battle of Monmouth and who in 1822 was voted a pension of eighty dollars a year for life. Some, however, took to adventure because they desired it for its own dangerous sake. Loreta Janeta Velasquez was of this type: she fought for the South in the American Civil War and did a small worthless bit of spying. She disappears from history travelling to New Mexico with her fourth husband. She was a restless tormented creature, a true ruffian in her determination to have her genius recognised—a fine of ten dollars with ten days imprisonment was all the honour the Confederates gave her when she confessed her masquerade—and who achieved nothing except a few children which could have been produced far more comfortably at her home in New Orleans. And we must not forget blue-eyed Belle Star, the outlaw queen, as good as any man with her gun, who died at last, shot in the back by a rejected lover, "Venus" Watson, and the fact that he shot her in the back is a compliment she would have appreciated.

These examples are mere infringements on a masculine world, women snapping the whalebone imprisonment of skirts, the physical counterpart of the intellectual battle waged by such as Mary Wortley Montagu, Fanny Burney, Mary Woolstonecraft, Emily Brontë, against man's smug indifference until Mrs. Bloomer made breeches respectable and the suffragettes forced parliament to realise that women possessed intelligence as well as legs. Women have won the fight but they have lost in the triumph, for the harem-system has always been the best breeding-ground for feminine genius. A comparison between the histories of east and west reveals that in the comparative freedom of Europe, women have had far less power than when shepherded by eunuchs behind the latticed walls of some seraglio where, cut off from the normal occupations that sublimate so much of our sexual energies, they were driven either to homosexuality or to consuming ambition that made them cunning mistresses of their lord's will. Even the great Suleyman the Magnificent lived beneath the dominance of red-headed Russian Roxana. In the west, woman, being given power in the home, satisfied her ambitions with petty tyranny, usually leaving the world-stage for the childlike posturing of men. She had no escape from her world, nor did she often desire escape; the laws binding her were—and still are—man-made, outwardly she has submitted, realising that in apparent submission lies her strength, her control of masculinity by subtle flattery and through the spiritual weakness that makes a slave of any man in love. Sometimes, in the strict past the woman rebelled, but if she did, man netted her in his laws, laws brutally created to make certain that, for the sake of property, women should not take lovers and bring the bâton sinister to his descendants. As outlet from this prison, which, if the woman were clever enough, could be turned into a throne, she had to become adventurer, blue-stocking or prostitute, and very often she combined all three. A woman murderer or thief, concentrating her energies into other outlets than sex, can be more brutal, more clever than any man. The barbarities of a woman in power are appalling, while a woman turned thug is incapable of understanding pity. One has only to remember creatures like Hell-Cat Maggie of the early Bowery days to realise that, however vicious, few men would go to the extent of filing their teeth to points and wearing brass finger-nails as was her game when out for killing; and Annie Christmas with her floating brothel on the Mississippi who could earn her living as a woman with the flesh, or as a man with her prodigious physical strength. I would far rather meet the entire Spartan army than a troop of Amazons, that merciless crew who lopped the right breast so that they could handle the bow with greater ease.

In comparing feminine with masculine brutality one is struck by an interesting point, the woman commonly prefers to torture and the man to kill. Perhaps this is based on the physical difference, but it cannot be entirely so, for in the records of sadism, the victims chosen by women are usually young helpless girls, servants or apprentices, feeble enough to be murdered easily. The male sadist acts quickly, stabbing or strangling his beloved, but the woman's pleasure apparently lies in inflicting pain. Our Sunday newspapers continually produce cases of this kind, in which wretched girls have been flogged and starved often to imbecility and occasionally to death. But the death is mainly an accident. Elizabeth Brownrigg is probably the most famous example of the woman sadist, and her husband and son were imprisoned only for six months each while she was deservedly hanged. Women murderers take an extraordinary low place in the Newgate Calendar. Apart from child-killing, a purely social crime that has nothing whatever to do with the desire to slay, and the occasional poisoning of a too-presumptuous lover as with Madelaine Smith, of an interfering parent as with Mary Blandy, or of an out-worn husband as in innumerable cases, women are not basically murderers. Being usually physically incapable of violence, it is natural that they should resort to poison, but even poisoning is comparatively rare. Men are so tortured by their neighbours' good opinion that often they would rather kill their wives than face a scandal; thus we see a respectable little man like Dr. Crippen of undeserved notoriety being forced to slay a bumptious over-bearing wife so that he might with a good conscience enjoy his mistress. On the whole, women are far more sane about such things; love being so vital a part of their lives, they have little compunction in deserting husband and even children under the stress of desire. The majority of cases of husband-killing are for money or, curiously enough, are perpetrated by ageing women in love with a younger man. Whether the impetuosity of youth, the defiant urging of the lover, drives her to getting rid of the legal impediment, or whether she acts in desperation before the appalling exposure of her mirror, is debatable; but I lean more towards the mirror as inspiration. A woman

unfortunate enough to love a younger man probably
suffers more anguish than any other living creature. In
frenzy at the sight of gathering wrinkles and slackening
throat, she is fully capable of murdering a husband so
that she can bind the lover securely to her by marriage.
We might almost say that the comparative dearth of
murdered husbands compared to murdered wives shows,
not tenderness on woman's part, but a certain callousness,
for while a man would sometimes prefer to cut his wife's
throat than to hurt her feelings by infidelity, the woman
hasn't the faintest compunction in walking from the
home. And there is another point: for so long have
women, netted in masculine laws, been made to condone
the husband's mistress, they are not so outraged when
they discover infidelity; man, on the other hand, tormented by his sense of property—wife being property—
and by the horror of rearing a bastard as his own child,
will kill in an effort to retain his self-respect, his honourable position before the world.

But murder alone is no passport into Ruffians' Hall,
madmen can kill, or cowards cornered and driven desperate with terror. We have no welcome for the Jack the
Rippers, slitting a woman to investigate the strange
machinery that makes her function; no Billy the Kids
shooting in the back for preference; or wolfish devils
like Sawny Bean with his hungry brood sucking the
marrow from a human bone; no Hell Benders smacking
their unsuspecting visitors on the head through a curtain;
no savage Harpes of the Natchez Trace, brooding beside
their women and listening for the crash of hoofs from a
lonely horseman; no Dr. Websters of Boston driven to
frenzied baking of lean sanctimonious creditors; no dope-
gangling gangsters or sadists like the demon of Dussel-
dorf . . . Ruffians' Hall is careful whom it permits to

enter, it has little chivalry and will shut the door against women, no matter how beautiful, who, like Mary of Scotland, slaughter a husband, or like Isabella of England destroy a king her husband with a red-hot spit in diabolic fashion; even the records of the Countess of Essex might be scanned with care, uncertain whether those poisons she sent to Overbury in the Tower are sufficient to let her pass . . . Or Lucrezia Borgia: what did she do? there is a rumour of poisoning, but a rumour that is so opaque that it reveals naught, and a suggestion of incest with her brother and father, the father tale being an obvious lie, yet perhaps with the brother . . . But incest will not let you pass, or all the Kings and Queens of Egypt, with the might of the Incas, must enter . . . Far more is needed. Not those who sat knitting around the guillotine during the French Revolution, nor the thousand Kurdish women under the Black Virgin who paraded for battle in Constantinople during the Crimean War. . . . Circe is the password for the woman-ruffian; Circe who turns men to snuffling swine at her little feet. Women driven by the splendid arrogance of their bodies, superb and conquering, with men forever pleading with them, men offering all gifts for one embrace—they are the true women-ruffians.

Even the German Princess, who was neither German nor a Princess, can enter, the triumphant rogue whom Pepys saw act her own life, "but never," writes he, "was anything so well done in earnest, worse performed in jest upon the stage." Her true name was Mary Carleton, and she was one of the first of whom we have record who used that popular game of having a man without breeches nabbed in her bedroom by an outraged husband whose honour only blood or gold could satisfy. She can enter the Hall because her life was one of set

ambitions from the moment she realised the simple truth
that she could escape a situation by walking out of it and
that a husband when squeezed of all cash can be discarded for a wealthier man by merely changing her address and telling one or two lies to a not too inquisitive
priest. So famous did she become that a play was written
about her exploits—that which Mr. Pepys saw—and in
which she acted the name-part and spoke an epilogue of
true ruffian-faith:

> " You think me a bold cheat, but case 'twere so,
>   which of you are not? Now you'd swear I know.
> But do not, lest that you deserve to be
> censur'd worse than you can censure me:
> the world's a cheat, and we that move in it,
> in our degrees, do exercise our wit;
> and better 'tis to get a glorious name,
> however got, than live by common fame."

" The princess," writes her biographer, surely with no
malicious intent, " had too much mercury in her con-
stitution to be long settled in any way of life whatsoever.
The whole City of London was too little for her to act
in. How was it possible then that she should be confined
in the narrow limits of a theatre? She did not, however,
leave the stage so soon but she had procured a considerable number of adorers, who, having either seen her
person or heard of her fame, were desirous of a nearer
acquaintance with her. As she was naturally given to
company and gallantry, she was not very difficult of
access; yet when you were in her presence, you were certain to meet with an air of indifference." There is the
woman ruffian, leashing her lusts under that mask of indifference, transmuting her sexual desires into desire for
gold, into power over men. Two gallants loved her, and
she " gave them encouragement, till she had drained
about three hundred pounds apiece out of them, and

then, finding their stock pretty well exhausted, she turned them both off, telling them she wondered how they could have the impudence to pretend love to a princess." True ruffianism, indeed, to empty their pockets, then to kick them out-of-doors with a reprimand, this arrogant little baggage, daughter of a Canterbury chorister! but by this time she had probably begun to believe her own lies. The tragedy is that they hanged her on January 22, 1673, not for any notable cheat, not for having married so many husbands that she couldn't count them all, but for returning from transportation; and she had been transported for the petty shame of stealing a silver tankard, a sentence she deserved at having thus degraded her talents, for thus betraying the noble code of high ruffianism.

This type, which to-day we call "gold-digger," is the most common of women ruffians; she is close to the whore, only she will sidle out of her bargain if she can, taking money and giving no return with Portia-like arguments about the promised pound of flesh. Not that the whore also would not avoid fulfilling her bargain were she able: practically all of them are thieves and entirely unscrupulous. During a time of extreme penury, I existed in a room of about ten feet by four in a house of more than dubious reputation near Maida Vale. Except for myself and wife and a musician friend who was generous enough to present us with this room rent-free, there wasn't a single tenant in the house not a prostitute, apart from a large floating population of part-time workers, some of them married, who earned a little booze-money on the side. One woman in particular should be mentioned, a not too unattractive creature married to a decent workingman who lived placidly under the delusion that his wife spent her days charing, and I

don't suppose a better euphuism could have been found
for her job; she had a daughter, then about thirteen or
fourteen, and far from all the nonsense one hears of the
maternal instinct glowing tigerishly in even the most depraved, that woman deliberately cajoled her daughter
into the business. Not that the girl needed any cajoling,
she was an over-fleshed, saucy-eyed wench who had
probably already decided that she might as well be paid
instead of wasting her charms unremuneratively on the
local riffraff. Not long ago I saw that girl again, about
six years after this period, and it took me fully five
minutes of hard thought before I was able to remember
who was the floppy whore that kept on smiling at me
from the corner of the bar. She looked about thirty, the
tired flesh having given up the struggle long before the
spirit flagged; it had lost its flexibility, it drooped on
bosom, belly and throat, while the parched skin could
only be made to appear appetising by smudges of paint
and layers of powder. Whatever illusions, born from
love of Francis Thompson and de Quincey, I might have
had of these creatures, they quickly went when I was
forced to live amongst them. There was no Sonia to
whom like Raskolnikoff I could kneel, saying, " I do not
bow to you alone but to all the suffering of the world
in you "; no Nancy boasting of lost virtue before the
goggling Rose; no sentimental maudlin lass like her who
seized Little Dorrit only to fling her away, wailing, " I
never should have touched you, but I thought you were a
child! " and who then " with a strange, wild cry," fled
into the darkness of London Bridge. No. There was no
sentiment in the ladies of Maida Vale, no remorse for a
virtue lost so long ago that they probably couldn't recall
the time, no envy for the pious and respectable, nothing
in all their talk except sex and drink. One has somehow

a romantic idea of the poor harlot selling her " beauty for a bit of bread " and yearning always for the luxury of being able to sleep alone. From my experience, this is entirely untrue, her work obsesses the prostitute, and in some peculiar fashion does not exhaust the body. There was one large bold-eyed Jewess, practically the queen of this house, who used to become as excited as a young girl when her lover visited her: he came roughly once a month and stayed a week-end, never for one moment suspecting his mistress's trade, for she had a discarded husband hovering somewhere in her past, and his existence—whether mythical or not I never discovered—explained her two children and her bank-balance. Altogether, that episode remains in my mind with a choking fusty smell and a sense of dirt, of unwashed frying-pans, filthy stoves, torn soiled feminine garments on the stairs, and windows from which the dusty curtains had never been lifted. Here is the woman ruffian at her lowest, her cleanliness and sense of decency gone with the selling of the flesh; most of the women were sexually abnormal —how irritating it is that sex can only be discussed with smutty words, with incomprehensible scientific terms, or in pious phrases that give a lying sanctimoniousness to the conversation, making one ashamed—but few really cared for the conventional love-making, practically all were homosexual, which is a perplexing point, and most of them were sadists or masochists. The latter can be easily explained as self-protective, for, apart from casual drunks picked up in the street or inquisitive adolescents, the whore's clientele is made up of sexual freaks. These women, I am certain by their talk, would have been puzzled had one of their clients suggested ordinary behaviour, they would have been suspicious and even perhaps afraid. For this reason, the prostitute serves a

A Harlot's Progress—Plate I
(William Hogarth)

useful purpose: but for her, many starved sadists would have to seek their game in normal suburbs and we should have a great many more murders than we have even to-day.

Lower than the prostitute, perhaps, we should place the bawd, she who entices servant-girls and waitresses and other easy prey into a brothel. This type, as with the harlot, is rapidly disappearing under our cleaner sexual attitude and the freedom of women which they are using nobly, but it still exists. Hogarth painted a famous woman of this profession in his *Harlot's Progress*. The fat old creature patting innocent Kate Hackabout under the chin as she alights from the coach is a portrait of Mother Needham who grew so hated for her tricks of corrupting young girls that when on April 30, 1731, they locked her into the pillory for keeping a disorderly house, the mob pelted her with such gusto that she died from her injuries a few days later. In this glorious world, that ecstatic panorama of life, that hurly-burly of exultant ruffians, male and female, Hogarth also gives us Sarah Malcolm, and although we have decided that murder alone is not sufficient guarantee for Ruffians' Hall she is worth a passing notice. She seems a hefty wench in the painting, half-leaning on the table as if about to spring up murderously; there is a wary alertness in her pose, in the tightly clenched grim mouth, the fierce staring eyes and wide animal nostrils. They hanged her opposite Mitre Court, Fleet Street, on March 7, 1733, for the murders of Mrs. Lydia Duncombe, Elizabeth Harrison and Anne Price; she was also suspected of being involved in the murder of a Mr. Nesbit, in 1729, near Drury Lane, for which a certain Kelly was hanged, protesting his innocence to the very end, saying that the bloodied razor found under the corpse was his property but that he had lent it to a woman whose name he didn't know. Whether innocent of this early murder or not, Sarah's trial aroused huge attention, and when at ten in the morning she was taken in the cart from Newgate to Mitre Court, the crowd was so great that a Mrs. Strangeways who lived near Sergeants' Inn crossed Fleet Street on the heads and shoulders of the spectators. Wearing a crêpe mourning gown, white apron, sarcenet hood and black gloves, the twenty-five-year-old Sarah made a saucy end, probably being drunk, and it was said that her face was heavily painted to hide the chalk of terror. Before being turned off, she gave a friend, not a confession, but a protestation of innocence—inevitable ruffian gesture—and promptly fainted the moment the rope was about her neck. At the undertaker's on Snow Hill, people paid freely to look their last upon the murderer, and one gentleman, at the cost of half-a-crown, was permitted even to kiss her mouth. After all this furore one expects a classic crime, but it was a very bungled affair, reflecting no credit whatever on Sarah's cunning. The bodies were found at noon on February 4, 1733: Mrs. Duncombe, a widow of about eighty, was lying dressed on her bed, evidently smothered; her companion, the elderly Elizabeth Harrison, was in bed, strangled, with two or three strange wounds in her throat, apparently caused by a nail; the servant, Anne Price, being seventeen years of age and lusty, put up a fight: she also was in bed but her cap was off, her hair tangled, and her throat cut from ear to ear. A trunk was broken open and rifled. The crime might have remained a mystery but for Sarah herself. That night, or rather next morning, at one, a Mr. Kerrell who had chambers on the same stairs as the corpses, returned to find Sarah, his laundress, still in his

rooms. He asked what she did and if the murderer had
been caught; answered Sarah, "No one had yet been
taken up; but a gentleman who had chambers beneath,
but had been absent two or three days, was violently
suspected." "Be that as it may," said wise Mr. Kerrell,
"you were Mrs. Duncombe's laundress, and no one who
knew her shall ever come into these chambers until her
murderer is discovered: pack up your things and go
away." Something in her manner and the sight of a
strange bundle on the floor, made Mr. Kerrell call a
watchman and have her taken in charge. The bundle
revealed some linen and a silver pint tankard with a
bloodied handle. His suspicions confirmed by this, Kerrell went into the street to ask the watchman what he
had done with the prisoner; the watchman calmly
answered "that she had promised to come again next
day, and he had let her go." She was soon found: as if
demanding punishment, she was discovered chatting to
two watchmen at Temple Gate and, on being taken to
Newgate, eighteen guineas, twenty moidores, five broad
pieces, five crown pieces and a few shillings were dug
out of her hair, altogether exactly eight shillings and
sixpence less than had been stolen from Mrs. Duncombe.
In true ruffian style, Sarah looked around for others on
to whom she could shelve her guilt and denounced
Thomas and James Alexander with Mary Tracy as the
murderers. At first nobody believed that these three
existed, but a seventeen-year-old boy confessed that he
was called James Alexander and said, "I have a brother
named Thomas, and my mother nursed a woman where
Sarah Malcolm lived." They were all taken into custody,
Sarah telling a complicated story soon blown away as lies
that nevertheless kept the three unfortunates in jail for
some time.

That is the history of Sarah Malcolm, a crude murderer immortalised by Hogarth, and its value to us lies only in her determination to tag the guilt on to others, in her amazing effrontery at not only remaining in the house of murder but later consorting with watchmen, and in her gallant end when she wrote her protestations of innocence which she asked to have published and which were actually sold for twenty pounds: you can read the lies in the *Gentleman's Magazine* for 1733. We have now watched the low-grade woman murderer at work— I refuse to write " murderess " as firmly as I would the insulting " adventuress" and "poetess," for there should be no sexual distinction in art—and noticed how appallingly savage she can be: as a privileged servant, it would surely have been simple for Sarah to choose an hour when the old lady was alone instead of having to murder all three for a little gold? Her bland refusal to consider danger is typical of the ruffian, male and female, as also are her efforts to entangle other people and the last defiant cry of innocence. Only at the end, when literally in the shadow of the noose, did she turn womanly enough to swoon, reminding us of Mary Blandy who poisoned her father at her lover's instigation and who went daintily to her hanging, " habited in a black bombasine dress, her arms being bound with black ribands. On her ascending the gallows she begged that she might not be hanged high, ' for the sake of decency '; and on her being desired to go a little higher, expressed her fear that she might fall. The rope being put round her neck, she pulled her handkerchief over her face, and was turned off on holding out a book of devotions which she had been reading." Yes! even to their hangings do the ladies bring a fragrance of femininity, a sweet almost naïve beauty that is found lacking in the more brutal and unimagina-

tive executions of the male. But if they give delicacy to
their end, women are liable to bring the most fiendish
brutality into their crimes, and innumerable are the
murders inspired by women. One of the most horrible
killings in the history of British smuggling was at the
instigation of women. An informer called Chater was
travelling to Chichester with one Galley, an officer of
excise, and on the way they stopped at the White Hart,
Rowland's Castle, where Chater talked too much and
soon found himself and friend ringed in by smugglers.
Chater got a punch on the nose but nothing else for the
time, the men were angry but they needed women's
tongues to drive them to actual murder. Two of their
wives came in and, on hearing the tale, cried, " Hang
the dogs, for they came here to hang us! " at which, one
of the smugglers leaped on their bed—for the informer
and friend were by now in drunken slumber—and
trampled on their faces, kicking them with his spurred
heels. The tortures that followed were truly diabolic,
obscene and unnecessarily cruel, and they are an intrusion into this chapter; but they might never have happened if those two women had not walked that night
into the White Hart. As Robin Green put into the mouth
of his Elizabethan she-cony-catcher, Fair Nan: " In my
high loving, or rather creeping, I mean where men and
women do rob together, there always the woman is most
bloody, she always urgeth unto death, and, though the
men would only satisfy themselves with the party's coin,
yet she endeth her theft in blood, murdering parties, so
deeply as she is malicious." There are innumerable
examples of this Lady Macbeth quality in the woman
ruffian, this murder-by-proxy, this holding of the candle
while the man wields the knife.

In Sarah Mitchell we have seen the crude she-ruffian,
o

whose skill reveals nothing feminine, and before dismissing the murderer, we will take one or two more examples of a far more common type, the husband-killer. There is one really strange case that comes to my mind, that of Ann Whale and Sarah Pledge who murdered Ann's husband for no apparent reason except that Whale forbade Sarah to enter the house and his sober habits rather irritated the females. "Nan," said Sarah, "let us get rid of this devil!" and said Nan, "How can we do it?" "Let us give him a dose of poison," said Sarah and dropped some roasted spiders into his beer. As spiders were not efficacious enough, poison was bought and that finished the husband off. I mention this case because of its sheer madness, its apparent lack of motive, for there is no lover in the affair. Putting aside the probable basis of homosexuality, it gives us another proof of the old wisdom of not permitting your wife to become too friendly with a woman. Many are the marriages broken, if not by killing, at least by infidelity, due to lewd inspiration from the bawdy urgings of a gossip. Medieval husbands had a great horror of this and distrusted their wive's women friends equally with the male, and very often they are more dangerous. This, however, is an irrelevancy, let us return to the ruffian-murderer killing her husband or employing men to kill him. The eighteenth century offers us an excellent example in Catherine Hayes, burned on May 9, 1726, that being the punishment until the thirteenth year of the reign of George III for husband-murderers, the crime being considered "petit treason." It was customary, however, to strangle the woman before lighting the faggots: Catherine was unlucky, the flames scorched the executioner's hands so that he prematurely let go the rope and the people saw her kicking at the wood, writhing in agony, and screaming for some time. It took three or four hours to burn the body.

She had been married many years before the killing, and her home-life was one perpetual quarrel, Catherine having been heard on occasions to say " that she should think it no more sin to murder him than to kill a dog." In their house in Tyburn Road—now Oxford Street—with them lived a tailor, Thomas Billings, whom Catherine passed off as her son by a previous marriage but who was without doubt her lover; also involved in the plot was a lodger, Thomas Wood, and one can perhaps conclude that he also was her lover. Her argument with both men, a very conclusive one, was that on Hayes's death she would be mistress of fifteen hundred pounds. The murder was arranged carefully by getting the husband so drunk that they had to put him to bed, and while he lay there, Billings hit him with a coal-hatchet, but so blunderingly that he only woke Hayes up and had to make quite unnecessary noise by hitting him a second time. The problem, the ever-pressing problem remained—a huge mound of flesh and apparently unlimited supplies of blood to damn them for ever. Catherine—the men were palsied with funk—suggested chopping off the head because without the head the body could not be recognised. She held the candle—true attitude of the steady-handed woman-ruffian—and the pail while " Billings drew the body by the head over the bedside, that the blood might bleed the more freely into it; and Wood with his pocket penknife cut it off." Having got the head off, Catherine now wanted to boil the flesh from it, but the men were too impatient, and they threw it into the Thames near Westminster. But in the darkness, with shaking hands, imagining phantoms in every shadow, they threw head and pail, not into the river, but on to the dock where a watchman found them in the morning. The body yet remained, so Catherine bought a box which was found to be too small; they cut off arms and legs, and yet the box was not large enough; so they chopped away the thighs and bundled the whole muddle in somehow where it was concealed for a time. Later they threw the remains into a pond in Marylebone Fields, but all was wasted effort: the head had been cleaned and put upon a post in St. Margaret's churchyard, Westminster, in the hope of identification. Evidently the murderers were afraid to be alone, the men slept—or rather tossed in torment— together, " and Mrs. Hayes stayed with them all night, sometimes sitting up, and sometimes laying down upon the bed by them." It is astonishing that they remained safe for so long with that accusing head becoming quite one of the holiday sights of London, but Catherine changed her lodgings and continued to live placidly above suspicion. The murder was committed on the night of March 1, yet it was not until the 28th that she was committed to Newgate. They caught her while she was in bed, with Billings " sitting upon her bedside, without either shoes or stockings on." Being told of the suspicions about her husband's murder, she implored them to let her see the head, which was granted, and she fell on her knees before it, wailing, " Oh, it is my dear husband's head! It is my dear husband's head!" and " taking it in her arms, she kissed it, and seemed in great confusion, begging to have a lock of his hair; but Mr. Westbrook [the chemist who had embalmed it] replied that he was afraid she had had too much of his blood already. At which she fainted away." Wood was next taken and the remains of the body discovered by accident in the pond. Wood confessed everything, saying that Catherine "was the first promoter of, and a great assistance in several parts of this horrid affair." When Catherine was told of this confession, the actress deserted her, her courage went, and she said simply that they must tell Billings " 'twas in vain to deny any longer the murder of her husband, for they were equally guilty, and both must die for it." But her ruffian-spirit came back after that first betrayal, and when arraigned she pleaded not guilty in a firm voice while both men pleaded guilty, merely asking that they should not be gibbeted in chains afterwards, a sentence that for some reason terrified the most hardened criminal. Witness after witness came forward to state that while in Newgate Catherine had said, " the devil put it into her head, but, however, John Hayes was none of the best of husbands, for she had been half starved ever since she was married to him; that she did not in the least repent of anything she had done, but only in drawing those two poor men into this misfortune; that she was six weeks importuning them to do it . . . she could hold up her hand and say she was guilty, for nothing could save her, nobody could forgive her; that the men who did the murder were taken and confessed it; that she was not with them when they did it; that she was sitting by the fire in the shop upon a stool; that she heard the blow given and somebody stamp; that she did not cry out, for fear they should kill her; that after the head was cut off, it was put into a pail, and Wood carried it out; that Billings sat down by her and cried, and would lie all the rest of the night in the room with the dead body; that the first occasion of this design to murder him was because he came home one night and beat her, upon which Billings said this fellow deserved to be killed, and Wood said he would be his butcher for a penny; that she told them they might do as they would do it that night it was done; that she did not tell her husband of the design to murder him, for fear he should beat her." In which confusion we see Catherine leaping from despair, from pity for her accomplices, to gradual faith in her own high destiny; slowly she discards compassion and tries to rouse pity at the mention of her husband's cruelty, to show herself as the distressed female defended chivalrously by two gallants, while the full blame she puts on Wood, Billings being her favourite. But it didn't work, women are not good liars in the sense that they talk too much, permit their minds to wander from the one purpose: " she herself confessed at the bar her previous knowledge of their intent several days before the fact was committed; yet foolishly insisted on her innocence, because the fact was not committed by her own hands." To the end her courage maintained her while " her fondness for Billings hurried her into undecencies of a very extraordinary nature, such as sitting with her hand in his in chapel, leaning upon his shoulder, and refusing upon being reprimanded (for giving offence to the congregation) to make any amendment in respect of these shocking ·passages between her and the murderers of her husband, but on the contrary, she persisted in them to the very minute of her death. One of her last expressions was to enquire of the executioner whether he had hanged her dear child [Billings], and this, as she was going from the sledge to the stake, so strong and lasting were the passions of this woman." All the same, she made one brave attempt to poison herself in prison, being foiled by a fellow-prisoner at the last moment.

Catherine reveals fully the strength and weakness of the woman-murderer, her deep sense of martyrdom under the restraining hand of marriage, the frustration of her will to freedom merging to hatred of the husband, unsatisfied even by having a lover in the same house. Undoubtedly she convinced herself that Hayes was a tyrant, yet he seems to have been an easy-going fellow, if intolerably sober most of the time, which apparently galled Catherine, who liked her pint in low singing company. Her feeling of being wronged would quickly justify murder, for the ruffian strains always to impress society with his or her own neglect and even victimization. Cold-bloodedly, Catherine urged her lover Billings to the deed, but he seems a weak creature and probably for this reason she dragged Wood into the plot. Having wrought the men up into a state of murder, she got them blind drunk and sent the stupid Billings to the husband with his axe: in the whole silly affair, she alone seems to have kept her head and to have calmly faced inevitable suspicion, and her mask must have been a bold one to have withstood the rumours for so long. It is, however, her behaviour in prison that shows the difference between male and female murderer and which justified Mr. Ahearn's mistrust of dames. It is not exactly that women talk too much but that they talk too loosely, contradicting themselves, admitting guilt without even being aware of admitting it. As an example of this, Katherine Howard's confession to Cranmer is a pathetic document for, while denying her marriage with Dereham, she forgets her denials in sudden terror and distractedly admits the truth in a negative fashion. So it was with this ruffian-Catherine: unable to squirm away from Wood's admission, she at one moment calls herself guilty and the next cries that the murder was done without her knowledge or help; then she skips to say that she had enticed the men to it, only to insist that she knew of their plot all the time yet feared to tell her husband lest he beat her. She entangles herself in her lies, for-getting what she previously said when some new trick of escape comes into her mind. But dominant in her heart, greater even than her own terrors, is love and apprehension for Billings. What man could equal such nobility, such passion, that it can usurp even fears at the prospect of a ghastly death? What man would cry like Kate Howard upon the scaffold, "I die a queen but I would rather die the wife of Culpeper"? or like Kate Hayes plead with the executioner for a lover's life when placed upon the sledge on the way to the faggots?

A woman's existence is bounded by this superb, this un-reasoning and ruthless love. She is admirable, terrifying. Consider Christiana Edmunds, condemned to death in 1872 and reprieved and sent to Broadmoor. She was a pathetic, middle-aged spinster destroyed by her mother, and mothers can sometimes be the most appalling ruffians, dominating the lives of their children until they squeeze all youth and happiness from their prey with omnivorous affection. "The caterpillar on the leaf," wrote Blake, "reminds thee of thy mother's grief." In that Mecca of the lonely, Brighton, these two settled, and poor Christiana's repressed existence rapidly drove her to such neurotic behaviour that her mother feared she would imitate her father and go mad. She called in a Dr. Beard, and Christiana fell instantly and passionately in love with Dr. Beard. This is a danger against which most doctors have to guard, for to the average respectable lady her medical adviser is her father confessor, and often, even with married women, he is the only man who knows not only the secrets of his patient's mind but of her body too. Dr. Beard was tactless, he was far too sympathetic with Christiana. He asked for trouble, and he got it. Christiana confessed her passion, and in those pre-Freudian days the man was perplexed and terrified, he tried to calm her with affection, he even stupidly wrote letters, although there is no suggestion whatever that he meant a word of what he wrote. Such was his misguided treatment, and the result was appalling. Christiana determined to murder Mrs. Beard so that she could marry the doctor. She bought some strychnine and she bought some chocolates and she went to tea with Mrs. Beard, who on biting a chocolate immediately spat it out again. Realising the truth, the doctor told Christiana what he thought of her and the unfortunate, despairing woman swore that she would convince him of her innocence. She picked on a small boy in the street, despatched him for a box of chocolates, inserted strychnine into the sweets and had the box sent back, saying that they were not what she required. This she repeated, stocking the wretched confectioner with deadly sweets, until on June 12, 1871, a small boy died in agony. Thus did Christiana justify herself, thus like a true ruffian did she prove her good conscience, revealing to Dr. Beard how cruelly he had misjudged her in believing her capable of a single wicked thought against his wife. The police, however, with small respect for the nobility of ruffians, soon had her up for trial and proved their case. This example is almost too perfect a specimen of the woman ruffian at work: Christiana did not care if she murdered all Brighton so long as the man she loved at least respected her, the innocent boy was of no account beside the doctor's good opinion.

This callousness, this amazing lack of conscience in most women, is often appalling, although of course Christiana's case is beyond average, for her years of repression under a bullying mother had driven her slightly insane. Insanity, however, only released the unconscious urge of the ruffian spirit. Christiana would believe that she had every justification because her will was naturally paramount, as God's is paramount. We cannot too often reiterate this ruffianly good conscience, this bland refusal to see another point of view or to feel sympathy. Can any ordinary soul, for example, appreciate the attitude of someone like the notorious Maria Manning who robbed and murdered her disdainful lover, doubling his legs back with cord and burying him in the kitchen with lime and a gallon of vitriol, and afterwards calmly ate a goose with her accomplice-husband over the remains? In court, Maria behaved like a good ruffian, throwing the blame upon her drunken cowardly husband, and gabbling all through the proceedings. She dressed for the tragic part in a black satin gown, with cap and ruffles of white lace, a plaid shawl, and primrose yellow gloves; she could not resist flaunting the corpse's one-time love for her and talked much of injustice, saying, " I have lots of letters from Mr. O'Connor (the corpse) to show his regard for me. I think, too, that, considering I am a woman and alone, and have had to fight against my husband's statements, as well as against the prosecution, and that even the judge himself is against me—well, I think that I am not being treated like a Christian, but like a wild beast of the forest. The judge and jury will have it on their consciences for giving a verdict against me. I am not guilty. I have lived in respectable families (she worked as maid once for the Duke and Duchess of Sutherland), and can produce testimonials of character. If my villain of a husband, through jealousy and revenge, chose to murder poor Mr. O'Connor, I really don't see why I should be punished." A delightful speech in the real tradition, for there can be no possible doubt that Maria shot her lover, although her husband confessed that he " saw O'Connor fall across the grave. He was moaning. As I never liked him very well,

I battered in his skull with a chisel." Maria has been doubly honoured: Dickens described her public execution and Madame Tussaud's took a cast of her face, although this was against her express wish. Before being turned off, she presented a handkerchief to the surgeon and asked modestly, "Please cover my face. I do not want the public to stare at me."

Maria's case, however, is not purely one of sex, there were other motives, including robbery and, very importantly, revenge. Revenge is a vital facet in the ruffian's make-up, for the slightest insult becomes to his or her dignity as assault on God. More truly and perplexingly feminine was Christina Cochran who loved John Anderson and yet was weak enough to permit her family to force her into marriage with one John Gilmour who died of arsenic poisoning six weeks after the ceremony, being most tenderly cared for by his wife while he shrieked and twisted in agony, for women murderers make the most admirable nurses for their victims. The jury's verdict in 1844 was non proven, but, as in the more famous case of Madeleine Smith, there can be no doubt of Christina's guilt, but the puzzling point is why she ever did get married. Apparently to her it was simpler to kill than to refuse her family's command, a common enough trait with very weak yet stubborn characters, who become often the most dangerous criminals. Of course it is foolish to pretend that only women-ruffians can be so entirely callous —William Palmer was the most cold-blooded of rogues, for one—but it is true that the woman-murderer usually shows far less consideration for her victim than does the male, suffers from no remorse and can act superbly the part of broken-hearted martyr. Yet for all this callousness towards the dying, there is normally a second side, passionate love for another, for him who is so often the unconscious inspiration of her deed. She can smile and pout kisses at her beloved over the writhing corpse of the husband, then the next instant become the broken-hearted compassionate wife. To attain the fulfillment of her love, nothing else is of importance, all can be kicked contemptuously aside. She can in her great self-sacrificing noble tenderness for one man calmly butcher the husband who bars her from the completion of her desires.

Love in a woman is so dominant, so all-consuming, that it awes one to reverence; yet it is the blade that kills them as true ruffians. Unless they can smother it, they are doomed, and how few are the women who can pluck love entirely from their lives. It must be sublimated into another lust of even greater violence, drink being a common substitute, or it must be twisted into resentment by some early tragedy, a frustrated first love is only too common a cause for frigidity or homosexuality in women, as also it is with men. I have a male friend, impotent for life because of a frantic wedding-night, and there was a girl I knew who was driven coldly within herself, to a hatred of men, because of a love-tragedy in which the lover was not even to blame, but her rage against God at being cheated became transferred in some queer fashion to a contempt for all men, whose love she accepted only at her command and that rarely, while she exalted as something spiritual her love for other women. A mutilated first love has destroyed many a woman's later life, has either chilled her sex or made her exploit it recklessly in the manner of a prostitute.

When, for example, the exceptionally beautiful Pauline Bonaparte loved Fréron, she was an unfledged girl, but her ambitious brother forbade the match. "I will chose lifelong unhappiness rather than marry without your consent," she wrote to Napoleon. "You, from whom I

expected happiness, you compel me to renounce the only
man I can ever love. Young as I am, I have a steadfast
character. It is impossible for me to give up Fréron after
all the promises I have made to love him alone. Yes, I
will hold to them. Absolutely no one can prevent me
keeping my heart for him, receiving his letters, answering them, and repeating that I will love only him." The
power of the Corsican family, dominated by the terrifying Madame Mere, was too strong for Pauline to fight,
it was so strong that eventually it was to prove one of
the main causes of Napoleon's own downfall: she discarded her lover, and in his place took uncounted men
to flatter her physical loveliness and the potency of her
charm. Her body, dedicated to Fréron, no longer became sacred, although it dominated all her life. She gave
herself completely to her own body, tending it with passionate solicitude. For hours she massaged, painted, per-
fumed, and dressed it; she had a negro to carry it in his
black arms to the bath, and she unfolded its glory to
Canova so that almost he could not finish the sculpture
with longing to use his hands on flesh, not marble. We
have her body in his stone but it is an uninspiring work,
exhaling none of her amazing fascination: she lounges on
a too-realistic sofa, showing small firm breasts and delicately muscled stomach. She is more adorable on the
medal struck in her honour by the Paris mint from draw-
ings by Baron Denon, "that faunlike amateur of
beauty": on the obverse, we have her profile under
Grecian curls, faintly smiling, the nose is straight, the
eyes heavy-lidded; but on the reverse she stands in all her
splendour of nakedness as the Three Graces, revealing
herself to us from front, from side, from back, a long-
legged miracle of perfection. But this body which she
pampered, for which alone she lived—save for adoration of

her brother—took its revenge, was ever ailing, driving her into neurasthenia and a frenzy of meaningless loves, shadows of the lost Fréron whom when a girl she had worshipped in Marseilles. He had been twice her age, and it is interesting to note in the chronicles of women how almost inevitably their first seducer is older than they: the early thirties and fifties would seem to be man's most fascinating ages, perhaps because the thirties combine youth, virility, with experience, and the fifties experience with the addition of fatherliness, and it is natural that a young girl should love a man who can act both the father and lover.

Into dispassionate use of her body, an early love can drive a woman to satisfying its urge as she satisfies the lusts to eat and drink, without real interest, the man being but the physical manifestation of her own desire for herself, discarded callously in the morning. Thus are many women ruffians created, for the first necessity is to destroy love or to fuse its passion into another desire, such as drink, political or social ambitions, or lust for money as an end in itself. Even that vice, usually more common with women than with men, snobbery, can replace love. Sophie Dawes is proof of that.

Sophie does not seem to have been very attractive. Her father, Dicky Dawes or Daw, was an oyster-catcher and part-time smuggler on the Isle of Wight, and in 1805 young Sophie, then probably thirteen or fourteen years of age, became servant to a farmer, from servant she rose to being chambermaid at an inn, and eventually reached London where she worked in a milliner's. For the first and only time in her life, Sophie allowed love to interfere with ambition, for being caught with a water-carrier in a compromising posture, she lost her job, and took the only alternative offering: orange girl in the playhouse,

that whore's seminary, from which she quickly graduated
to being in keeping to some gentleman. He dismissed
her at last with fifty pounds, and her subsequent adventures for a time have been left in decent obscurity until
we discover her working as a servant in a brothel. She
kept self-respect enough to retain skirts in that temple
of nudity, and was not for any casual client's buying.
One of these clients was servant to the Duc de Bourbon,
a wealthy émigré, and at Sophie's request the man in-
troduced her to his master. Probably youth was Sophie's
fascination, for in the miniature painted of her at this
time I can trace no real beauty, although the artist would
naturally exaggerate any charms he could find. The large
eyes seem the mostly lovely feature, they are of a bright
blue, but the brows are rather straight and heavy; the
mouth is thinnish if well-shaped; the dark brown hair,
parted in the centre, ripples into the fashionable curls about
the round face, showing one little ear. She was, we are
told, tall and graceful, and certainly the miniaturist has not
forgotten the feminine loveliness of shoulders and breasts.
The simple muslin gown does not hide the full glory
of those breasts pushed upwards by the sash, and
probably her very coarseness may have fascinated the
aristocratic Bourbon. There is something of an animal-
attraction in the sturdy bodies of peasant-women, something that draws one with a sense of thrilling danger,
like submitting to the fury of a leopard; to a sated appetite like Bourbon's, Sophie's virility with the bloom of
youth would appear desirable, and in young girls, in the
pastel-shading of their skin, there is an urge that pulls at
elderly men, so peach-like and virginal seems the flesh
unstained by age, tempting to bitings and caresses. There
is nothing peculiar in Bourbon's desire for Sophie, but
the mystery lies in her complete domination of him in

later years. He did make one effort to escape her, but that was near the beginning of the affair, before her grip was unbreakably on his soul. When the Bourbons returned in triumph to France, the duke went to Paris and forgot Sophie, although she hurried after him. He even had the temerity to instal a rival, another Sophie, Sophie Harris, in Lisson Grove, but Sophie Dawes's determination was such that the Bourbon, now titled the Prince de Condé, gave way and, to hide the affair, Sophie spread the lie that she was her lover's illegitimate daughter. The one real passion of her life seems to have been a desire to be received at court, but under Louis XVIII and grim Madame Première this was no easy matter: hence the illegitimacy tale and Sophie's determination to marry. It was here that she failed lamentably: instead of choosing either a fool or a knave for husband, she married an honourable soldier, M. de Feuchères, who fully believed that she was Condé's bastard. Sophie's behaviour was now typical of her upbringing, this sudden power made of her a tyrant, the penniless oyster-catcher's daughter bullied her servants almost to suicide, threw things at them at the least murmur of disobedience, and in her miserliness, would ostentatiously count the faggots brought for the fire and lock her door against thieves in the house; the people detested her so thoroughly for her overbearing cruelty that stones and curses would follow her carriage when she flaunted herself in the streets. Only one decent feeling can we find in her, and one strangely at variance with her militant snobbery: she never ignored her relations and settled her mother comfortably in a Paris house; to Condé's relations she was merciless, his illegitimate daughter, Madame de Rully, who refused to sit at the same table with her, she bundled out of the Condé establishment, together with her husband, a peer of France, and had her dowry taken from her. Her power became really incredible, and with it grew vanity. She wanted to act and therefore arranged private theatricals, and although she was a hefty woman of thirty or so, she insisted always on taking the part of the ingénue, and if she happened to forget her lines she would rush into the wings and kick the unfortunate prompter. M. de Condé, usually the only audience, being an old man, managed to sleep comfortably through these performances. A repellent creature, over-eating, over-drinking, over-made-up, Sophie could yet do what she liked with her lover, and one can but stand in puzzlement before the amazing situation. It is true that Condé was growing old, he was about fifty-eight on his return to Paris in 1814, but Sophie's control of him was through some sexual domination, one of those secrets which men never confess. She satisfied in Condé something he could find in no other woman, he was entirely her slave, and when his friends protested he could but meekly reply, " If you only knew how she treats me! she beats me! " as if this admission of serfdom were an explanation of it. And perhaps it was: how can we tell what masochistic desires in the old man were assuaged by the brutality of this coarse arrogant vixen? He gave her not only his body and soul, but his wealth, and she sold all his property she dared, pocketing the money, even contemplating getting rid of the Palais Bourbon and only being restrained by her desire for ostentation. But her one great ambition was not satisfied, she had not been received at court. She even got into touch with King Charles X and hinted that, as Condé was entirely in her power, she might entice him to will his money to the royal godson. Failing here, Sophie next made the same offer to the Duchess of

P

Berri, mother of the heir-apparent to the throne, who replied haughtily that she didn't wish to hear of the subject again. Through Talleyrand she now turned to Louis Philippe, Duc d'Orléans, who, being by no means well off and possessing a large family, responded instantly. But he found the task by no means simple: the king refused to let Sophie enter the palace, nor could bribery or cajoling entice any of the royal family to have anything to do with her. Years before, she had been fully exposed as Condé's mistress and was unable any longer to boast of her royal, if bâton sinister, descent. The husband could not be deceived indefinitely, and his suspicious attacks at last in 1824 drove Sophie to a probably drunken confession, whereupon M. de Feuchères, having his whip with him at the time, soundly flogged his wife and left her house, never to return. M. de Condé wrote pleading with him not to expose the scandal, but de Feuchères, tormented by the idea that Paris had been jeering at him as a knave or a wittol, resigned from the Prince's household and asked the War Office to transfer him to the army in Spain. Had it not been for this open disgrace, Sophie might have entered court, but the King could not possibly receive so notorious a woman. Therefore her bribery of Orléans, but here she found for once that de Condé's will was not utterly destroyed: the Prince loathed the Orléans family, he would have nothing to do with them, and even Sophie's hysterics and physical assaults could not induce him to make one of Louis Phillipe's younger sons his heir. The wretched old man became so tortured that he could not sleep and even abandoned hunting and shooting, while he crept through his palace in terror, like one expecting an assassin lurking around every corner or hiding behind the curtains on the window. Sophie surrounded him with her creatures, some of whom were her lovers, and gradually she got rid of as many of the Prince's faithful servants as she could. So feeble had grown de Condé that he could scarcely walk and had to be helped up and down stairs— this was not only advancing age, he was lame from a broken thigh caused by being thrown from a horse, and only with difficulty could he lift his right arm as high as his shoulder because of an old wound, and was therefore unable to dress his own hair or tie his cravat—and now his mind began to weaken under the constant terror of his violent mistress, he hid from people and shuddered at the bare suggestion of gossip. Terrible quarrels raged in his apartments, the servants heard Sophie abusing him, heard the Prince yelling insults in reply. His mistress followed him wherever he went, carrying the will, pushing it before him when he sat down, and he was appalled by the continual dinning of death, death, death. But he could not resist for ever. On August 30, 1829, he signed the will, making Orléans's son, the Duc d'Aumale, " his universal heir." But he was tortured even yet: driven to his bed with dropsical legs, he was not permitted hot foods and liquors, and Sophie immediately fed him to the gullet and smuggled to him the richest of wines. But tenaciously he clung to a world that returned him nothing but misery, and he was heard to say that " now they've got what they want, my life's probably in danger." The awful part of this affair is the old man's realisation of Sophie's schemes, he had no illusions, no hopes, only terrors. But Sophie had achieved her ambition: on Sunday, February 7, 1830, she was received in the Tuileries. It was all very unexciting, for the widower King kept little state, being subdued by priests and virtuous females into weariness of pomp. He smiled at the vulgar Englishwoman when she slid into a curtsey, and remarked on the coldness of the weather; and the Dauphin didn't even know who she was: he asked Madame de Noailles who answered lightly, " It's easy to know those who are branded, Monseigneur "; while the Dauphiness was so agitated that she almost waved Sophie away with her fan, a gesture that even Sophie couldn't misinterpret. At last, however, she had been received! yet even in her deep satisfaction Sophie did not stop from plaguing her wretched lover, he was obviously near death and she was determined not to be cheated out of a single sou, she pestered him to make over to her his estates as a deed of gift. These were already willed to her but, true miser, she wanted actual cash not future promises and perhaps she feared lest the Prince secretly make a second will. Besides, she was gambling on the Bourse with extreme cunning and amassing huge sums. But she had gone too far. Charles X was now in exile, and the old Prince plotted to follow him, he arranged for a carriage to call secretly one morning. Surrounded by spies, however, the plot was soon known, and Sophie determined to prevent it. There was only one safe way —by murdering the Prince.

On the morning of August 27, 1830, the Prince was found hanging from his bedroom window, a handkerchief about his throat, a second handkerchief joined to it and fastened to the top of the window. The suggestion of suicide was absurd. The Prince was unable to lift his arms and therefore could not have hanged himself, and it was noticed that a door to a secret staircase reaching to the ground-floor was unbolted. Sophie was, of course, acquitted, Louis Philippe now being King of France, and the only judge who showed any honesty was immediately forced to resign. Acquitted though she might be according to law, society judged and condemned her, she had no friends left and was driven to lonely brooding on that one day of glory at the Tuileriès. Her only escape was travel, and eventually she returned to England to fall ill of dropsy, being suddenly struck down on December 15, 1840, with angina pectoris.

Most ruffians demand our admiration for their courage and determination, but nothing other than disgust can be aroused by the contemplation of merciless Sophie Dawes. Her ambitions were so petty, miserliness and snobbery, and it sickens one to read of her incessant persecution of the feeble terrified old Prince, her lover. It is foolish to contend that no man could behave in quite so inhuman a fashion, but it is true that very few men indeed could combine such system with such patience, and for so many years. Sophie is the woman ruffian at her most selfish worst; almost beautiful beside her seem those lowest of she-ruffians, the whores, who after all can shift the moral blame on to the shoulders of a persecuting and vigilant society. There is the doxy whom that tolerant Elizabethan, Thomas Harman, spoke with over his gate. She was " surelye a pleasant harlot," he tells us, " and not so pleasant as wytty, and not so wytty as voyd of all grace and goodnes. I founde, by her talks, that shee hadde passed her tyme lewdlye eyghttene yeares in walkinge aboute." He asked her plainly how many men had been her lovers and what were their names, and at last she told him that they " for the moste parte, are deade. ' Dead!' quoth I, ' howe dyed they, for wante of cherishinge or of paynefull diseases?' Then she sighed, and sayde they were hanged. 'What all?' quoth I, ' and so manye walke abroade, as I dayelye see?' 'By my trouth,' quoth she, ' I knowe not paste six or seuen by their names,' and named the same to me. ' When were they hanged?' quote I, ' Some seuen yeares a gone, some

three yeares, and some within this fortnight,' and declared the place where they were executed, which I
knewe well to bee true, by the report of others. 'Why'
(quoth I) 'dyd not this sorrowfull and fearefull sight
much greue the, and for thy tyme longe and euyll
spent?' 'I was sory,' quoth shee, 'by the Masse; for some
of them were good louing men. For I lackt not when
they had it, and they wanted not when I had it, and
diuers of them I neuer dyd forsake, vntyll the Gallowes
departed vs.' 'O, mercyfull God!' quoth I, and began
to blesse me. 'Why blesse ye?' quoth she. 'Alas! good
gentleman, euery one muste haue a lyuinge.'"

After this refreshing interlude from one of the poorer
ruffians, living honestly according to her ideals of what
Harman names a "bolde beastly lyfe," we must return
to the true woman ruffian, seeking power, if not through
her sex, through poison or magic, and the witch gives
us numerous examples of the ruffian, of some bullying
old hag tramping the countryside with fearsome power,
crooking her fingers at a neighbour's cows or subduing
a whole village to sycophantic terror by the sound of her
voice. At the same time there were many sincere witches,
and a study of this question will arouse in the most
sceptical a sense of uneasiness, a doubt of his rationalism.
I find myself torn in this way, having experimented a
little on the edge of magic and seen its inexplicable
potency; men like Paracelsus, Forman, and Nostradamus,
were not charlatans, and although it can be insisted that
they were the dupes of their own cunning, hypnotised
by their own cheats, what retort can be given to conscientious investigators like W. B. Yeats, or even Bulwer
Lytton who became an adept? Unquestionably there are
some forces which the magician controls, and whether
these be natural electrical forces or supernatural ones,

cannot be decided; many of the conclusions of modern
scientists would have dragged them to the stake not many
years ago. For all that we can tell, the magus may still
be far ahead of modern thought, and that which we
damn as evil or as trickery might yet become the accepted beliefs of a wiser generation. The witches remain
on the outskirts of magic, they are the followers of a
religion older than Christianity, the worship of Diana,
and just as Christianity absorbed much of paganism, so
did witchcraft absorb much of Christianity, accepting the
devil—a creature unknown in Roman and Greek times
when divinities were human enough to combine good
and evil and did not need this severing of personality,
this creation of God and Satan. Reading witch trials,
again and again one is struck by the sincerity of the
witches, and hallucination alone cannot explain much of
what they tell; nor can torture be given as reason for
the confessions, although in many cases that would be
true, for in all ages, in all countries, the witches repeat
strangely similar experiences: tales of Sabbat nights, of
the rituals undergone, they vary but little. Always too,
strangely enough, they deny any sexual pleasure in the
contract, which does away with the theory of some sexual
possession, for the devil's embrace is a brutal thing; in
the words of the *Compendium Maleficarum*, written by a
great witch-chaser in 1631, " witches confess that the
semen injected by the devil is cold, and that the act brings
them no pleasure but rather horror," and from this it has
been deduced that some leader of the coven would disguise himself and carry an imitation phallus, a theory
I cannot accept, for there was no such organisation in the
average coven and many witches lived in loneliness; some
ectoplasmic coition might have occurred, and yet continually the doubter reaches that frightening wall which

logic cannot scale: from all countries, in all periods, ignorant women have repeated almost word for word identical experiences of Satan and the Sabbat. Apart from the genuine worshippers and those innocently accused of occult power by neighbourly malice or ignorance, amongst the witches lived many a good ruffian, lured to the coven by desire for power. When the witch offered her body to her familiar so that he could mark her for his own, nipping her, sucking her blood, she might become his slave yet also she demanded his obedience, the reward of power over others. Many of the women—and men too, for there are men witches, although comparatively rare: thus says Philomathes, " there are twentie women giuen to that craft, where ther is one man "—and subtle knowledge of herbal poisons, and when the lusting girl came for a love potion to attract some lad, often enough she carried away a villainous concoction made, according to knowing cynical Reginald Scot, of " the haire growing in the nethermost part of a woolves taile, a woolves yard, a little fish called *Remora*, the braine of a cat, of a newt, or of a lizzard: the bone of a greene frog, the flesh thereof being consumed with pismers or ants; the left bone whereof ingenereth (as they saie) love; the bone on the right side, hate. . . Besides these, manie other follies there be to this purpose proposed to the simple; as namelie, the garments of the dead, candels that burne before a dead corps; and needels wherewith dead bodies are sowne or sockt into their sheetes; and diverse other things, which for the reverence of the reader, and in respect of the uncleane speach to be used in the description thereof, I admit; " but he does tell us that many of these " confections prepared by lewd people to procure love " are " meere poisons, bereaving some of the benefit of the braine, and so of the sense and understanding of the mind. And from some it taketh awaie life, & that is more common than the other." The Sire de Burzet, wanting to re-awaken his wife's love, asked Jeanette Neuve—later burnt —for a potion and she gave him a drug that killed the woman within a few hours. Poison was one of the witch's principal tools, but a curse also is sometimes strangely effective—inevitably so if the one cursed knows that he or she has been bewitched.

The most famous cases of witchcraft in this country are given us by a Lancashire coven in 1612: this was a strong group, terrifying its neighbours, and some of them at least used poison to consolidate their power. Alison Device gave evidence that being one day " in the house of *Anthony Nutter* of Pendle aforesaid, and being then in company with *Anne Nutter,* daughter of the said *Anthony*: the said *Anne Whittle,* alias *Chattox,* came into the said *Anthony Nutters* house, and seeing this Examinate, and the said *Anne Nutter* laughing, and saying, that they laughed at her the said *Chattox*: well said then (says *Anne Chattox*) I will be meet with the one of you. And vpon the next day after, she the said *Anne Nutter* fell sicke, and within three weekes after died. And further, this Examinate saith, That about two yeares agoe, she, this Examinate, hath heard, That the said *Anne Whittle,* alias *Chattox,* was suspected for bewitching the drinke of *Iohn Moore* of Higham Gentleman: and not long after, shee this Examinate heard the said *Chattox* say, that she would meet with the said *Iohn Moore,* or his. Where-upon a child of the said *Iohn Moore,* called *Iohn,* fell sicke, and anguished about halfe a yeare, and then died: during which languishing, this Examinate saw the said *Chattox* sitting in her owne garden, and a picture of Clay like vnto a child in her Apron; which this Examinate espying, the said *Anne Chattox* would haue hidde with her Apron: and this Examinate declaring the same to her mother, her mother thought it was the picture of the said *Iohn Moores* child. And she this Examinate further saith, That about sixe or seuen years agoe, the said *Chattox* did fall out with one *Hugh Moore* of Pendle, as foresaid, about certaine cattell of the said *Moores*, which the said *Moore* did charge the said *Chattox* to haue bewitched: for which the said *Chattox* did curse and worry the said *Moore*, and said she would be Reuenged of the said *Moore*: whereupon the said *Moore* presently fell sicke, and languished about halfe a yeare, and then died. Which *Moore* vpon his deathbed said, that the said *Chattox* had bewitched him to death. And she further saith, That about sixe years agoe, a daughter of the said *Anne Chattox*, called *Elizabeth*, hauing been at the house of *Iohn Nutter* of the Bullhole, to begge or get a dish full of milke, which she had, and brought to her mother, who was about a fields breadth of the said *Nutters* house, which her said mother *Anne Chattox* tooke and put into a Kan, and did charne the same with two stickes across in the same field: whereupon the said *Iohn Nutters* sonne came vnto her, the said *Chattox*, and misliking her doings, put the said Kan and milke ouer with his foot; and the morning next after, a Cow of the said *Iohn Nutters* fell sicke, and so languished three or foure dayes, and then died. In the end being openly charged with all this in open Court; with weeping tears she humbly acknowledged them to be true, and cried out vnto God for Mercy and foregiuenesse of her sinnes, and humbly prayed my Lord to be mercifull vnto *Anne Redfearne* her daughter," a plea of which my lord took no notice, daughter with mother and eight others—two only being men—was hanged at Lancaster.

All this sounds extremely flimsy, gossip in the dark forest of Pendle, the malicious lies of a girl—herself a witch—against a woman she hated, but when all the evidence—and the above forms a very little part of it—is considered, one must agree that the Lancaster jury's verdict was a rightful one. Those women were witches. The two leaders, Anne Chattox and Elizabeth Demdike confessed completely, and they might never have been apprehended but for one quarrel between the two groups, that of Chattox's and Demdike's. The original Demdike who started everything died before she could be brought to trial, but she had first persuaded Chattox into the cult, bringing to her house the devil " in the liknes of a Man, about midnight," who said " that hee must haue one part of her body for him to sucke vpon." At first Chattox coyly refused this sacrifice, then she asked " what part of her body hee would haue for that vse; who said, hee would haue a piece of her right side neere to her ribbes, for him to sucke vpon: whereupon shee assented." Both families were now involved in the craft: old Demdike had in her clan, her daughter Elizabeth Device, and her grandchildren, Alison and James Device; Chattox had her daughter Anne Redfearne, while many of the neighbours also were initiated. Strange indeed must have been the scenes in that Lancashire forest: we find James Device on the day before Good Friday sneaking into church to receive communion, " not to eate the Bread the Minister gaue him, but to bring it and deliuer it to such a thing as should meet him in his way homewards," but he swallowed the bread, and when a hare stopped him on the way back and demanded God's flesh, it threatened to tear James to pieces for his disobedience; whether this was a devil or a human being dressed like an animal must be left to the reader to decide, but it must be understood that it was common for the witches to wear animal-masks and queer disguises for ritual purposes. Quarrels flashed amongst the groups: Robert Nutter tried to seduce Anne Redfearne and when she would have naught to do with his kisses, swore that "if euer the Ground came to him, she would never dwell vpon his land," and later he died. This was normal witchcraft, but real trouble began when Demdikes and Chattoxes quarrelled, for the Demdikes were robbed and Anne Redfearne was later seen wearing a band and coif which had been part of the stolen property. Anne's father thereupon, in terror of bewitchment, bribed the Demdikes for years until, forgetting the blackmail for one year, he died. The brawling between the families grew so outrageous apparently that the law intervened and when the witches were brought before a justice of the peace their hatred for each other was such that they confessed the truth, each accusing the other of witchcraft and murder. Other witches as yet unsuspected met excitedly in the Malking Tower, old Demdike's home, on Good Friday, and swore to blow up the castle in which their comrades were imprisoned, and one Jennet Preston "craued assistance of the rest of them that were then there, for the kiling of Master *Lister* of Westby; because, as she then said, he had borne malice unto her, and had thought to have put her away at the last Assizes at Yorke; but could not." Shortly afterwards, Mr. Lister died in great agony, wailing "*Iennet Preston* lyes heauie vpon me, *Prestons* wife lyes heauie vpon me; helpe me, helpe me: and so departed, crying out against her." She was sentenced to death at York in July, 1612.

Close to the witches one sees the sinister figures of professional poisoners, those men and women who combined the trades of pander, poisoner and often astrologer;

women such as the mysterious "Wicche of Eye; the
whiche was brent on the even of Symond and Jude in
Smythefeld" for aiding Eleanor Cobham, the Duchess
of Gloucester, in her alleged witchcraft; and Mrs. Anne
Turner, "of a low stature, faire visage, for outward
behaviour comely," bawd and "lay-mistress of poisons,"
who encompassed the death of Sir Thomas Overbury in
the Tower of London at the command of Frances, Lady
Essex, that gay ambitious wench "of a lustful appetite,
prodigall of expence, covetous of applause, ambitious of
honour and light of behaviour," who so madly loved
King James I's minion, Sir Robert Carr, that she would
kill to possess him utterly. Into that tangled drama also
appears another of these wise dangerous women, Mary
Woods called Cunning Mary, a Southwark laundress,
who said that the countess had offered her £1,000 for a
quick-moving poison to rid her of her first husband, the
Earl of Essex. Mary Turner was tried and sentenced to
death on November 7, 1615, and when magical papers
and little images given her by that great wizard, Dr.
Forman, were produced in court, "there was heard a
crack from the scaffolds, which caused great fear, tumult
and confusion among the spectators and throughout the
hall, every one fearing hurt, as if the devil had been
present and grown angry to have his workmanship
shewed by such as were not his scholars, and this terror
continuing about a quarter of an hour, after silence was
proclaimed the rest of the cunning tricks were likewise
shewed." As she was the inventor of yellow starch, or
at least the introducer of it into England, Lord Chief
Justice Coke sentenced Mrs. Turner to "be hanged in
that dress, that the same might end in shame and detestation," and at her execution, even the hangman and his
assistants donned yellow ruffs, thereby banishing the

abomination from the country. The whole of this
" Great Oyer of Poisoning " is a fascinating scandal, the
most astonishing part being Overbury's power of absorbing numerous poisons for so long with such little effect,
but perhaps many of them neutralised each other. " Sir
T. never eat white salt but there was white arsenick put
into it. Once he desired pig, and Mrs. Turner put into
it lapis costitus. The white powder was sent to Sir T.
in a letter he [a Dr. Franklin, the wizard who supplied
the drugs] knew to be white arsenick. At another time
he had two partridges sent him from the Court, and
water and onions being the sauce, Mrs. Turner put in
cantharides instead of pepper; so that there was scarce
anything that he did eat but there was some poison
mixed. For these poisons the Countess sent me rewards;
she sent many times gold by Mrs. Turner." What evidently finished the poor devil was a clyster, an enema, of
some corrosive sublimate so violent that it even blistered
the skin.

Apart from Mrs. Turner, a petty ruffian, we have an
excellent example of a real woman ruffian in this case,
the Countess of Essex. When thirteen or fourteen years
of age, she was married to Essex, about a year her senior,
and he immediately travelled abroad on the customary
grand tour to complete his education; such marriages
were not consummated, they were a business bargain, a
seal on property. With her husband away, Frances was
brought up in the corrupt court of James I, " she was
hatch'd up by her mother, whom the Sour Breath of that
Age (how justly I know not) had already tainted; from
whom the young Lady might take such a Tincture, that
ease and greatnesse, and Court Glories, would disdain
and impress on her, than any way wear out and diminish.
And growing to be a Beauty of the greatest Magnitude in

that Horizon, was an object fit for Admirers and every
Tongue grew an Orator at that Shrine." And James's
court was incredibly licentious. In such an atmosphere
was the girl-bride reared until she loved King James's
" dearest bedfellow", handsome, stupid, vain young
Robert Carr, although it is more than hinted that Prince
Henry was her first lover. Probably it was the honour
of being loved by the Prince's mistress that seduced
Carr, for he was one of those narcissist youths incapable
of loving anything but himself. Anyhow, he had his
counsellor, the brilliant Sir Thomas Overbury, to write
love-letters for him, and if Overbury wrote them in the
style of his charming *Characters* it is a pity they have
not been preserved. Then Essex returned and carried
his bride into the country. At first she refused to live
with him, but he called on the aid of her parents, and
her stout mother, Lady Suffolk, was not the one to
tolerate such nonsense. Frances had to leave her lover
and act the wife. Desperately, she called on Mrs. Turner
of Hammersmith, and from Dr. Forman, Mrs. Turner
bought various poisons for the husband and amorous
potions to inspire the lover. It is probable that wizards
deliberately gave harmless drugs to their clients: none of
Forman's poisons worked any more than Franklin's
were later to work on Overbury, but the love-philtres
were far more successful. Carr returned to his mistress
but, as Frances wrote furiously to her " Sweet Father "
Forman, " My Lord is lusty and merry, and drinketh
with his men; and all the content he gives me is to abuse
me, and use me as doggedly as before. I think I shall
never be happy in this world, because he hinders my
good and will ever, I think. So remember, I beg for
God's sake, and get me out of this vile place." Poison
failing, Frances had recourse to law, and found that

again her husband baulked her, for naturally enough he objected to the suggested charge of impotency. Somehow the divorce was shuffled through, a jury of " seven noble women ", including Frances's mother, examined her and swore she was " a Virgin uncorrupted." Another and likely enough tale says that, owing to Frances's alleged modesty, she went veiled to the examination and " one mistries Fines, near Kinswoman to old Kettle, was dressed up in the countesses cloathes, at that time too young to be other than *virgo intacta*." Meanwhile the quarrel with Overbury had started. Overbury despised his master and grew over-bearing, he even insulted Frances, probably afraid lest the King grow jealous of her, telling Carr that if he " went on in that business he should do well to look to his standing," to which Carr haughtily replied that his " legs were strong enough to bear him up; and that he should make him repent those speeches." When Carr repeated this to Frances, Overbury was doomed: she hated him, and was determined to destroy him, and somehow managed to have him committed to the Tower on the charge of refusing an embassy to Russia which James had offered him. The divorce finalised, Frances at last married her beloved —now raised to the earldom of Somerset—and then poisoned Overbury through Mrs. Turner. She had gone too far in her great arrogance, the murder was too obvious, and soon the truth appeared. Following the arrest of her servants, Frances was taken, and shortly afterwards, Carr. The behaviour of James is really horrible. By this time he was weary of his favourite, for had not George Villiers, later Duke of Buckingham, appeared to be appointed the King's Cupbearer like a second Ganymede? When messengers arrived to arrest Carr, " the king hung about his neck, slabbering his cheeks, saying

'For God's sake, when shall I see thee againe? On my soul, I shall neither eat nor sleep until you come again.' The earle [Carr] told him, on Monday (this being on the Friday). 'For God's sake, let me,' said the king, 'shall I, shall I?' then lolled about his neck. 'Then for God's sake give thy lady this kiss for me.' In the same manner at the stayres head, at the middle of the stayres, and at the stayres foot. The earl was not in his coach when the king used these very words (in the hearing of four servants, of whom one was Somerset's great creature and of the Bed-Chamber, who reported it instantly to the author of this history), 'I shall never see his face more.'" Both Carr and Frances were found guilty and sentenced to death, sentences which James later commuted to imprisonment in the Tower during his pleasure. It is likely that Carr was innocent, but whether that be true or not, there was no happiness left for the Earl and Countess of Somerset. Released after years of imprisonment, " they lived long after, though in one House, as Strangers one to another."

Frances's course was a swift and violent one. The poisoning of Overbury seems a futile act, but it is probable that he possessed some secret, perhaps knowledge of her attempts to kill Essex, that drove her to this otherwise stupid murder which was to drag her into lifelong misery. Yet in their very brevity a certain splendour stirs us in those few years as we watch the restless hoyden urged by her lust for Carr into murder. Love usually unsteadies the ruffian, but in Francis's case it was different because, to her, nothing else mattered but the satisfaction of her own uncontrollable desires. It is James who shows as the greatest ruffian of them all, slobbering over his favourite while deliberately sending him to his doom.

Q

Frances came of good ruffian-stock, for her mother, the Countess of Suffolk, was a dominant woman. Regardless of her family's private opinions, she kept her feeble husband clamped beneath her skirts and pushed her children into marriages. Suffolk was Lord High Treasurer, and bribery and corruption became so common through his wife's sticky fingers that Bacon compared the treasury to a shop in the Royal Exchange with Lady Suffolk as tradeswoman and with some treasury official acting as apprentice, calling the people in to buy. Not content with stealing public monies, the countess was also in the pay of Spain. Women in politics often show this venality, for to them a nation's honour is of little importance compared to their own great comfort; many a man has been destroyed beneath their influence in this field. Even strong social movements, revolutions, have suffered by feminine intrigue. Take for example, Theresia Cabarrus.

A very lovely creature indeed was Theresia. In Mlle. Bouldard's portrait in the flashy Rubens style, there is a warm beauty of silkily textured flesh, big yet firm: plump shoulders and heavy breasts to which the cloth seems sluggishly to cling, half unfolding as if it were sensuously alive and exhausted by the too-great glory of such an embrace. Thick black hair that seems to drink the web of pearls enclosing it, falls slumberously down her back, gliding over the left shoulder. The skin is flawless, the eyes dark and bright with vitality and health. Yes, a very lovely creature, and Mlle. Bouldard's brush was no liar, for even in the harsh stippling of an engraving Theresia's beauty shows. There is an engraving of her dressed in some peculiar Grecian masquerade; the hair seems here to be of a lighter shade, banded in plaits like a turban about her head, framing the round, plump face on which there is a lazy, retrospective smile. She is toying with some flowers in a vase, and has that startled yet expectant smile usually found only in photographs. But it is her figure that catches the eye: the sturdy almost masculine legs, the rotund buttocks and half-seen breasts over-swelling the corsage. That Theresia was beautiful in the Spanish fashion, vital and tantalising, her body so permeated with sensuality that the slightest movement would seem an amorous invitation, cannot be doubted, and cunningly did she use that beauty. Daughter of the Spanish banker, Cabarrus, she was bred to accept money as one of the natural products, as the benediction of God upon her class, raising her above the dirty, common sweating people working blindly like moles to create that gold for her delectation. And wisely she hoarded her real capital, herself, to see what percentage she could obtain by investing it, like a banker with his gold or a prostitute with her sex. Theresia was reared on this banking principle of giving loans without capital: the banker would, on good security, present an I O U, acceptable only because of his bluff that he had vast sums at his command, when very often he hadn't enough to cover the IOU itself. There are always people so hypnotised by the suave tongue and well-bred manners of the ruffian that they will pull out their pockets and force money on him. The banker played—and to a certain extent, still does play—upon this pathetic faith of a sycophantic people. Theresia carried the principle into society, promising with her eyes often far more than her body intended giving, although she was apparently sensual enough to choose lovers occasionally at her pleasure. Nevertheless, her mind betrayed her body and her schooling, she fell in love—the equivalent of a banker lending without security. Theresia, when she arrived in Paris in 1780 to complete her education, was rapidly taught the exquisite falsities of romantic passion. It was an ugly world, this world of aristocratic refusal to take things serious when unwashed men and women covered their dirt with expensive clothes and powder and cropped their hair to get rid of lice. Theresia adored it because the whole basis of that society was an exaltation of external things, love being the exploration of the physical nerves and never of the delicate vibrations of the spirit. She was worshipped, the men jostled each other in eagerness to enjoy her vivid hetaeric charm, but she was foolish enough evidently to fall in love with de Méréville. Her father was having none of that nonsense—lovers were safe enough, but husbands were a liability unless carefully chosen—so she married instead the handsome, debauched twenty-six-year-old Marquis de Fontenay. There was no pretence of love in the contract, but he was an aristocrat and financially well off. Theresia was content to accept him with his noble name and beautiful town-house and dutifully to produce his children so long as he did not interfere with her gallantries with other men. It was now that the French revolution was beginning to stir, when even ox-like Louis considered rebelling against the strangle-hold of the bankers and, under the prompting of Mirabeau, dismissed the banker Necker, father of Madame de Staël. Seeing the mightiest of them depart, other bankers thought to frighten the king into obedience, to stop him from suppressing private banking and issuing state money known as assignats, and they worked on the people. Agents provocateur went among the starved people and their propaganda resulted in the storming of the Bastille. That terrified the king right enough, but the bankers had released a force which they found rushed beyond their control, they had reckoned without Robespierre, who was no corrupt debauchee like the gross, pock-marked Mirabeau. The real revolution came to Paris, and simultaneously almost, Cabarrus collapsed in Spain. For the first time, Theresia understood what it was like to be without money, she wailed and wept to Lafayette, crying that if only he could march on Madrid as he had marched on Versailles. As the revolution grew more powerful, the voice of the people being heard in the cold precise tones of little Robespierre, Theresia became panic-stricken. "This seems so false," she cried, "so hysterical. Those horrible signs, this chatter of equality and power, this detestation of aristocrats, to what fearful end will it lead? Truly, my friend, I am afraid." She thought it best to escape from Paris, and made for Bordeaux; then Tallien came in the name of the revolution, eager to twist money from the wealthy by setting up the guillotine. Those who could not pay him lost their heads. Theresia was arrested, imprisoned, when Tallien visited her: it was not money she offered in return for life, it was her luxurious pampered body that Tallien took as ransom. Openly she became his mistress.

It is absurd to contend that Theresia cared twopence for Tallien, he was coarse and ugly, and his embraces must have revolted her patrician mind and shivered her delicate body with disgust. But deprived of de Méréville, of the man she loved, the man for whom she believed her body had been ordained, she was able to degrade it without that degradation spiritually affecting her. Flesh and soul were separate, for only in love can they unite, and Theresia loved nobody. Her ambitions were her one desire, and she accepted the brutal caresses of Tallien without being in the least mentally shamed by them, just as she accepted his children with the acquiescence of an animal. There is something of the animal in Theresia's perpetual childbearing. Like a savage, she produced child after child, gestation seeming curiously unimportant to her, a kind of temporary annoyance that was no drain whatever on her superb physique. Tallien appeared as her one escape from this dangerous corner. She was in jail and the massacre was at its height, engineered by such as Tallien so that they could make money by terrorising people into paying to keep their heads, she did not want to die, and the sacrifice of her body was a small matter, after all, compared with the sacrifice of her life.

The only occasions in which it is possible for a woman to choose death rather than what is popularly known as dishonour—apart, of course, from religious neurotics—is when she is completely in love with one man. For only then is her body of real value, it becomes sacred as the vessel for his children. Theresia was not in love and therefore had no false notions about purity. She threw herself at the butcher, and in an insane fashion she became almost happy, her sex being sublimated into the ruffian passion for dominance. She played the good fairy to the aristocrats and managed to make her lover permit a few to escape, at a price, including a troop of actors she wanted for her amusement. She performed ostentatiously the part of a true Jacobean, a mænad of the guillotine, but all the while she was cunningly seeking ways to destroy the revolution and to bring back the rule of her own class, the bankers.

As Goddess of Reason she was jubilantly worshipped in a church, but despite her revolutionary jargon and behaviour, she did not impress the quiet, clear-sighted Robespierre, the noblest figure of his age. He was not deceived for all her voluptuous posturing, no woman's beauty could affect the cold determination of that man; hating all bloodshed, realising that the slaughter was Tallien's dirty way of making money, he sent spies to

Bordeaux, and Theresia, in desperation, wrote to the Convention a patriotic letter suggesting that women be trained to work in the hospitals to help the revolution. Already she was picturing herself as the Compassionate Angel of the sick and wounded, but Robespierre tossed her letter aside and ordered her to leave immediately for Orléans. She fled at once to hiding, helped by the secret agents of the counter-revolution, but all the while Robespierre watched her, knowing exactly where she lurked, and eventually she was taken to the Petite force and remained there until the Incorruptible was destroyed, dragged down by one of the dirtiest ruffians in history, Joseph Fouché. And, unwittingly, Theresia helped in her enemy's death. Fouché knew that he was doomed, that he, Tallien and the other racketeers of the revolution had not deceived Robespierre and that he was ready to impeach them for treachery; their only hope was to strike first, but Fouché had no good material with which to work, and his own methods were always underhand, the way of a rat that burrows and attacks only when the victim is helpless. He had not the courage personally to impeach Robespierre, but he worked on the terrors of Tallien until he had the man almost hysterical, ready for murder. He faked a list of names of the corrupt ministers—and save for Robespierre's party nearly all were corrupt—and he carried it around, insisting that it was a copy of Robespierre's list of those about to be condemned. It was now that Theresia became useful. She was still in prison, having had to suffer the indignity of being stripped naked before the soldiers who searched for concealed weapons or money, and under Fouché's cunning lies she became quite a romantic figure, a helpless and beautiful woman jailed without trial, separated from her lover. Fouché made much of the story for the sentimental hearts of the rabble. He even found a Spanish dagger which he presented to Tallien so that he could brandish it melodramatically and swear that he was going insane through the loss of his beloved and would stab the tyrant Robespierre to his death. The dagger was excellent propaganda. Tallien waved it about and sobbed and ranted, but Robespierre smiled and waited. He waited too long. Desperate and frantic with fear, on the 9th of Thermidor, July 27, 1794, Tallien impeached him before he could speak, and instantly the terrified wolves were on him, they did not give Robespierre a chance, they howled him down. Then came Theresia's triumph. The mob shouted exultantly while Tallien led her out of jail. " *Vive Notre Dame de Thermidor!* " they yelled, and like a queen she smiled upon them. It was all very beautiful, the romantic tale had its fitting end, and Fouché's dagger could at last be sheathed, for Prince Charming had rescued his Princess from the Ogre and nothing now remained to do but to live happily ever afterwards. Theresia became the Queen of Paris, and she was happy in her dominance, in this worship, and back trooped her old friends, strangling the revolution. At her parties, the bankers mingled with the new leaders of the people, with Paul Barras, Tallien, Fréron, and others. The assignats were gradually destroyed and private banking took their place. The revolution died with the death of Robespierre, and in the place of Liberty, Theresia sat enthroned upon all-powerful gold. Theatres, cafés, dancehalls, appeared again, the easy money of corruption was thrown on gambling-tables and into fashionable debauchery. Meanwhile the poor grew as hungry as in the days of Marie Antoinette, that being the privilege of the poor— to watch their betters enjoy themselves on the warm side of the window. Now that Robespierre, Marat, and Saint-Just were dead, who was to remember the poor wretches in whose name the revolution had been fought? Forget them quickly, these skeletons in the conscience of humanity, for gold was trickling again into the vicious circle, there were gay lights to sparkle against women's skin, on women's bodies that seemed even more beautiful than ever in these new costumes of freedom, the straight-skirted high-breasted Grecian gowns. Theresia's salon was the throne-room of this gutter-aristocracy, and it was upheld by groups of young men organised by Fréron in the manner of modern fascisti, armed to beat anybody insensible who dared even mention that he was hungry. When these bands decided to clean up the last Robespierrist stronghold, the Jacobin Club, they asked Theresia to lead them and, de-lighted, she agreed. The Jacobins had fled at their ap-proach, and amidst cheers and laughter the triumphant Theresia turned the key upon the revolution, locking for ever the Jacobin Club. Then Tallien blundered, England was threatening invasion and he found that he had sold himself to the bankers for nothing. They did not trust him, and he lost his head—trying to revive the spirit of the revolution, he called on the patriotism of the disillu-sioned people, massacred hundreds of English prisoners, and denounced royalty. That was enough for Theresia, here was her opportunity to get rid of the ugly Prince Charming who had served his purpose. She pretended to be so shocked by the massacre that her love for Tallien was killed, and she began to seek a more powerful lover. There was only Barras, and he was living with her best friend, Rose de Beauharnais, known to history as Josephine. Brutally, Theresia ejected Josephine, took her place with Barras and then pushed Josephine into the arms of a promising young soldier called Napoleon Bonaparte. Josephine protested, she wept and wailed to have her lover back, but Theresia was determined. Josephine must accept

Bonaparte and see that he did not prove dangerous, while herself, as Queen, would take her rightful place beside the master of the day. Here is one weakness in Theresia. She who was so cunning, so coldly ambitious, was yet blind enough to choose the weak-willed Barras, not recognising the genius in Napoleon's eyes. She made Barras appoint her friend's lover General-in-Chief of the Army of the Interior, so she must have appreciated something in Napoleon, but she was too interested in the obvious emblem of success, gold, to see greatness beyond a faded coat and a rather boorish manner. Here her upbringing was to blame.

Then Napoleon became surprisingly important. He began to conquer Italy, and growing afraid, Theresia sent the reluctant Josephine to spy upon him, for Barras was in a ticklish corner. Parties were being formed against him in the chamber, and if this young soldier were to take the enemy's side all Theresia's ambitions would come to naught. She was determined to strike quickly. On the night of September 4, 1797, she gave a party at the Luxembourg, and while Barras fidgeted with impatient terrors she remained calm and gracious, for at that moment her fascist groups were arresting Barras's opponents: fifty were sentenced to transportation. For a time Theresia was safe, but she was disillusioned about her lover, he was feeble, a coward, and she began to desert politics, realising that there was one thing mightier than the word or the sword —wealth. She might possess a golden bed in Barras's country house at Grosbois, but it was not often that nowadays she slept in it. The banker Ouvrard had become her new lover, and under his cultured outlook and graceful manners whatever remained in Theresia of the temporary sans-culotte gradually vanished. Ouvrard's genius fired her genius, and when war broke out, although Napoleon was now in power, she became again of great importance, because wars cannot be fought without money. Chafe though he did at having to give way before the detested moneylenders, Napoleon was forced to turn to Ouvrard, but he even now would not permit Theresia to visit his court. Ouvrard was a married man, Theresia had divorced her first husband, but was still the wife of Tallien, and Napoleon, whatever his own amorous investigations might have been when campaigning, was very strict about the morals at his court. Finding that she was impeding his rise, Ouvrard began to avoid his mistress, and lonely save for her brood of children, Theresia saw all that she had fought for with ruffian callousness slide from her fingers. She attempted to capture Napoleon, but in vain. Then suddenly came the strange and great adventure that makes her of such importance to our thesis. Her next lover was a young nobleman of thirty-three, François-Joseph, heir to the principality of Chimay. Theresia was now thirty-one, but her fierce life and abundant child-bearing had told upon her beauty, had made cushiony her flesh and lined the plump face, but nevertheless François-Joseph loved her. To her amazement Theresia suddenly realised this, and apparently it came as an astounding revelation. She who had discarded love for ambition, accepting men's caresses as purely physical sensation, discovered herself adored, almost reverenced, and in gratitude for this miracle she forgot all ambitions, forgot everything in a passion for her husband—for, having divorced Tallien, she now married François-Joseph. Her life was spent in trying frenziedly to out-lie the past. Josephine was forbidden by Napoleon to see her and Theresia was hurt, not for her own sake but for her husband's, she wanted him to be respected, and to her astonishment she realised that even her being ostracised did not affect his love, it made him in truth even more tender towards her. He adopted all her children and greedily, exultantly she bred for him, at last finding her salvation, knowing the holy joy of procreating for the beloved. She told romantic lies about the past, she repeated the dagger story, although none believed it but François-Joseph, she swore that Tallien had treated her abominably and had deserted her to follow Napoleon to Egypt, she said that she had never been Barras's mistress but had used her influence with him only to help prisoners. Pathetically, she tried to convince people, and grew old and ugly but madly happy in the peace and spiritual fulfilment of François-Joseph's love. She became a noble creature, and here we have a fascinating portrait: the ruffian tamed by love. It is a magnificent spectacle, and shows clearly that the woman-ruffian automatically ceases to be a ruffian if her emotions can be directed into their rightful course; or rather, let us say that the woman ruffian is one whose natural sex has been directed into the wrongful course, that she becomes a neurotic perversion of herself, her normal desires distorted and seeking some ambitious orgasm that leaves her eventually unhappy and old before her time.

We have given quite a large space to the woman ruffian, but after all this chapter is her one annexe, practically the whole of the remainder of the book being devoted to the male-quarters, and before we conclude there are one or two ladies who should be glanced at if only for the paradoxical reason that they are not ruffians. There is, first of all, Maria Dolores Eliza Rosanna, alias Lola Montez. At first glance Lola would seem the perfect example of a ruffian, but a brief survey of her adventures will prove the opposite. She has ruffianly qualities, of course, being an adventuress: for example, we find her determined to give romantic colour to the commonplace event of her birth in Limerick in 1818, for she states that her father was the son

of Sir Edward and Lady Gilbert and that her mother was
the descendant of a noble Spanish house who had fled
from a convent for love of her father. Everything apper-
taining to Lola assumed heroic stature in her eyes, she was
not a liar in the strict sense of the word, she was an artist,
a creator, and her creation was herself. In a way this is true
of all women, but with Lola, as with the ruffian, it was
the mainspring of every act. She performed always before
the audience of her mirror. Her father dying in India and
her mother marrying again, Lola was treated very kindly
by her stepfather, and in that warm rich land she grew to
vital maturity until shipped to Scotland. That childhood
of Lola's is of importance, it rang the romantic note,
giving the bizarre backcloth against which she was
proudly to strut her insolent way. Trouble first began
when her relations tried to force her into marriage with a
" gouty old rascal "; Lola instead eloped with and married
a handsome young lieutenant. The marriage did not last
long. Back in India, the husband ran off with another
man's wife and Lola was soon on her return voyage to
England, amusing herself scandalously on the way. After
a legal separation, she adopted her famous Spanish
pseudonym and attempted to go on the stage. Here she
failed because she refused the amorous suggestions of Lord
Ranelagh who, in revenge, had her howled off the boards.
This is the point that raises Lola beyond the ranks of
ruffianism, for no ruffian would consider the pawning of
her body of any importance if it were a necessary prelude
to her material success. Nothing matters to the ruffian but
the satisfaction of his or her ambition. Lola wanted to be
an actress, and even to-day it is tragically true that sometimes a woman's career on stage or screen is begun by
what is commonly called her ruin. Such cases are rare
enough, yet they do exist, and when ordinary girls with

ordinary ambitions succumb, it is natural that a ruffian should think nothing of it. Yet Lola respected her body, only to love would she surrender its magic. Therefore she failed both as ruffian and actress. Lola never sold herself, she kept the vital core of her being inviolate, pure and sacred, she gave only to those whom she loved. She sang for coins in the streets, she pawned her clothes, rather than degrade her womanhood with loveless caressings. She had many love affairs, but they were usually unhappy ones because restlessly, vainly, she sought a companion as proud and as strong as herself. Then after failures as an actress, after a lonely fighting courageous voyaging over Europe, she met Ludwig I of Bavaria. His passion for her was so violent and all-consuming that there was nearly a revolution about her in his country, and Lola was even forced to defend herself with her whip in the street. " My kingdom for Lola! " cried Ludwig, and he meant it. But rather than destroy her lover, Lola fled from Bavaria, disguised as a boy: would any ruffian throw aside this possibility of uncrowned queenship for the sake of a lover? No; as a ruffian, Lola was a magnificent failure. She was too impulsive, too generous, too essentially noble and pure in spirit, to use her sex and beauty deliberately for the advancement of herself in power.

We find the same with the lovely actress, Adah Menken, who, " with the little end of a dimity nothing fastened to her waist," horrified all London in the 'sixties by being strapped to the back of a galloping horse in the portrayal of Byron's *Mazeppa*. Like Lola Montez, Adah always lied about her birth, she lied so continually and with such conflicting statements that now it is impossible to get nearer to the truth than to presume that she was born in New Orleans about 1835 and that it is more than probable that her father was a Jew. She certainly looks Jewish in her photographs. The fantasy of these women is such that they begin to believe their own lies, even though those lies change from day to day; like the basilisk that can only be caught by seeing its own reflection in a mirror, they become hypnotised by themselves. Yet Lola and Adah, despite this ruffian quality, were not true ruffians because they were unselfish and always eager to give far more than they received. They were romantics and the romantic is necessarily a liar because he or she refuses to accept the truth lest it demolish the glorious fantasy they create about themselves. Adah was astonishingly beautiful with that vivid excitable beauty of the passionate young Jewess, highly strung and sensitive and eager to explore this frightening miracle of the flesh that caged the vital spirit struggling for profound satisfaction in the mystical union of love. She was dark and bigly built and amorous. In the photograph showing her as Mazeppa, far from being covered merely by the little end of a dimity, her strong fleshy limbs are so thoroughly draped that she would be laughed off the most respectable bathing-beach in respectable England to-day, but the legs are powerfully made and perfectly formed in their stout silk fleshings, with gently puckered knees, broad hips, and little feet with slender ankles; her dark head on which the black curls tumble in provocative disarray is well shaped, the face rather childishly yet attractively plump, the eyes large, intelligent and alert. Her eagerness to investigate love brought her when quite young into the arms of the pugilist, Heenan, for she had not yet had experience enough to reach the wisdom of Isadora Duncan who warned girls that athletes make the least satisfactory lovers, their muscles absorbing all that vitality of the spirit which is love. Heenan married Adah and promptly drank and wenched away all her stage earnings. Adah fought him, for she had the temper of a devil, and at last furiously she deserted him for good. Later, after this excursion into pugilism, she turned hungrily to the arts in search of the completion she craved, she even scrambled after that feeble little red-headed drunkard, Swinburne, probably excited by his hysterical hymns to passion, and the photographs of the pair together are charmingly ludicrous, for she towers like a benign goddess over the tiny poet who gazes up with pride and apprehension at her like a naughty boy in dread of a spanking.

Neither Adah nor Lola are ruffians, and I include them here only to point that fact, for they are the type, like Isadora Duncan, whom the world damns as adventuresses —a truly honourable title, meaning a free woman—and are usually accepted as illustrations of ruffianism. They are actually tormented souls seeking peace in love. No ruffian would waste her time like Adah on the little Swinburne or on the huge gross Alexandre Dumas *pére,* nor like Adah would she attempt to write poetry in imitation of Walt Whitman.

This poetry is pathetic because it is the poetry of despair; its artistic qualities may be of small importance, but the tortured soul it reveals brings instant sympathy. Here we see the violent, strongly-sexed woman groping ever for a spiritual satisfaction that is denied her, ending always in anguish, in tears because the tormented demon of her heart can find no worthy master.

Such women are indeed pathetic, they are rebels defying an intolerant society, but they are not ruffians because they are forever seeking the peace of love and often dying, like Lola, frustrated in the arms of the church, that last resort of despairing souls who seek elsewhere a fulfilment they have failed to realise on earth. It is in the painted strident ranks of the harlots that we shall find the genuine woman ruffian. There are debased examples on every side in every city, whispering " Dearie " from the shadows of Maida Vale or flashing large eyes in coloured lids at you from the cubby-holes of shop doorways in Piccadilly or around Leicester Square.   But these are the outcasts, the hopeless ones, pandering not to man's healthy desires, but to such weird impulses that most of us have met only between the covers of Krafft-Ebing or Havelock Ellis. We must go beyond them, to the army of women so beautiful and vitally desirable, yet essentially cold, that the normal man will think the world well lost to die in their arms. It is a type rapidly disappearing, the emancipation of women having taken away the need for such: theirs is a profession, as the old jest puts it, destroyed by amateurs. For which, all we who love decency and freedom should be truly grateful. Woman at last has escaped from the nemesis of motherhood and is therefore capable of loving without restraint. Yet for all her freedom, she has greater respect for her body than had her timid grandmothers torn between racking curiosity and morbid terrors. Woman has not become promiscuous—except for a certain young neurotic type who considers it somewhat clever to forget the name of her lover of last night—her respect for her body is greater than ever because it is no longer a dirty mystery to be shuffled away in swathes of flannel, hooped with whalebone or steel, or clogged with innumerable petticoats, her respect is no longer based on fear of consequences or on cheap moral maxims, but on the knowledge that to degrade her body is to degrade her spirit, for both are fundamentally allied, both are facets of the same truth, the ego.

For specimens, therefore, of the woman ruffian at her best we must ignore the present century. Greek and Roman days give us illustrations enough, medieval times too can be explored—let us not forget our own Alice

R

Perrers greedily plucking the rings from the fingers of her dying lover King Edward III as he tries to croak the name of Jesus—while the seventeenth century under Charles II and Louis XIV offers such a bewildering array of caressable cold-blooded ladies that it is better to hurry forward lest we grow confusedly verbose by their very number; let us pause at the last century, the nineteenth, that wealthy epoch when Imperialism was flowering so gaudily in decay, spilling the blood of gold into the feckless hands of a debauched aristocracy.

These girls sprang mainly from poor families and by the sheer force of their beauty became more powerful queens than any who sat on thrones. The lovely Caroline Walters was typical of them. She started her profession in a Liverpool pub, the Black Jack, where she earned her famous nickname:

> In Liverpool, in days gone by,
>   For ha'pence and her vittles,
> A pretty girl, by no means shy,
>   Was made to set up skittles.

Seduced at seventeen, she soon found herself in London, the pride of the rowdy, brazen Piccadilly Saloon. I mention skittles particularly because one of her remarks might well be accepted as the credo of this type of woman-ruffian. She would say truculently:

" I'm not a lady but I mean to be treated like one."

VIII

Cora Pearl

In her garret in the Rue de Bassans, she would sit, ugly and fat and old, and her scaly fingers would touch with angry wonderment this skin once beautiful, or she would stare, tearless and defiant, upon the plaster model of her breasts when young. That cast at least was deathless, it would remain to prove to after generations who had not known her magic that there had once lived a goddess so beautiful that lords and dukes had spilt Danae-showers of gold into her lap for the exquisite privilege of temporarily possessing her. And her bust remained still beautiful if not quite perfect; yet what could one expect? She was forty-four and not many women of that age could boast a figure such as hers, even though time had mauled the face; but her face had never been the loveliest part of her, it had been impish, vital, but not really beautiful. Recently a fool had laughed when she spoke of her triumphant past, and she had ripped open her bodice and shamed him and the others with the practically unspoiled purity of chest and shoulders. Why should time scribble on her face, nipping her under the ears, loosening chin and jowls, squeezing ridges at the corners of her mouth and wrinkling up the eyes, yet leave secure and still desirable limbs that none could see, that no man now cared to see?

In this dark room, musty with that peculiar sweetish odour of old and unclean flesh, Cora Pearl would fondle treasures of the past: an Indian china tea-set as fragile as flower-petals, silver asparagus-tongs—almost she had forgotten the rich savour of asparagus, but the sight of the tongs nevertheless watered her mouth with sensuous memories—a fish-slice and silver napkin-rings, and soft crinkling undergarments of faded silk webbing into age. These were her past, here lay the booty of a lifetime's merriment. These few derelicts were all that remained, these pathetic souvenirs from the hands of dead lovers, when once she had lounged in velvet in salons of gold, glittering and blinking with jewels, with pearls sullen upon the whiteness of her chest. She had always loved rich things to see, to eat, to handle—she loved tall painted vases like the torsos of dead ladies gaping for gifts, solemn-faced ormolu clocks, garishly coloured fans, tapestries, and mirrors, mirrors everywhere so that when she walked a hundred Cora Pearls walked with her. She liked to spend —five hundred pounds was not too great a sum for a dinner to twenty of her admirers—yet herself scarcely ate or drank, keeping thereby her superb youth until cancer pressed its hand upon the unblemished skin and brought her low.

She had spent, but she had been careful even in her extravagance. Every louis received was entered into her account-books. Living on about two hundred and fifty thousand francs a year, Cora nevertheless did not ignore the business side of her profession. Down each page of the ledger she ruled two lines: the first space for the man's name, the second for the date of his visit, and the third for the amount he had paid. It had looked neat and sensible, yet now all was gone, her creditors had grabbed everything; in those days of vital youth how was she to realise that the first column would one day suddenly finish and that the third column would show sums she would blush to record? It had not seemed possible that an end must come when she watched men fight amongst each other to touch her hand or stare into her small grey eyes, when men threw money under her shoes while she clattered and

tinkled a can-can amongst the plates and glasses on the
table. That bitch Marie Colombier had called her bow-
legged. A lie, a lie . . . Even now, brooding alone in her
fireless garret, Cora pressed her nails into the palms and
stamped her feet to think that there could live such liars.
Why, but a few days since she had shouted at some irrever-
ent scoffers: " If I could only go undressed, I'd soon show
you! . . ." But she had to dress, hiding her remaining un-
faded loveliness. In the past she had usually worn pull-
over gowns to parties so that at any moment she could
strip away the cuirass of cloth—beautiful cloths from
Worth's, but not so beautiful as the torso they concealed.
She who had loved ostentation and gaudy colours, had surrendered to her dressmaker's judgment and always dressed
most simply. Exquisite clothes: soft flowered tea-gowns,
provocative delicate deshabille, creamy caressing under-
wear. Once at a party of women there had been argument
about the perfections of each, and a comparison took place
with giggling solemnity, but there was silence when Cora
Pearl unlaced her stays, and all agreed, hushed in reverence
or jealousy, that her figure was the most faultless they had
ever seen. One spiteful shrew insisted that she used pink
paint, but Cora had only laughed. She could afford to
laugh, knowing that it was a lie.

Now, only memories . . . memories which she had tried
to compress into a book. When writing her memoirs, she
had found it difficult to disentangle the past, to make a
pattern from that dazzling kaleidoscope. How to begin had
been her problem. " *Il y a des femmes qui envient notre
sort; hôtels, diamants, voitures! . . . Quels rêves dorés! Je
ne veux pas me poser en moraliste: je serais mal dans ce
rôle.*" She could not play the moralist, even on paper, for
she had loved each moment of her past, she would act the
same if the chance offered, if this wrinkled face should

miraculously smooth and the cancer cease gnawing into her body. Yes, a difficult task to mirror yourself with pen on paper, and besides she had not been able to use real names. She had sold her right to that and had therefore to invent pseudonyms for the famous men who had worshipped her. That was why the book had failed. "A catalogue of dull love affairs," one critic had called it, " a basket of exceedingly dirty linen." Dull love affairs! Those men at whom he jeered, those passionate lovers, would have whipped the life from such a sneerer. She'd have whipped him herself in the past. She had been afraid of no one. Goddesses never were afraid, and she had been in truth a goddess, with her perfect body and the cold heart of Diana. That book of hers had given her greater trouble than any other task she had attempted. When, for example, was she born? Where? " *Donc, je suis née* 1842, *à Plymouth, dans le Devonshire.*" Her memories were very vague of that insane childhood home with her drunken musician father, Frederick Crouch, composer of *Kathleen Mavourneen*, and her fifteen brothers and sisters. And here she could not tell the truth. Impossible for a man to leave even the mother of Cora Pearl. She could not write that her father had fled to America, she simply stated that he had died and that her mother had married again, not from love but from practical morals, to have someone to look after her children. Following a brief education in France, Cora went to London to live with her grandmother. She had found this part very difficult to write, for whenever she realised that vile beast of a satyr she had met one Sunday after church she always wanted to spit. The pen had trembled in her pudgy fingers. He had been about forty years of age, she but fifteen or sixteen, and he had spoken to her. This episode bred in her, Cora had always insisted, an instinctive loathing of men, a raging hatred that made her incapable of loving any of them. The man said: "Where are you off to, my little girl?" and she told him—to her grandmother. "I am sure," said he, "that you like cakes." She blushed a little, smiled, but could not answer. "Come with me," he said, "and I'll give you some." How kind! she thought, what very nice people one does meet, and how her grandmother would laugh. After this, surely she would be allowed out alone, for there was no danger, she was so big! So she followed the kindly gentleman, not, she wrote, because she was vicious—decidedly not; She was not even curious, she merely thought, "This will be amusing." He took her to a great house, and on the way she noticed a ragamuffin of a boy, and in her gaiety and superior grown-upness, she slipped a penny into his hand. They entered a low-ceilinged room crowded with men and women drinking and laughing, and the smoke and vile air almost stifled little Cora, while the gentleman pulled her down into a chair beside him and offered gin, but she wanted cakes and insisted on having them. As his rum did not arrive he left her and went to seek it, and for a moment Cora grew afraid. The stink, the noise, the dishevelled women and drunken men accentuated her prim isolation and brought temporary semi-conscious realisation of her peril. Afraid though she was to remain, she was yet more afraid to leave. What would the gentleman think if he came back to find her gone? He would take her for a silly little child, and she was so proud of her newly discovered grown-up dignity. Therefore she waited, and soon he returned with a glass upon a saucer. As he offered it to her she nearly laughed aloud, for most peculiarly he reminded her of an under-mistress at her school. She took the glass and drank, and when the cakes were brought she felt too drowsy to taste them. She fell asleep upon her chair.

In the morning light she awoke to find the man beside her. She gaped in horror and despair while he dressed, and then he suggested that she live with him as his mistress. "I have never forgiven men," she wrote, "not him nor any other, not even those not responsible for this." She sat watching, stupefied, it was like a nightmare, incredible and terrifying, and she knew that never again would she dare return to her grandmother. Her childhood was suddenly, brutally finished, ravished from her in a night of which luckily she could remember nothing. No, she told him when he asked her, she would not go away with him. "Often," she wrote, "when I think over this episode, the most banal in the world, I feel that I suffered more in my coquetry as a woman than in my virtue as a young girl."

Very quickly did Cora—soon she was to call herself Cora Pearl, her real name being Emma Elizabeth Crouch —take to her new exciting life. A Bill Blinkwell, owner of a dance-hall, became her lover, and he was fool enough to carry her with him on a trip to Paris. When he had to return to London, Cora refused to go back with him. She had found her world at last. A sailor became her first French lover, but he had no money and was soon forgotten when wealthier admirers came. Cora was never exactly beautiful; her figure she knew was perfect, but her face was round and fattish, the eyes small, and her voice rather harsh, but her hair was lovely, dark reddish hair crinkling with gold lights that glittered under candleflame more brightly than the jewels about her throat. As one man wrote of her: "She had a tremendous gift of amusing horseplay and, above all, an almost superhuman knowledge of the art of love." She was vital, she drew men by the untamed demon smiling through her eyes, by the swift animal movements of her firm, well-fleshed limbs; she was irresistible, being spiritually inexhaustible. Noisy, cursing, shouting, she swaggered about Paris, and she rode so superbly that they nicknamed her La Centauresse; she passed through the broad streets, lounging in her rubber-tyred coupé or in her carriage with the two footmen on the box; or she sat in theatres, or danced at dinners in precious silks and muslins, her dark-stockinged legs vividly shaped against swirls of white lace; she never returned home before four or five in the morning, and she spent from two till four o'clock in the afternoon seated at her dressing-table. Every man in Paris implored her kisses, but always lightly she replied, " No cash, no favours."

" Cora upon ice! " cried the Duke of Hamilton, seeing her skating in the Bois de Boulogne, " what an antithesis, you hot one! " " Well," said she, " now that the ice is broken, won't you give me something warm to drink? " And she grew to love the duke, if she was capable of loving anyone, but he was a perfect gentleman, she noted, and she liked to listen in awe to his brilliant ironic wit. Other lovers followed when the duke, blind drunk, fell and cracked his skull at Baden. There was Daniloff, who insisted upon wearing his hat in a restaurant until Cora, who never could abide bad manners, hit him over the head with another man's stick and broke it. " I was sorry afterwards," she said, " because the stick was a valuable one." Khalil-Bey came next: he had fifteen million francs in a Paris bank when he met Cora, but it was not long before he had to sneak back to Constantinople without a penny. Napoleon III, Cora always insisted, adored her, but many doubted it because there was no proof except her word, and that was scarcely reliable. But none could deny that she was loved by the Emperor's cousin, Prince Napoleon, nicknamed Plon-Plon. He worshipped Cora, all gold on which he could get his fingers he squandered for her delight, and once when he sent her a box of the most expensive orchids, she considered the gift so insultingly trivial that she tossed it to the floor and danced a can-can on the dying flowers.

Lover after lover, and all so generous—they had to be generous, otherwise they would never have got her, for above all Cora was a shrewd tradeswoman. Grasping she was, mean as a peasant in gathering money, yet she tossed it away with magnificent scorn, for she knew that so long as she remained desirable there would always be fools of men to give her more gold, and the higher she put her price the more eager they were to pay. It was not the money she desired, it was the subjugation of men, it was to extract all from them, to make them sell their estates, bankrupt their families, and then contemptuously to waste a fortune on a dinner. Gold was the symbol of her power. With it she made men pay again and again for the wickedness of the stranger who that day in Covent Garden had decoyed a conceited little girl and broken her vanity to shreds. No, she despised riches. . . . After she had cracked Daniloff on the head for not taking off his hat, he one evening weighed in his hand the string of pearls about her throat because a man had praised them, punning upon her name. " Will you take his words for these pearls? " said Daniloff, and when Cora asked what he meant, he answered, " Because they are both equally false." Cora ripped the pearls from her throat and hurled them to the floor. " Pick up the pearls, my dear," said she, " and to prove they're real I'll give you one for your cravat." But Daniloff would not move and the other guests scrambled on the floor, and when they returned the pearls Cora ruefully noticed that although there were no pearls left on the floor neither were there any on her necklace. But it was worth the loss to make the gesture. And, after all, what were a few jewels? One smile, one nod of acquiescence, one invitation from lowered eyelids, and jewels by the hundreds were hers.

Gay days . . . and gayer nights . . . Once at dinner they served her up in a monstrous pie at the Café Anglais, and what man could desire a tastier dish? She had a cast made of her bosom, just as it was said that Pauline Bonaparte had done, and she had had her hands cast as well, one hand upholding one breast like a cup while the other hand and breast formed a lid, all in onyx, like those cups at Versailles made for Marie Antoinette so that in her dairy she could drink milk from the sacred image of motherhood. But a gentleman, turned thief of love, stealer of memories that he would retain for ever in cold onyx, stole Cora's cup. She was sometimes easily taken in by men, her vast contempt making her underestimate their cunning. A Serbian posing as the Prince de Hersant, robbed her of her jewels. " He was a Prince all right," she said airily, " but a Prince of the Order of Rogues."

Such merry memories for this tortured dying woman in her attic, under the grimy sloping roof. Herself in the sculptor's studio, and Madame Desmard pressing her ear into her cold breast and whispering sadly, " What a pity the chisel can't repeat those throbbings which are life." Pity indeed that the chisel could not bring the beat of the heart behind the stone so that eternally Cora Pearls might come, fresh Galateas for each succeeding generation. That night when she had been cajoled into acting on the stage as a counter-attraction to the popular Adah Menken! She smiled ruefully when she remembered the fiasco, it had been a jest, she had never taken herself seriously as an actress or singer, but she had been always ready for any devilment. It was in 1867 that she took the appropriate part of Cupidon in *Orphée aux Enfers*. She had been far from a success. Covered with diamonds, with a vivid blue cloak sliding from her plump shoulders, with glittering blue feather-wings and yellow sandals, she had pranced dazzlingly to the footlights, " wearing a corsage far too low," as one liverish critic put it, " and not sufficiently adhesive to the bust." She lasted twelve nights, which after all was quite a triumph for an actress who had only her figure to commend her. At first her friends' applause kept her going, but after a few nights their hands got tired and their voices hoarse, and then, as she wrote herself, she " was hissed at last; and I left the boards without regret or the wish to return to them again. Such is glory." As a matter of fact, she left the boards under a bombardment of rotten fruit and vegetables, and her only retort was typical—she poked out her tongue at the turbulent audience. They sang a song afterwards about the apples flung at her:

Like Paris and Helen of Troy
—an old story told anew——
a second Paris has given
Cora Pearl an apple too!

Then into this fantastic gaiety, this world of magnificent irresponsibility, tragedy suddenly came, came in a fool's mask, in the body of a fat, conceited, serious young lout. Cora should have known better than to tolerate the protestations of an idiot like Alexandre Duval, for youth takes itself with preposterous solemnity. Besides, he was no gentleman, and Cora always did like gentlemen. Wealth could please and buy her, but only the manners and talk of a gentleman could really impress her, could give her a frightening yet delightful sense of her own inferiority and a pride in her conquest of such a clever and well-bred lover. Duval's father had started as a butcher and had made a fortune out of restaurants, nevertheless Cora forgave Alexandre his degraded social position. Because of his eight million francs, this noisy yet fastidious girl permitted Duval to embrace her who was worthy only of princes, and her friends and old admirers were quite scandalised. She had acted in bad taste, and that was unforgivable. All the same, her Napoleon was far away and she needed money; besides, Plon-Plon had given her full permission to amuse herself if she got bored or hard-pressed for cash. And she spent so much that she was always hard-pressed for cash. She charged Duval seven thousand francs a week, and joyfully he paid: she was cheap at the price for such a fat young lout as he. But his money began to fail and his mother interfered to rescue her boy from the clutches of the siren, she refused to lend him anything. Cora then told him plainly that this was the end, the bargain was finished, he had got his money's worth and should be grateful. But the wretched idiot insisted that love should be included in the agreement, and when Cora pointed out that she was a business woman and not a sentimental fool, he became desperate with hurt vanity. He pushed his way into her boudoir while she was having her dusky red curls arranged by a hairdresser. That was intolerable, unforgivable, it proved he was no gentleman, and apart from these appalling manners, the young fool had neglected to bring the promised diamond necklace. Cora threw him out, and in the best tragic manner he pulled a revolver from his pocket and shot at himself on her doorstep. Even in this he was a bungler, he aimed six bullets at his chest and only one hit him, wounding him slightly. Although Duval was soon up and out of bed again, the scandal was too great for Cora: although she hoisted the Union Jack on her roof and demanded British protection, she was expelled from France. That was the end. They sang about the affair at the *Vaudeville*,

Cora being the heartless courtesan, Duval the pathetic dupe of love; this fat young fool, sodden with obese vanity, basked in the easy favours of the bored yet ambitious young ladies of the chorus and listened smugly while they sang of his martyrdom.

Later, when Cora did go back to Paris during the Franco-Prussian war, she thought to recover her position by offering her house in the rue de Chaillot as a hospital for returned soldiers, paying all expenses amounting to about twenty-five thousand francs. The government accepted the offer, but gave her no official recognition. Raging at this insult, she began proceedings for the recovery of her money: they returned her fifteen hundred francs, and when the official brought the gold she threw it in his face. Hers always was the splendid gesture: she scorned money yet ever needed it for the luxuries her pampered body craved, luxuries that were but the symbol of her body's animal-power. For she had never loved aught but herself, her life had been one battle to rehabilitate the degradation of herself in her own eyes; haunted by memories of the kindly gentleman in Covent Garden, she lived only to prove that she was no man's dupe; and never loving, never being weakened by the terrors and jealousies and irresistible desires of ordinary people, she had been able to remain cold and strong and fearless.

Few now came to visit her, few remembered Cora Pearl. Even the streets no longer wanted her; not for a few louis could she sell what had once been beyond all price. Yet she did not complain or repine, she understood that she must pay for that gaudy past. And it had been worth it. What use were tears? They would be an insult to her body. She didn't really live nowadays, except for hours of excruciating pain when cancer clawed at her, reminding her that there was yet something sensate in her aged flesh.

She who had cost ten thousand francs was grateful for a louis from a drunkard whose eyes were too dimmed with wine to see the face he kissed. Venus had discarded her for younger, more supple limbs. Her recondite knowledge of amorous play, her still firm figure, were no longer assets when one looked into the pouchy face with its skin dried by cosmetics, wrinkled with lascivious memories, and saw the lewd demon behind her eyes. Yet she was not old, she was only forty-four. So suddenly had age gripped and twisted her, punching her traitorously with this disease, disease of the flesh, that she could not truly believe she was no longer young. And always had she hated men. Often she muttered to herself how greatly she hated men, that beast in Covent Garden who had drugged her and those who had followed with gifts to lay before her, none had she really loved, although one or two she had respected and even feared a little because of their gentlemanly manners and cruel wit. What right had any of them to grumble, hands in empty pockets? She had given them rarer wealth than gold or jewels. " Although to men on the whole," she wrote, " I was cold, I sometimes melted." Sometimes . . . but always at her will, never at his. No man could buy that moment when the artful harlot became the passionate woman, no man could conjure that woman into life with words or caresses, he could but pray that in his arms she might create some image of herself that would bring desire. Never the man did she want, he was a fool she despised, it was herself she loved, this body which she loved to adorn. Men were the worshippers, slaves before Circe, they paid and paid heavily to be vouchsafed a glimpse of a heaven that was indisputably hers and hers alone, and which could not be shared save in one of those moments of unexpected charity when goddesses condescend to look with haughty compassion upon a sleeping Endymion or a wary Adonis. Then, then in that rush of glory, in that blinding rapture beyond all imaginings, the man, even though he threw a fortune at her feet, need have had no regrets, for he on honey-dew had fed and drunk the milk of paradise . . .

Strange that the glory should shrivel to this, that curves of subtle magic should sag like tired balloons, that the smile which had turned men's hearts to scared desire, should disgust them now . . . Strange . . . The wages of sin, they said . . . Well, she had been given her wages and had earned them fully. She accepted without sorrow, without anger, and with a certain defiance. Life had been good. Her memories were worth a hundred years of other women's lives. Therefore, it did not matter that this room was dark, that her fortune had dwindled to a few unpawnable mementoes, that her body was loosening from the skeleton and that the rat cancer was eating her into a grave. She had her ghosts for company, rare, laughing, drinking, roistering, most loving ghosts . . . there were none better . . .

IX

The Art of the Ruffian

At the end of her memoirs, that tedious, involved and often inaccurate work, Cora Pearl summed up her faith. She wrote: " At all times there are fascinating women, just as there are always princes and diplomats, workers and capitalists, men of honour and rogues. If I had to live my time again I should perhaps display less folly and more sense, not that I should be less esteemed but I should be more maladroit. Ought I then regret the conditions that have made me what I am? Yes, if I think upon my poverty, but not if I look back upon those things which have prevented me from losing my serene quietude. If gold is made to spend and diamonds to glitter, you will never be able to reproach me with not having put those things to their proper uses. I have sparkled with the one and parted with the other. That was as it should be, and I have never failed to put back into circulation everything that came to me. Honour and justice were satisfied. I have never cheated anyone because I have never made myself a slave to anyone. My independence was everything to me. I have known no other real happiness, and it is still that which most attracts me to life: I prefer it to the richest jewels, for I believe that the most valuable things in life are those which we cannot sell because they do not belong to us." Her independence, that she kept at least, and apparently it satisfied all her desires, for everything else she lost, her wealth and her charm. Cora is a strange creature and her fascination was apparently immense, although, apart from that classic figure of hers, there seems little evidence that she was beautiful. " A clown's head on a body worthy of Diana de Poitiers," one man said of her, but that is undoubtedly a libel. We might also reject the continual insults about her voice, which could not possibly have been so harshly jangling as many insisted. There are always people only too eager to speak insultingly about genius, small spiteful jealous animals will ever lie about their superiors with envious malice. Nevertheless, Cora's charm could not have been in her face or voice, nor purely in her body. But how is one to pin down the inexpressible attraction which some women possess, to explain the supple animal caged in a vital body which draws men even against their will? A modern woman novelist has tried to express this fascination by the one idiotic word " it," and others have slithered aside with the vague phrase, " sex appeal." " It," with its insulting non-gender flavour, as if desire were some kind of beetle, misses the point badly, while " sex appeal " does not even attempt to explain it. Normal desire of one man for one woman is understandable on the theory of the Hermetic marriage commanded by the *Zohar*, the fusion of opposites to form a perfect unity, a psychological balance, the I and the Me metamorphosing into one complete and indivisible personality. On this basis we see why certain men and women are mutually attracted and yet can appear repulsive to others who do not need the same spiritual counterpoise. But there are ruffians outside this area, there are the Casanovas and the Cora Pearls who can retain the balance within themselves; while acting the perfect lover, they are yet themselves never satisfied in love. Cora was a genius of sexual in- genuity purely because she could remain coldly aloof, for excitement turns man or woman into a blunderer: Cora

never blundered because, except in the rare moments of
which she speaks, she felt no sexual interest in any man.

   She reiterates again and again her hatred of men and
she places all blame for this upon the rogue who drugged
her in Covent Garden.   We have only Cora's word for
this episode, yet there seems no reason to doubt it, and on
examination it loses a great deal of its hideousness.   She
was not a child, she was fifteen or sixteen, and more than
likely a hefty, strapping wench.   Nor was she averse to
being spoken to.   She accepted the offer with alacrity and
insists that she went for the cakes only because she thought
that it might prove an amusing adventure, she was neither
afraid nor even curious.   In fact, she was obviously a
bumptious young girl determined to show her grandmother that she could look after herself, and in a sense she
got what she deserved.   It was her prurient upbringing
that helped, the shameful hiding of truth that gave her
this stupid courage, because only dimly was she able to
comprehend that there might be anything for so important
a little person to fear.   And at least she is frank enough to
confess that the horror which overcame her in the morning was not at the loss of her virginity, but at the blow to
her self-esteem.   Therefore her hatred of men cannot be
based on the sexual brutality of this one man, but on her
realisation of his physical superiority and cunning.   She
had been cheated, so she dedicated her life to the rehabili-
tation of her bruised egoism, only by the betrayal of men
could she prove to herself her own uniqueness, could she
blot away the shameful memory of that morning when
she awoke to realise that, for all her insouciant smugness
of the day before, she was in truth only a vain, stupid
girl.   Nor is her refusal to return home wholly convincing, she accepted her situation with amazing complacence
and with only the five pounds left her by her seducer,

tackled the difficult world of whoredom without fear. She took too swiftly to the life for us to waste time in weeping over her lost maidenhood. The blind morality that insists on blaming the act of seduction for the harlot will of course refuse to see this point, it will insist on sentimentally contemplating her ravished innocence and damning the man as a devil in the guise of a whiskered philanthropist. But if he had not been the means of leading Cora over the threshold one cannot doubt that she would have found another inductor soon enough. The harlot makes the act of seduction, and no act of seduction can possibly make a harlot. If it could, there would be far less honest women in this world, for many a wench at an early age of innocence has surrendered from much the same motive as Cora—the same motive that causes small boys to smoke at too early an age, or to drink bad wine and snigger over smutty stories, so that they may appear grown-up—and has swiftly pushed the episode far back into her subconscious, settling placidly into innocence again as if the seduction had never taken place. It is on the point of the drugging that the kindly gentleman remains damned; for that, there is no excuse. But I doubt if the drug were really necessary. In her determination to prove herself a woman of the world, Cora, like many another silly girl, would more than probably have submitted to anything he suggested.

Cora's hatred and contempt for men is typical of the harlot, but it is likely enough that the germs were settled in her long before she met the kindly gentleman; they probably began their work in her childhood, for an unsettled home-life, particularly a home-life in which the husband is either of no importance or from which he decamps, often creates this angry dissatisfied state, both in men and in women. Isadora Duncan is a case in point,

so also is Lola Montez, but with them a confused upbringing sent them in passionate search for security, for a sound
love-basis on which they could reconstruct their spiritual
outlook on life. On Cora, as on many others, it drove
her coldly to a hatred of men, of the brutal betrayer of
her mother, with whom she automatically associated herself. Her revenge on men was revenge upon the father
who had bullied her mother and not even bothered to
love her, his daughter. Children are emotionally so sensitive that the least jar likely to knock aside their parents'
haloes is likely also to upset their whole sexual balance;
any thought of favouritism, of an alteration in a parent's
affections, will make them as jealous as a dog who sees his
master pat another dog. Childhood is the vital age, and
should we examine carefully the upbringing of many a
good ruffian, male or female, we should soon trace the
causes of their hatred of society. With Cora Pearl, I feel
that it was unquestionably the irresponsible atmosphere of
that Plymouth household with her innumerable scantily
dressed dirty brothers and sisters, an exhausted mother and
a drunken sentimentalist of a father weeping musically
over Kathleen Mavourneen, that sent her into the world
as a preordained courtesan. The gentleman in Covent
Garden was but a necessary accident, the inevitable prelude to her unconsciously chosen life.

The transition from this gay annexe of Ruffians' Hall
into the study and studio of the artist is but a small step,
for the artist is extremely feminine in many ways. While
the woman creates with her body, he creates with his
mind, and both are continually posturing, lying, cheating
themselves in an illusory world. Yet rarely do we find
the artist behaving in an anti-social manner, save very
often in drinking or wenching far too much, but neither
of these exhilarating pastimes can be considered purely

attributes of ruffianism. There have been artist ruffians, of course, and many an artist has been a man-of-action: Chaucer fought in France, Ben Jonson trailed a pike in Flanders, Thomas Churchyard spent thirty years of continual fighting in Ireland, Scotland, and the Low Countries, Lodge sailed round the world with Cavendish, but such exploits have nothing to do with our thesis. There were men like George Borrow who must have seemed the incarnation of Satan himself when he strode into some Spanish peasant's hut with that diabolical work, a Protestant Bible, or like the superb Doughty, or Sir Richard Burton, or Herman Melville, but these are adventurers, not ruffians; there were roaring, insulting old bears such as Dr. Johnson, crushing senseless with abusive words any pathetic inoffensive man who dared speak in his presence, or like the raging Swift, torturing two tragic women and dying eventually, in his own words, " like a poisoned rat in a hole," or like the delicately ironic Pope, squeezing venom into his *Dunciad*. There is nothing ruffianly in their lives, no destroying only for the sake of greater power, their ruffianism is expressed mainly through the iconoclasm of their work. Rarely indeed are the two combined, ruffianism in art and action, although musicians curiously enough of all artists probably lead the most violently anti-social existences. Wagner is an excellent illustration of this ruffianism of mind expressed in word and deed. He demanded unceasing adulation from those around him and chafed if people did not listen open-mouthed to his often preposterous remarks, fretting should they speak to others when he stood by. His boastful and occasionally lying autobiography is a fine piece of sneaking ruffianism, bristling with spite, and written on the understanding that it would not be published until many years after his death so that those whom he abused would be unable to answer back. We see him strutting pompously through life yet pettishly stabbing at poor wretches like Meyerbeer at every opportunity; and there is that shameful scene when he gave a supper in honour of Laube after the production of his play, *Karleschüler*, and sat wriggling with impatience until the opportunity came to sneer at the work he was celebrating, and the embarrassed guests crept out in silence while the miserable Laube stole off, crushed and in despair. It was the same with Gounod: while smirkingly receiving and repeating Gounod's praise, he refused noisily under any circumstance even to listen to *Faust*. When he was present, no other man must be considered to possess a spattering of intelligence. He would cheat men of their money or their wives, then scream with outraged fury should they upbraid him for it. His malice towards poor Minna, his first wife, is appalling: like Shelley, he was unable to understand why she should become jealous because, while sharing her bed, he told her that he needed a spiritual affair with another woman and no subtler insult could be offered a woman with its implication of Minna's lack of intelligence and spiritual comradeship. To his second wife, Cosima, he dictated for his to-be-published-posthumously autobiography the most childish lies about Minna, even hinting that she poisoned his dog because she was jealous of the woman who gave it to him. These are examples of a petty-minded ruffian, striking maliciously at shadows that do not even threaten so that he might keep intact his billowing egoism. It does not make pleasant reading—particularly to one who loves Wagner's music as greatly as I.

Here we see the artist-ruffian exposed at his blackest, with his small-hearted jealousies and cheap godhead-illusions, and it can be duplicated in many another musician—and in many an actor too, if it comes to that.

The other arts give similar examples, but never quite so perfect. Rabelaisian men like Titian's friend, Pietro Aretino, are the ones usually damned as ruffians, but they shine nobly beside such as Wagner, for Aretino was merely an open-armed lover of beauty and laughter, maintaining a private harem of five or six women in his house, adoring them all so completely that he either could not or dared not choose a favourite.

It is a curious thing that when we begin earnestly to seek for a combination of artist and ruffian we are reduced to minor painters or writers, to men like Richard Savage, a brawling braggart, pimp and cheat, who accidentally killed a man in a drunken brawl in a Charing Cross coffee-house; his work is practically valueless, and he is recalled mainly because he was the friend of young Sam Johnson, who thought him worthy of inclusion in his *Lives of the Poets*. Thomas Griffiths Wainewright is another example of the type we must accept to find this combination. There was dirty blood in Wainewright, for his maternal grandfather had published one of the most idiotically disgusting books in English—John Cleland's *Fanny Hill*. Wainewright was of the order of dandies, he liked boasting of his military experiences, which were exceptionally brief: in later life he explained this brevity by shuddering at the colour of the clothes he had had to wear, and murmuring that no artist should become a soldier unless allowed to design his own uniform. He wrote not badly, and he painted not badly. Most of these paintings are simple portraits without character, or are rather voluptuous yet conventional Victorian ladies, scarcely better than the average magazine illustration. But he lived as an artist is supposed to live, taking opium and dressing exquisitely, and he had the same peculiarity as his contemporary, Lacenaire—he adored cats. Then suddenly, for no explic-

able reason, he got married. He must have been in love
with Eliza Frances Ward, his landlady's daughter, for she
brought no riches beyond her beauty, but it is difficult to
imagine Wainewright in love with anybody except himself or a cat. He decided that he must sell his annuity of
£200 a year, and when the trustees objected, he blithely
forged their four signatures and drew £2,259 out of the
Bank of England. Succeeding so well at forgery, he
essayed the more subtle art of murder and poisoned his
uncle, Mr. Griffiths. Again he succeeded and, having
spent this inheritance, poisoned his mother-in-law for a
miserable £100 and the hopes of getting her £10 a year
pension. This was a petty reward, so he next insured his
sister-in-law, Helen, and poisoned her, but when he asked
for the payment of £16,000 the insurance companies
refused to give him the money, not being able to understand why so poor a girl should be valued at such a rate.
Wainewright fled to France, and on being eventually
captured, had the astounding good luck to be charged only
with forgery. How he got away with the murders is inexplicable, but he suffered nothing worse than transportation for life. At the age of fifty-eight, he died in Hobart
in 1852, and we learn that " his later days in the sick ward
were employed, I am told, in blaspheming the pious
patients and in terrifying the timid." To the end he kept
his arrogance undimmed; he boasted in Newgate—" I
have always been a gentleman, and I am a gentleman still.
Yes, sir, even in Newgate I am a gentleman. The prison
regulations are that we should in turn sweep the yard.
There are a baker and a sweep here beside myself. They
sweep the yard; but, sir, they have never offered me the
broom." And when he was asked how he could have had
" the cold-blooded barbarity to kill such a fair, innocent,
and trusting creature as Helen," he replied, " Upon my

soul, I don't know, unless it was because she had such thick ankles."—a reply worthy of the Marquise de Brinvilliers, who attempted to poison her daughter for the logical reason that she was growing too tall. Of Wainewright, Barry Cornwall, who knew him well, wrote: "He was not entirely cruel. I imagine that he was perfectly indifferent to human life, and that he sacrificed his victims without any emotion, and for the purpose simply of obtaining money to gratify his luxury": an excellent ruffian epitaph!

Wainewright was an excellent ruffian, but a poor artist. The same, however, cannot be said of Michelangelo Merigi, famous as Caravaggio (1569–1609), whose revolutionary attitude towards painting broke the fetters of the too-romantic neo-classical school, for he insisted on painting realistically, directly from life. His work nevertheless is dull, static, but the man himself was as fiery a ruffian as we will meet in any profession. With dirty face and uncombed hair, he strode through life, dressed in the richest of clothes that hung about him in tatters with neglect. He was a racketeer who would not tolerate a rival, and with a burly architect friend, Onorio Longhi, he libelled and persecuted any painter who dared challenge his position. One poor wretch, Baglione, who thought to seek legal protection was chased down the street by Longhi, wearing a steel-shirt, who hurled stones and insults after him. Gloomy and raging against life, Caravaggio was quick to answer any slight upon his dignity, and when, failing to pay his rent, his landlady seized his clothes, he smashed all her windows; and on one occasion he tried to kill a tapster in a tavern; he stabbed a man in the Piazza Navona, and was eventually banished for murdering a player at tennis. Seeking refuge in Malta, he was nobly received and worked conscientiously until he fought a Knight of St.

John and found himself in jail. He escaped at last, only to die of fever after being shipwrecked on the coast of Spain and losing all his goods. Belisario, a Greek (1558–1643), was of the same type. He lived in Naples and murdered any rival painter, even poisoning one of his own pupils who showed promise of excelling the master; he told Guido Reni either to get out of Naples or die; and if threats did not work, he would mix dirt with his rivals' paints or throw acid at their frescoes. It is a strange thing that, like Caravaggio, Belisario was not a great artist—in fact he was by no means Caravaggio's equal—while the man who expressed ruffianism superbly in art was Salvator Rosa (1615–73), who, although he lived with brigands for a time, was a gentle romantic, depressed by his own tempestuous dreams and his visions of a dark and violent earth.

Perhaps this is the explanation we seek, for Salvator Rosa in paint created a real ruffian world which Caravaggio and Belisario could not express save in their violent behaviour. It is the same with Cellini, an admirable ruffian who was merely a cunning goldsmith without genius. Is it that the artist's ruffianism becomes sublimated into paint or words? That would seem to be the truth. Cervantes, for example, began life as a splendid man of action. At Lepanto, he was ill with fever and his comrades tried to keep him below-deck, but he insisted upon taking the most dangerous position in the fight and received three gunshot wounds— two in the chest and one which maimed his left hand for life. Later, in 1575, captured aboard the *Sol* by three Turkish galleys, he was carried to Algiers and locked into a dungeon under the false impression that he was a valuable catch because he had with him a letter from Don John of Austria. For five years he remained a prisoner and four times he tried valiantly to escape, and even under the threat of torture refused to confess the names of his accomplices, insisting that he alone was the plotter. Hassan Pasha, Dey of Algiers, is said once to have cried: " So long as I have the maimed Spaniard in my keeping, my Christians, my ships—aye, and the whole city!—are safe." His wounded hand kept Cervantes at home when at last he was ransomed, and for it we must thank one of the greatest masterpieces of the world, *Don Quixote*. And can one doubt that if Sir Walter Scott had not had that withered leg, we would now possess our incomparable Waverley novels? He'd have galloped off after Wellington and probably got himself killed. And we should be grateful to Byron's club-foot; more than likely it gave us *Manfred* and *Don Juan*. Sir Thomas Malory too was always in trouble, being twice accused of " feloniously raping Joan, the wife of Hugh Smith "—but we cannot accept this as rape in the ordinary sense: *raptus* probably meant breaking into the house and throwing Joan out of it—and it was only because Edward IV locked him into jail for his Lancastrian plots that he found leisure enough to write that superb swan-song of chivalry, the *Morte d'Arthur*. We will, however, find no better illustration of this confusion of artist and man of action than in the great Rimbaud, who in 1873 finished the last line of *La Saison en Enfer*, threw his pen away, and went adventuring, joining the Dutch army after five years tramping over Europe, starving, begging, peddling in the streets. He was shipped to Java, but hating army discipline, deserted and struggled through the jungle until he reached the coast and found a ship. He worked at Suez and by the Red Sea, and was foreman of a gang of labourers at Cyprus, but he could never hold a job for long, he always quarrelled with his employers, his arrogance refusing to accept another's authority. He started to explore Abyssinia with a capital of £16, and he might have performed great deeds had the French government helped him. As it was, he became a failure, but a brave and splendid failure.

In most artists there exists this continual struggle, the need for action that becomes translated into paint or music or stone or words. Villon never made a good ruffian. It is true that he killed a man, but it was in self-defence, and it is true that he stole and committed sacrilege and even acted the pander in a brothel, but all through his superb poetry one feels a half-hysterical terror of death, a rage against the dirty, dying, medieval world breaking through his malicious laughter. He was unhappy because he could not reconcile the two impulses of art and ruffianism, they fought against each other, torturing him. So, too, it was with the mighty Marlowe, boozing and blaspheming in Elizabethan taverns, acting the government spy until Frizer's shilling dagger killed him in Eleanor Bull's Deptford inn. His poetry expresses the violence of his age, the hunger for new things in a rich earth; always the peacock-east intrigued him, he dreamed of outlandish countries with gorgeously dressed turbaned kings with scimitars, and dark, bright-eyed naked ladies in nets of gold. He remains one of the greatest of poets, but one tortured always by this conflict expressed in bitter railings against God and the Queen. After all, there is small difference between ruffian and artist, they are facets of the same emotion: one being the master of the physical world, and the other of the spirit. Was it a coincidence that our greatest era of poetry should arrive with the adventurous opening of the New World? Do not Drake and Shakespeare spring from the same impulse, one voyaging the dangerous seas of earth and the other adventuring through the timeless and perilous lands of the spirit?

Artists are not the only adventurers of the spirit, arrogant creatures hiding from the world and revealing it afresh through the prism of genius. There are scientists also spurred by the same passion, but of modern science I understand very little; of the science of the past I can speak more safely. I know it is the usual custom in these thinly rationalist days to smile contemptuously upon the researches of the alchemists and astrologers, and if astrology were limited to the puerile nonsense printed in modern newspapers that contempt would be deserved. But real astrology is a profound and disturbing science, and some of the discoveries of alchemy are of genuine importance. Paracelsus may seem a buffoon, boozing and brawling and waving his sword and chattering about the great Azoth, but his philosophy is definitely worth studying, and his determined efforts to bring the vagaries of contemporary science to earth by exposing a plate of excrement as the greatest secret of medicine to the scandalised academy was by no means an act of stupidity—it was a lesson those airy metaphysicians well deserved and needed. He is, however, outside the ranks of ruffianism, but there is one great man who might be included—both a scientist and poet of the Elizabethan age—Edward Kelly, or Talbot, we are not certain which is right. Kelly's ruffianism is apt to overshadow his genius, but he knew deeply about alchemy, and his patron, Dr. Dee, admired and believed in him, and Dee was a very great man indeed. Seamen like Humphrey Gilbert, John Hawkins and Hugh Smith would consult him on abstruse questions of navigation, and he had drawn official horoscopes of Edward VI, Queen Mary, and Queen Elizabeth. Elizabeth also consulted him about the most auspicious day for her coronation and had acted upon his astrological advice with what results we know. When Kelly came to him, Dee believed

his tale at once. We really don't know all the truth about
Kelly, but it appears that he was born at Worcester on
August 1, 1555, and had been an apothecary's apprentice
and is believed to have studied at Oxford. He is alleged to
have been a forger and to have had his ears cut off and to
have been pilloried: of all this we have no actual proof,
but it appears that he was once wandering through Wales
when he put up at a Somerset inn near Glastonbury. The
landlord, seeing that he was a learned man, produced a
manuscript which, during the religious persecution of the
early Elizabethan days, had been found in the rifled
sepulchre of a bishop, together with two small ivory
caskets, one containing red powder, and the other white
powder, but half the red had unfortunately been lost when
the box was being dug up. As nobody could read the
manuscript, Kelly bought the lot for a guinea, having
noticed that it was a profound treatise on magic, probably
the Book of St. Dunstan. Together with Dee, he began to
experiment with his find, but alchemy took second place
when Dee discovered that Kelly could read the crystal, and
night after night was spent in conversation with spirits
through the glass. The British Museum possesses one of
Dee's crystals, and we have his notes on these séances and
they are interesting but, to me at any rate, unrevealing,
being most involved in symbolism. Kelly at the time was
in his early twenties, and Dee was about thirty years his
senior, and both were married—Dee to Jane Fromond,
once lady-in-waiting to Lady Howard of Effingham, and
Kelly to a girl nine years younger than himself called Joan
Cooper. Then in May, 1583, the Earl of Leicester intro-
duced Dee to Albert Laski, Count Palatine of Siradz, and
as he was deeply interested in alchemy he insisted upon
taking all four back to Poland with him. They settled in
Laski's palace at Cracow and sweated at their researches

until the count began to despair of results and passed them on to the Emperor Rudolph of Bohemia, and here in Prague, Kelly obviously cheated, for with one single drop of red oil he transmuted a pound of mercury into the purest gold; and so powerful was his metaboliser that the residuum produced a small ruby in the bottom of the crucible. Unable to perform the experiment indefinitely the four next appeared again in Poland, at the court of King Stephen, only shortly to decamp for the patronage of Count Rosenberg, who sought, like Ponce de Leon, the elixir of eternal life. Kelly promised to keep him alive for five hundred years, but it was not long before they were back in Prague. We are, however, not interested in these alchemical investigations; although it cannot be questioned that Kelly was defrauding his benefactors, it is doubtful if Dee was a part of the trickery, and Kelly might, while extorting money from credulous fools, have been using that money for legitimate experiments. Of this we cannot be certain, but where this strange household assumes extraordinary interest is in Kelly's behaviour as a " skryer ". Dee could not see into the showstone and had to rely on his friend's eyes until there came the astounding revelation when the spirit, Medina, a pretty girl child, told them that they must " share all things in common ", including their wives. " After all these," wrote Dee, " and many other things told me by the same Mr. E. K., we departed each to his bed, where I found my wife awake, attending to hear some new matter of me from Mr. Kelly, his reports of the apparitions, continued with him above four hours, being else alone, I then told her, and said, ' Jane, I see that there is no other remedy, but as hath been said of our cross-matching, so it must needs be done.' Thereupon she fell a weeping and trembling for a quarter of an hour. And I pacified her as well as I could; and so, in the fear of God, and in believing of His Admonishment, did perwade her that she shewed her self prettily resolved to be content *for God, his sake, and his secret Purposes,* to obey the Admonishment." It does seem as if this was all a plot between Kelly and Jane to delude the elderly Dee, for a day or so later Kelly said he saw two men fighting and told Dee that one was speaking to him, saying, " I sent a thing to thy wife by my man, and this fellow hath taken it from him." The other man, being then wounded in the thigh, produced " a yellow square thing," whilst the victor cried, " Hast thou laid it under the right pillow where his wife slept yesternight? " Dee adds: " Hereupon we went away: and I coming to my Chamber, found my wife lying upon her bed (where I lay yesternight) and there I lifted up the right pillow, upon which she lay resting herself (being not well at ease). And in manner under her shoulders there I found my precious Stone, that was taken away by Medini: Whereat E. K. greatly wondered, doubting the verity of the shew. But I and my wife rejoyced, thanking God." Surely a queer household! and we still possess the solemn document they drew up, surrendering to each the other's wife. It is too long to quote in full, but the beginning and end are well worth inclusion. " We four," it runs, "(whose heads appeared under one Chrystalline Crown, in one pillar united, and inclosed) do most humbly and heartily thank Thee, O Almighty God (our Creator, Redeemer and Sanctifier) for all Thy mercies and benefits hitherto received, in our persons, and in them that appertain unto us: And at this present, do faithfully and sincerely confess, and acknowledge, that Thy profound wisdome *in this most new and strange doctrine* (among Christians) . . . Beseeching Thee, as Thou art the onely true Almighty and Everlasting God, Creator of Heaven and Earth, Thou wilt, in Thy infinite mercies, not impute

T

it unto us for sin, blindness, rashness, or presumption, being not accepted, done, or performed upon carnal lust, or wanton concupiscence; But by the way of *Abraham-like faith and obedience*, unto Thee, our God, our Leader, Teacher, Protector and Justifier, now and for ever. And thereunto we call the holy Heavens to be witnesses, for Thy honour and glory (O Almighty God) and our discharge, now and for ever. *Amen*." But this blissful Eden did not last for long. The Emperor lost his patience with Kelly at being unable to produce anything other than glib promises, so he pushed him into the castle of Zobeslau to see if solitude would induce him to manufacture that alchemistical Stone which is the Waters of Life. Unable to manufacture any stone except his written masterpiece, *The Stone of the Philosophers*, at the age of forty-two Kelly tried to escape in 1597 by knotting his bedsheets together and climbing out of his window; but the cloth snapped, and that was the end of Edward Kelly.

It is difficult to estimate Kelly. He was, like many a ruffian, a confusion of charlatan and genuine seeker after knowledge, but whether the search was the first impulse or whether by continual talk he convinced himself of his sincerity we cannot tell; his works, however, have definite value, and he was quite a good poet. Whatever doubts, however, we may feel about his ruffianism, we can certainly have none when we contemplate probably the most famous so-called magus of all, Joseph Balsamo, who rechristened himself Count Cagliostro. He would tell great lies about his birth and childhood, whispering romantically of the East and of the mysteries he was taught in far Arabia, but the truth was that he came of lowly parentage, being born at Palermo, in Sicily, on June 8, 1743. His father died when he was quite young, but it does not seem that Joseph made any attempts to help his mother, he was

F. Bonneville del.

CAGLIOSTRO.

lazy and liked the carnal things of life, so an uncle placed him in a seminary where he could be given a much-needed religious education. This did not suit the precocious lad, and he continually ran away until, to keep him at his work, they locked him into a Benedictine monastery, where he chiefly studied herbs and the art of healing. At last he managed to escape even from these high walls, and although only about fourteen years of age, busied himself with gusto in all possible debaucheries. He did occasional sketches, but most of his time was spent in stealing, drinking, gambling and wenching, and when one of his uncles was kind enough to take him home, Joseph retorted by filching everything on which he could lay his hands. He acted the pander to one of his friends, coaxing a girl-cousin into seduction, and keeping all the presents the lover sent his mistress, while he forged a will for the Marquis Maurigi, for which he was well paid, and made good money by selling fake theatre-tickets. Then, toying with magic, he fooled a miser called Marano into the belief that he could conjure gold from the ground, and, getting the man alone on a dark night, robbed him and beat him nearly to death. This scandal was too great for Joseph to ride, so he fled to Messina, where he adopted the superb title of Count Alessandre Cagliostro, and it was now that he met an alchemist, Altotas, from whom he learned at least the outward symbols of magic and the high-sounding patter. When Altotas died, Joseph's trickery was clever enough for him to find dupes prepared to stuff gold into his pockets until in Rome he met and married the beautiful Lorenza Feliciani. Until now, his ruffianism has been but common charlatanism, but it soon began to take on mighty proportions, for he had no sooner married Lorenza than he began to teach her the art of harlotry. At first she was aghast when he attempted to force her to sleep with his friends in return for cash down, but either his influence over her was so strong or her own inclinations led in that direction, for she quickly became expert at the game. This is according to her own confession and would otherwise be almost incredible. Joseph first produced two men for her to seduce, with only one of whom did she succeed, and then after her first essay had been fumbled so clumsily, probably owing to her shame and terror, that Joseph had to give her a very stern lecture on the art, explaining that adultery was no crime when committed for ambition and not for lust, and adding that he behaved in similar fashion with ladies so old that he had to drink aphrodisiacal Egyptian wine before visiting them. He had now a perpetual source of income, so long as Lorenza remained attractive, and together they wandered about Europe until, on reaching Paris, Joseph's reputation grew so high that when Lorenza wearied of this remorseless prostitution and threatened to rebel, he had her locked up for several months on the authority of the King. It was in London, however, that he first discovered the perfect way of making money; it was after he had been initiated into freemasonry that, back in Paris, he decided to institute a kind of female freemasonry. There can be no doubt that he had studied the researches of Mesmer, which had then become fashionable, and became an adept at hypnosis, for he made undoubted cures with the laying-on of hands—psycho-analysts tell us that they have experimented with hypnosis, but found that although the results are at first surprising, the cures are but temporary—and could apparently conjure images in mirrors and vases of water. It was now that time took its revenge, for becoming old, this man who had forced his wife into prostitution, grew jealous when he found she cared for other men, and having grown habitual to the profession, Lorenza naturally found it difficult to abandon it, for it had probably caught her physically, become like any other drug, a necessity to over-excited nerves. Joseph's masterpiece, however, was his fake-masonic idea, his Egyptian Lodge to which only thirty-six women were admitted as postulants with Lorenza as Grand Mistress and himself as Grand and Sublime Copt. Each woman had to give one hundred louis for admission and had to swear to remain chaste and obedient. The initiation ceremony began just before mid-night on August 7, 1785, and when the women entered the first apartment they disrobed and dressed themselves in simple white garments with various coloured girdles, being then divided into parties of six according to the colours of these girdles. Heavily veiled, they were next taken into the Temple, which was lighted from above and had thirty-six armchairs draped with black satin, while Lorenza, dressed in white, sat upon a throne. Gradually the lights were lowered, and in the gloom, Lorenza gave the command for each to uncover her left leg up to the thigh and to rest the right arm on a nearby pillar. Then carrying swords, two girls entered, and with silken ropes they bound the ladies together by arms and legs. There was a profound silence before Lorenza spoke about the shameful bonds which held women down as slaves to men, and symbolically the silken ropes were taken away again. They had now to pass through the temptation, and separately each passed into a different compartment lead-ing on to a garden: here they were assailed by lovers, some by force, some by sugary pleadings, and after proving their indomitable virtue, they returned to the Temple to be re-warded with the vision of Joseph, stark naked, being lowered from the roof poised on a golden sphere with a serpent in his hand and a flaming star on his forehead. He demanded that, having proved themselves, they henceforth go as naked as truth, whereupon, following Lorenza's example, they stripped themselves, and Joseph was hauled up to the ceiling again. The fun came next: a table rose out of the floor and was spread with a royal feast, then lovers joined the ladies, and all was eating and drinking and dancing and suchlike merriment until three o'clock in the morning. Joseph and Lorenza were making excellent money out of these gullible ladies until the scandalous affair of the Queen's necklace sent them scuttling out of the country into the arms of the Holy Office that charged them with the terrible sin of freemasonry. Joseph was sentenced to perpetual imprisonment in St. Angelo, and Lorenza to perpetual seclusion in a penitentiary.

Unlike Kelly, there is no suggestion that Cagliostro—to give him his more famous name—had any genuinely profound knowledge of magic. He was a cheat, and a particularly dirty cheat, ruffianism at its basest. No. There is an even baser form of ruffianism, that which like the reptile Zaharoff lives on carrion, on the slaughter of others; and the financiers too are worse than Cagliostro, for he had at least given foolish old women some return for their money, he staged a show to excite bored and elderly ladies, exhausted with normal delights; but of financiers frankly I know little. Money to me is something to spend, and I am constitutionally unable to understand the mentality of those who exist, like dung-beetles, purely to gorge themselves on glittering refuse. They are ruffians right enough, and with their power they have often destroyed ruffians far nobler than themselves.

X

William Walker

In Nicaragua, the Indians had evolved a legend pampering to their broken pride, threatening revenge on their centuries' old oppressors; this legend prophesied that one day a grey-eyed man would come from the north to drive out the detested Spaniard and bring freedom to the rightful owners of a lovely land. And when William Walker stepped on to Sonoran earth soon after de Boulbon's first expedition ended in bloody tragedy, and gazed silently upon this vivid world of tropical luxuriance, it seemed that now at last had the Indian dream come true. At least his eyes were grey, grey almost to steel that could quieten the most uproarious of his followers that in later years were to follow him to his death—his shouting murderous yet romantic followers, filibustering Americans raising aloft the hazy flag of Freedom for Whites and Slavery for the Niggers. He was not tall, this William Walker, merely a little above five feet, and he had not one grain of real humour in all those five feet. Thin-lipped, with large round forehead, he was an Ishmael carrying a gun—lawyer, doctor and journalist. He looked upon the fecund world of Central America as sensual men would look upon a voluptuous woman, he meditated rape while he watched de Boulbon resting after the empty victory of Hermosillo, and he offered him a lieutenantship in his own adventure. But de Boulbon, with gaudier dreams, refused the offer. "I go to death a gentleman, and I die a Christian," he said later, facing the firing-squad.

Walker stepped after him on to the fatal soil of Central America. There was no buccaneering instinct in him. He was a business man seeking new markets, a lawyer more keen on the items of law than on its principles, he was a politician desiring only his own aggrandisement; but above all, he was a brave man and a gallant leader. Under his banner—blue-white-blue with a red star in the white—strode the Texan rogues, exultant after winning their new home; and the never satisfied diggers of California, sniffing gold in every mountain; and the wanderers and the eager adventurers from every corner of the world. Nicaragua didn't want to be saved. The natives were content to be serfs, although ill-treated: they knew no other life. The land was too lavish to fight about with any religious sincerity, for there was more than enough food for all; true, there were constant uproars, practically a yearly revolution—they had had in fact sixteen presidents within six years—but such commotions did not trouble the people. Fool politicians shot themselves, as was only right. Yet these extraordinary Americans strode down from the north, they chartered a brig, and the U.S. marshal seized the brig. That was in July, 1853. Three months later, forty-five wary rogues set out in the barque *Caroline* under Walker and Emory and landed on lower California, at Cape San Lucas; then off they went to La Paz, which they captured with scarcely a shot and grabbed the governor, Espanosa. Then they grabbed the Mexican colonel, Robollero, who arrived just at the wrong moment to supersede Espanosa. After that, Walker held an election and chose himself president.

From California, the adventurers came running. New worlds to explore, new sufferings to encounter, a more violent death to be met than simple dying. They shouldered their guns and set out it seemed with the deliberate intention of getting themselves killed, for little else could they hope to gain. Most of them succeeded in meeting a bullet or two, but some lived to fling their lives into the faces of damned interfering Yankees in the slavery war. Against such men, the greasers had no hope. They fell before every step of Walker's mahogany-faced scarecrows until desertion, starvation and disease combed his ranks, and thirty-four tattered skinny barefoot men staggered over the border and surrendered to Major McKinstry, U.S.A., at San Diego, California. Those thirty-four were all that were left of the president and the cabinet and the army and navy of Sonora, the new republic. And contentedly the natives watched them go, puzzled a little perhaps that men should want to die for words like Freedom. Central America could now continue its fraternal revolutions, and up and down went Nicaragua's political see-saw. It had a population of roughly 260,000, one half of which was of mixed Spanish-Indian descent, a third pure Indian, about ten per cent white, and the remainder negroes.

Walker came back. He was a man with one relentless determination. He was mad with dreams, and he brought his raggletaggle ruffians with him, those Californians who boasted that California was the pick of the world and that they were the pick of California, sometimes adding with a wink—" Aye, California's the sewer of the world and we are the refuse of California." Criminals and gun-fighters marched side by side with politicians and business-men. A son and a nephew of Senator Bayard ran from school one night and stole two of his muskets; but Walker sent them home again. A sergeant fell heir to 100,000 dollars, but he burnt his boat-ticket back and stayed to die in Nicaragua. Such were the men whom Walker drew about him. Later, Burbank, Henningsen's lieutenant, was worth a fortune, but he never lived to spend it, Henningsen would say in after years that he'd heard two dirty privates quarrelling over the correct reading and comparative merits of Æschylus and Euripides, while he'd seen a soldier scribble a translation of Dante as he stood on guard. Surely the strangest army that ever followed a crazy leader into the jungle?

Most of them were doomed, of course. Everybody knew it, except themselves and Walker, that small, thin, tight-lipped man in his blue frock coat, striding aloof in dreams, striding ahead of starved ruffians with eyes bright to kill. They marched with broken arms and cracked ribs, and if their wounds became too painful to permit them moving, they put the pistol to their filthy ears. There was one of them once who was sentenced to death, and the greasers asked him fool questions about the next world and this damned world while he lay with a broken leg, until suddenly he howled at them to " Cut the fooling! If you mean to have this funeral, bring on your mourners and let's go through with it!" And one of Walker's lads slid off to China, where there are still two temples in his honour and you'll find his name in their list of gods.

Walker came back with more men and better guns. He came at the call of the banished liberal leader, Castellon, who sought revenge on the conservative president—the legitimate, as the party was called—Fruto Chamorro. When Castellon first asked Walker to join his democratic army, that lawyer, who could be cautious when he wished, insisted that he and his men be given colonisation grants, thus making the invasion legal, and three hundred so-called colonists signed up on December 29, 1854, and many of them did in fact later become naturalised. Vanderbilt, who wanted his steamers running to schedule through the lakes dividing the continent, helped with the loan of his ship, the *Virgen*, and afterwards added twenty thousand dollars to help certain Wall Street manipulations. Walker knew nothing of Wall Street, and he didn't care a damn

Wm Walker

about it, but he did care greatly about Nicaragua. His men were organised into the American Phalanx, and Castellon sent them off to die for his democratic cause at Rivas. Colonel Ramirez joined Walker with two hundred natives —there were fifty-six Americans—but when they embarked on the *Vesta*, half the natives didn't answer the roll-call and the other half were just good-natured animals even too lazy to run away: besides, their uniform was very pretty. This small troop of Americans and natives—one hundred and fifty-five all told—landed close to Rivas and began their march. They marched bowed under blinding rain through a rich new world, through tumultuous tangles of knotted shrubbery, slithering ankle-deep in muck, and hugging ammunition against the damp. They cursed the rain until, after a day and night's march, they crept through its fierce drumming on to a picket at Tola. Dawn: and through its smudged crystal, Lake Nicaragua beat its reflected lights on their hot eyes. Dreams faded in Walker's ambitious mind while he gazed in wonderment upon that shimmering splendour, that flashing blade of water; and he shuddered with deep happiness at the sight. Birds thrashed the air above him with flaming wings, clashing dark leaves together; green, scarlet, azure and gold, the macaws screamed harsh welcome to the sun; and the sodden, weary Americans gaped at the dazzling glory of the water under a tropic dawn that polished it to quicksilver. It was the most lovely sight that Walker had ever seen, he wrote later in his memoirs, more beautiful than anything that Switzerland, Italy or California could reveal. He smiled upon the sight, disdainful of the five to six hundred legitimist troops barring the lake from his fifty-five Americans and useless natives.

The Phalanx led the attack. Under Kewen and Crocker,

they charged. They did not waste their shot, they marched quietly at the enemy, into the rain of lead. Mouths set, guns at the hip, they marched, until but a few yards off; then they stopped and sent forth a volley, carefully aimed. Yelling, they rushed the advance guard and hurled the greasers off their feet. Bowie's curved knife was out and bright with blood. Back into the narrow streets, into the plaza, stumbled the enemy. Crocker, wounded twice badly, arm broken with musket-shot, yet gripped his pistol in his left hand and never lowered it, never lost aim, until a clean shot got him in the skull and flung him to the ground to be trodden by friend and enemy. Walker shouted for reserves. His shout was clear, shrill with triumph. He shouted again, and turned his head. And he was alone with his Phalanx. Almost as his full rage struck him momentarily blind, the greasers rallied; their very numbers pushed the maddened Phalanx back into little adobe huts. Achilles Kewen swung suddenly on his heel and was down; and tough old Doubleday abruptly jerked his gun into the air and clapped both hands to his head. Walker called for a sortie. Six of his men were killed and a dozen wounded, but a hundred and fifty greasers were dead and wounded and their morale broken; General Boscha drew back, exhausted, and let the Americans go free, contenting himself with butchering the wounded and throwing them into a bonfire, alive or dead.

All this time, the U.S.A. watched with relief yet apprehension its dangerous pests desert prairie and forest. Out of the sewer of California flowed the refuse; the remnant of gallant Texan defenders gave up chasing bears and Indians, and instead, shipped for Nicaragua to chase the greasers. Colonel Charles Gilman—every American who could load a gun and dared defend his title was an honorary colonel in those days—came hobbling on his wooden leg with thirty-five lizard-eyed scoundrels at his side. He was but one of many heroes who forsook wives, booze and ploughshares to have a peek at death over Bill Walker's little shoulder.

At Rivas, Corral—a sleek savage scoundrel who deserved his name, for the corral is a venomous snake, though beautiful—the enemy general, was collecting his army and ranting superbly with his rival, Guardiola, the most notorious rascal in Nicaragua—and that's saying a lot. He was a Sambo, half Indian, half African, a man who never killed save in the back, and was called the Tiger of Honduras—in polite circles. These were the two generals whom Walker faced with his little Phalanx, with about two hundred and fifty worthless natives, and two small cannon. On the cool morning of October 11 he began the march, and American feet trampled assuredly upon the dew as if the earth sweated beneath their tread; sternly disciplined, guns shouldered, they strode the white Transit Road to Virgin Bay. Four hundred of them. They had no uniform: only a red ribbon about their hats to show that they were fili-busters. Most of them wore red or blue flannel shirts and had heavy trousers jammed into huge leather boots. But in their belts the polished butts of revolvers gleamed like gouts of quicksilver, rifles were over their shoulders, and Bowie knives were like smears of sunlight at their sides. Davy Crockett, the valiant backwoodsman and politician, who had died in that little doomed city of heroes, the Alamo Garrison in Texas, would say that a mere squint at that knife would give you the colic, particularly before breakfast. The tale went that Colonel James Bowie, fight-ing a mob of greasers at Gonzales, shivered his sword on their thick skulls, but kept on at them with the stump and came away unharmed. So useful had he found the weapon

that he whittled it down and curved the blade, and thus
the Bowie was created. But the colonel's name is not per-
petuated merely because he discovered a new weapon, he
was one of Texas' bravest, and you can scarcely say higher
praise than that. He died, as did many of the noblest
Texans, in that terrible Alamo, with Dave Crockett and a
handful of other heroes. He was sick in bed when the
greasers smashed their way in after months of siege, but
he was not too sick to kill. Heaving himself up in bed,
he aimed clean and shot four of them, then he stuck a fifth
with his own beloved Bowie before a dozen of them got
him. Out in the courtyard, Crockett, with five others,
clubbed with his rifle until he smashed it; then he stood
back, sweating, panting like an animal, while they talked
warily of quarter. And while he stood alone, defiant and
fearless in the sunlight, Santa Ana slipped his sword from
its sheath. Crockett jumped for one last crack at the
rogue, but he had no chance of reaching him. They
hacked his body into little pieces. Over the vanished
Alamo, Texas raised a monument: *Thermopylæ had its
message of defeat; the Alamo had none.* The monument
is not needed, for the tale of that splendid siege will endure
for ever. Those men went boldly to their death, and they
knew that it was their death. A fortnight before the
garrison fell, when they realised that relief was impossible,
their tired eyes saw friends struggling among the horde of
Mexicans. For a moment it seemed that the incredible was
true, that help had come, that Houston perhaps had
managed to flog his weary horses to the rescue. But, no!
These were friends, but there were only thirty-two of them.
Thirty-two heroes had raced for the glory of being slain
beside their comrades! That was the spirit behind Walker,
the imperious spirit that would rather die a thousand times
standing next to friends than rot lonely into the grave.

While the filibusters marched merrily through the dust towards Granada, Granada itself was clanging bells and drinking and dancing and waving flags. For the people were celebrating their hero, General Martinez, who delayed with them a while after slaughtering the Leonese at Pueblo Nuevo. They wasted their powder in celebration, they banged off rockets and guns and cannons and bombs. They guzzled their kill-me-dead aguardiente, and they sang to guitars, drunken fingers lurching amongst the strings beneath trellised windows of purring senoritas. They danced in the plaza, they laughed and kissed and were gay, and they hoped to God that Walker would only arrive, that Corral wouldn't kill him before their brave, their noble, General Martinez, kicked him off the map of Nicaragua. When they couldn't drink any more, they slept, and the abrupt tropic night closed like an ebony shutter over the land, until all the lights snapped out in Granada; no lights to be seen except a faint rash of yellow on the water where, with muffled windows and furnaces well shielded, a small steamer roved along the shore like a languid bee flitting from petal to petal before it sank into the rich golden heart of the flower. Granada slept until the dawn tinctured the mountain-tops with silver haze and set the silly bells clang-clanking again, and woke up the city to drinking and singing and blowing off its guns and bombas. Then suddenly the bells clashed out of tune, jangled in abrupt terror when firing sounded near the walls, the vicious snarl of rifles and the zing of bullets spattering against adobe walls. Sentries staggered into the city, white-faced and trembling, followed by the picket with the van of the Americans hot behind them, firing from the hip and never wasting a shot. Walker and Valle were at the head, their horses rearing as shots came from the beasts on their backs and singed their manes. In the plaza, wiping the sweat of last night's booze from their faces, the garrison mustered and piled up furniture and rubbish for a brief stand. They fled at the first charge, and one hundred and ten filibusters had conquered Granada with only the loss of a drummer-boy.

Then began the usual diplomatic squabbles, interrupted by a *faux pas* by one of Walker's new recruits, Parker H. French, who tried and failed to take Fort San Carlos after pirating a lake steamer. Fort San Carlos retorted by murdering innocent westbound travellers; and some legitimists slaughtered half a dozen peaceful Californians awaiting their ship at Virgin Bay. Mr. Wheeler, U.S. minister, was slung into prison by Corral, so Walker immediately shot the legitimist secretary of state just to even matters a little. At any rate, it brought Corral quickly to heel and he howled for peace. Once again then did the bells of Granada peal out in festival, once again did the people drink and tinkle their guitars, when Corral rode towards the city. Walker and staff galloped out to meet him and, side by side, they rode through the streets to the Grand Cathedral. Little Walker seemed almost a boy on his great horse as the flower petals drifted down from the loving hands of senoritas, his cropped sandy hair looked practically white in the sun when he swept off his wide-brimmed hat. Beside him, the flamboyant Corral was like a macaw: beautiful to gaze upon, he pranced on his polished horse, smiling with wet mouth and long-lashed eyes, the dream of every girl that watched . . .

Peace was made, was carefully drawn up, and the liberal Rivas was elected president, Corral made minister of war, while Walker kept the power in his hands as generalissimo of the army of twelve hundred men scattered in isolated garrisons about the country, receiving a salary of five hundred dollars a month. The peace didn't last. Corral was caught breathing on the embers of rebellion and Walker immediately had him shot. Then he quietly gathered his Americans about him until, within four months, he had an army of twelve hundred. He showed himself a stern master, and being well-nigh owner of Nicaragua, thought himself the equal of any king or president in the world—ready to fight Great Britain and the U.S.A. lumped together, by God! But he did not realise that every step he took led towards disaster, he walked in dreams amongst the stars and did not see the careful plotting of Mr. Cornelius Vanderbilt in far New York. Vanderbilt had sworn to destroy Walker, and on such questions as that, he kept his word. It was all actually Walker's own fault. Vanderbilt controlled the Transit Company of steamers which carried passengers roughly twelve miles along the San Juan River and over Lake Nicaragua. This was an important trans-isthmian traffic, for passengers were transported by ocean from New York to Central America, then passed through river and lake to the Pacific to re-embark for San Francisco. When in 1853 Vanderbilt took a trip to Europe he left two men in charge, Morgan and Garrison, who immediately began systematically to rob him. When he returned and saw their tricks, he merely remarked, "I won't sue you, for the law's too slow. I'll ruin you." Walker was dragged into this business fracas because he considered Morgan and Garrison his friends, for they had helped him with men and reinforcements, and when they suggested that he take away the Vanderbilt charter to traffic and give them another in its place in return for the money they had lent him, he agreed. Already Rivas had started to delve into Vanderbilt's behaviour for, according to the charter, Vanderbilt had to pay the government ten per cent on

U

profits, but on the face of it, there were no profits. The explanation was simple: while the oceanic rates were very high, the trans-isthmian rates were astoundingly low, almost below cost. Rivas's investigators therefore decided in some involved fashion that the government was owed $35,000; they were offered $30,000, which they refused, so Vanderbilt passed the matter on to a special commission which was very expert in delaying decisions. Walker, with the incredible explanation that he did it to get rid of a nuisance, sent French—who had made the *faux pas* at Fort San Carlos—as Rivas's representative at Washington, and he was soon arrested for some act of criminal diplomacy. Walker called it a violation of diplomatic privilege and kicked out the U.S. minister to Nicaragua. That didn't help matters, and meanwhile Vanderbilt had discovered the treachery of Morgan and Garrison in their negotiations with Walker, and he demanded that Secretary of State Marcy take action against the filibusters, to intervene to protect the property of American citizens in Nicaragua, meaning, of course, his steamers, but he could not be obeyed, for Vanderbilt himself, in Walker's early days, had been one of the most flagrant violators of the U.S. neutrality laws. Vanderbilt acted on his own, he stopped his ships, and for six weeks Walker was unable to obtain reinforcements or supplies. Then he decided to seek allies in other Central American states and found a ready tool in Costa Rica, where there was a powerful legitimist government and a volatile gang of Nicaraguan refugees kicked out by Walker. Its president, Mora, issued a virulent proclamation, warning his countrymen that the hungry filibusters were ready to swoop upon them to steal their land and ravish their women. Great Britain next took a hand, for it had a good seventeen million dollars invested in Costa Rica bonds that were later defaulted to the last dirty dollar: it shipped arms to Mora, and Mora declared war on Nicaragua. With an army of nine thousand he marched on Guanacaste. Walker gathered his troops together in the plaza of Granada and talked bombastically at them, exciting their blood if not their intellects by shouting: " We have sent them the olive branch: they have sent us back the knife. Be it so. We will give them war to the knife, and the knife to the hilt! " Which they did—with a Bowie knife.

Three thousand Costa Ricans crossed the border in southern Rivas. Walker was in bed, red-hot with fever, but somehow he got on his feet, was lifted into the saddle, and with a horse between his legs, set out to deal with things himself, his subordinates being either fools or traitors. His grey eyes, always bright, were like diamonds with the fever behind them and with the rage that was like a demon in his heart. And his slim, blue-coated figure, red ribbon around the slouch hat, silenced the terrors in the democratic cabinet. He gathered his troops into Granada and stayed quietly, awaiting his chance. Occasionally he sent out small bands to see what the enemy was doing, and Lieutenant Green, with fifteen others, came across two hundred Costa Ricans at the mouth of the Serapiqui; he contented himself with killing a mere twenty-seven of them. Then at last, Walker came face to face with the invader. He met von Bulow squatting with three thousand regulars at Rivas. Von Bulow was astounded. He had been solemnly pondering when to begin wiping out these undisciplined Americans, when the Americans came for him. He made a gallant stand, but he was too bewildered to keep it up longer than four hours, after which he retreated, leaving two hundred dead and twice as many wounded. Although he had lost only fifty men, Walker had lost heavily. Almost all his officers were gone, and of his staff only himself and Captain Sutter remained.

Politics replaced the Bowie knife, and in the general elections Walker received over twice as many votes as all rivals, and on July 12 he was officially inaugurated President of Nicaragua. This was scarcely a free election, it was without question a faked one, but dictators when they know the people are against them beat the people either into submission or silence. Walker was determined to get power, and he got it. His ambition was to unite all the five Central American states into one union with himself as boss, and he added Slavery to his platform in the hope, not realised, of arousing sympathy in the south of the United States. But there were many battles yet to be fought, his dream remained only a dream, and he had innumerable foes to meet. Under General Belloso, the allies, Walker's enemies, had dug themselves into the town of Masaya, on top of a volcanic upheaval, a thousand feet above the world. So he marched out to crush them. His troops were now bright with uniforms and they carried their new flag which flaunted the filibusters' five-pointed star with the words *Five or None*—meaning that they intended to grab all the Central American states and not only Nicaragua. Ten o'clock that night they camped by Lake Masaya, halfway up the volcano, and the first twitch of daylight showed the allies but a few hundred yards away in front of the town, and Walker ordered a general advance under cover of his battery of howitzers. He scuttled the enemy from the main plaza, but there he had to pause, for it was impossible to continue without fearful losses, as he would have had to fight in the open while the allies held two further plazas and all houses between. He was not an impatient man, except when thwarted grossly, yet he showed impatience now. He grumbled and, although never a curser, being most God-fearing, he was heard occasionally to mutter behind his teeth when he thought that nobody listened. Then even worse came to chafe his patience. Zavala, the enemy general, marched on Granada. Only a hundred and fifty men—mainly invalids—were all that stood to hold him back. They locked themselves into the church, the armoury and the hospital, taking neutrals under their clipped wing, with Fry in command.

As Walker sapped quietly and muttered to himself on the slope of the volcano, the news reached him. He stood aghast. To-morrow he would be able to take Masaya, and behind him a couple of hundred non-combatants, a few sick and wounded men, held off an army. Their loss meant nothing to his ambition compared to the loss of Masaya, but there was the question of prestige, so essential to a dictator . . . Walker faltered only for a moment. He was an idealist, a dreamer. Already his men were gathering their baggage and mounting horses. He stood alone on his imminent victory, he gave only a last raging look at those adobe walls, at those mere dried bricks that had kept him at bay, then he leaped on his mustang and galloped over the lava desert, the Hell of Masaya, off to Granada. He had barely started when he met another courier who had slithered through Zavala's lines, and the news he brought swept the mad blood into Walker's head and prickled his skin. That handful of sick and wounded men and of men who had never touched a gun before, had fought for twenty-four hellish hours, answering all offers of quarter with—"Americans never surrender!" The patients crawled or hobbled from their beds and clung coughing and gasping to the rifles, trying to make their blurred eyes focus along the sights; the women and children snatched the hot guns from their hands and slipped in another charge when empty. Priests were there

—for Walker had an alliance with the church, the property class—and even the judges lost all civic thoughts and grabbed the bandolero. And actually, a newspaper editor threw away his pen, seized a sword and got a broken leg for his insanity. All night they stayed by windows, thinking that Walker had been slaughtered, they held their rifles and waited patiently for death. Then Walker came. His vanguard swerved in the Jalteva before the battery; and for a moment, the Americans fell back. But Walker's little figure on the big horse was suddenly at their head, his words rose above the thunder of cannon; he was pointing at the Lone Star flag above the church: a mere rag it was, ripped to a multitude of pennons with the shot, yet lazily it waved defiance above the sick and wounded. Walker shouted for volunteers and scarcely had he spoken before every man behind him answered and, Walker still at their head, they charged the battery, over-turned it and galloped to the plaza in front of the church, straight at Zavala and his army. And that army ran. The very sight of little Walker with his filibusters squeezed all courage from their hearts, and they ran, struggling amongst each other to escape those rifles that never missed, those Bowie knives which gave you the colic on sight, and they ran straight into a detachment sent round to meet them. . . .

Why continue? Why tell of the rise and fall of this lonely little ruffian, William Walker, a wasp in the gay lazy world of Central America? I have said enough to show the courage of the man, his indomitable purpose and insatiable ambition; I have said enough to reveal the unbreakable spirit of those Americans who considered all the Americas as their birthright, who tore Texas out of the hands of the greasers, then turned their hungry lizard eyes upon this land of Nicaragua. Why should we follow this lonely, almost pathetic figure to his inevitable doom? He could not win. How could he possibly win? Battles he always won; when it came to a straight fight, hand to hand, gun to gun, the Americans took it as fair game. But there is something bigger than fighting that overshadows all adventurers—fate. They are fate's darlings until eventually she tires, protests against their unceasing demands, and seeks another lover. And Walker's fate was growing weary of his importunity. He could not fight the world with a handful of filibusters; above all, he could not fight money. Mr. Vanderbilt had an eye cocked at him and Great Britain waited her chance.

He burnt Granada, and the men he left behind got drunk. The moment Walker's iron hand lifted they got drunk. They were nearly murdered as they staggered the streets, and but for Henningsen and a few sober officers they would all have been butchered. Then Mr. Vanderbilt sent a couple of scoundrels to start trouble and Great Britain despatched some gunboats. Then came an opportunity for Walker to make his peace with Vanderbilt, but in his violent arrogance he would not listen, and Giocouria, who had handled the negotiations, abandoned him in despair, telling him that he was deliberately shutting his eyes to the truth, that either he looked upon himself as divine and infallible, determined to pursue his course at all hazards, or he was being guided by rascals or madmen. Walker was so certain of himself and of his god that he would not listen, although Vanderbilt and Britain were cutting off his reinforcements. With his small band of filibusters he darted from battle to battle; but America and England edged closer, watched and waited. Walker gritted his teeth and made a last fling at destiny. He charged with four hundred men against two thousand five hundred Costa Ricans. Every inch had to be fought solidly, it was impossible yet insanely glorious.

And Walker pushed back the enemy to within three hundred yards of the main plaza of San Jorge. After that it was too hopeless even for him to continue, for the Costa Ricans had those damned adobe walls to lurk behind. Walker was almost crazy with rage. He saw his dream going; his country, the country he had seized sliding from his clutch. Tears blurred his sight as he gazed on the adobe walls. What can a man do with bricks except to put his back against them and die? He called for volunteers to storm the plaza, he asked for only forty. Fifteen came to him, and he stared at them with feverish eyes, his hand shaking as he clenched his fingers on the gun. Then he cheered them, and charged. Fifteen men against an army!... Lunacy—of course it was, but it was the lunacy of despair. His horse was shot beneath him, but he grabbed another and spurred forward. Again he fell, but even as he fell he was clambering on a third horse, just in time to get a ball straight on the Adam's apple. He clutched his throat and swayed in the saddle, stuttering with rage—but he kept on. He kept on furiously, magnificently, and the greasers fled before this sinewy little demon whom even a ball on the throat couldn't kill. His men were as mad as he, firing, clubbing, stabbing; they were bloody almost from head to feet. But even in his crazy suicidal despair Walker saw the greasers thick before him and realised that he could not destroy them all. They were so many, and he had but fifteen. With a gulp of sudden realisation, of sanity, he knew the hopelessness of his task, and he fell back. The tired troop fell back, staggered back to Rivas. Head bowed, Walker led his men over the dusty earth, Henningsen covering the rear with his guns; back, back to Rivas, over the earth that should have been his by right of conquest. Then as he and his staff rode slowly abreast of a planter's house at Cuatros

Esquinas, musketry blazed not forty yards away. The column of filibusters paused, startled; the ranks broke, tired horses and exhausted men springing away with the energy of sudden terror. But Walker did not flinch. His calm almost inhuman courage never deserted him. He was pleased perhaps in finding danger to rouse him from dark dreams. Grimly he sat his horse and drew his revolver; he emptied all six chambers into the house, then spurred on contemptuously, as stiff in his saddle as if on parade. Major Dolan, a long-haired Californian, rode directly behind him, imitating every gesture. He emptied his gun to the last cartridge, flung it at the house when empty, and cursed as he slid from the saddle, riddled with shot. His trousers caught in the trappings and his horse dragged him out, still cursing, holed with bullets, yet living to fight again.

It still kept on, the same terrible round of fanatical courage thrown into the face of death. Then the U.S.A. put an end to it, temporarily. They stepped in just as Walker seemed on the point of success, when the enemy was starved for powder and food, threatened with cholera, and with the rainy season just ahead. Commander Davis, of the U.S. Navy, demanded Walker's surrender to the United States. Walker almost burst a blood-vessel when he heard. What right had a mere subordinate naval officer to demand the surrender of the president of a friendly government! But what Walker did not know was that Davis was under Marcy's thumb, and that Marcy was under Mr. Vanderbilt's thumb. Walker marched out of Rivas under the impertinent protection of Davis. His sword was still at his side, the pistol shone in his belt, and his grey eyes were quietly introspective in the shade of his wide-brimmed hat. He turned in his saddle for a last look at Rivas, then swung forward and would not turn again. Big Henningsen towered behind him, and then followed the others, the true filibusters leaving their adopted country, their hard-fought-for, their detested country that held the bones of many a well-loved comrade; they trooped out of Rivas, back to the U.S.A. And in the U.S.A., Walker was fêted. All New York fought to see the hero. And still with the cold half-smile on his lips, the same blank stare in his grey eyes, he rode through the wide streets, ambition yet alive within him. Nothing could kill that ambition. He was determined to go back.

Again and again he tried to go back. His ships were stopped and the men disembarked. Once he did make a start, only to be dragged off to the U.S.A. again by an American frigate. Two years of frenzied effort passed before he did succeed. Then again the little hero returned to his destiny, once more he came to Nicaragua, while the two biggest navies in the world longed to blow him sky-high. He was as crazy as ever with dreams, he was going to his death—but what did that matter? He was going to his country, for one last fling at Alvarez, his enemy. He landed at Ruatan and issued a proclamation—without which nothing can ever get done in Central or South America—and half an hour's hard work made him master of Trujillo, himself getting a slight wound on the face. Then came the British man-of-war, *Icarus*, Captain Salmon, cruising into the harbour, and Walker was told truculently that England held a mortgage on the port's revenue, and that Salmon was there to protect those revenues by taking command of the town. Walker retorted that he had declared it a free port, and that they could get to hell out of it. So Salmon threatened to open fire if he didn't surrender. And Walker hid his face in his hands. Alvarez was hurrying over, he knew, with seven hundred men to attack him and the British were training their guns on him from the sea. There was only one thing for Walker to do: he retreated with seventy men, abandoning all accoutrements and carrying but two barrels of flour for them all and thirty pounds of ammunition each. In a mighty rage, Salmon took Alvarez and a horde of greasers with him and steamed after Walker.

He found him at the small Indian village of Lemas, fever-stricken and half-starved. The British boats came slowly up the river. Walker was tired. He sat and watched the enemy kick his few possessions over the ground and sneeringly ask him to surrender. The dream was gone. He was painfully tired, too tired even to move. He looked back upon the glorious past and clenched his little fists and shut his pale eyes at the memories. Then he stood up, looked these grinning bluejackets in the face, and asked to whom did he surrender—to British or to Hondurenos. To the British, most decidedly, said Salmon, most decidedly indeed. He even repeated it just before he handed Walker over to the Hondurenos. With martial generosity he offered to plead for him if, as an American citizen, Walker would ask his help. But the spirit was not dead. Those grey eyes hardened to stare this interfering lying British naval officer out of countenance. America! the country that had destroyed him! Never! Better to die a Nicaraguan than to sneak off as a living American.

He was court-martialled and condemned to be shot on September 11, 1860, and he revealed nothing of his thoughts, no glimpse of fear or despair, when the sentence was read to him. Then they pushed him back into his cell, into the very room that had once been his commissariat. And he sat there, never saying a word except to the priests, listening inside himself to memories of past glory, hearing again the crack of rifles, the shouts and the laughter of filibuster comrades; he felt the stir of all triumphs, old dreams . . . all gone.

At eight o'clock in the morning of the 12th., he stepped into the street amidst a detachment of soldiers and with two priests at his side. Excitedly, gaily, the happy people cheered to see that terrible little Walker die at last; they hung out flags to fête him to death, they drank to his death, they ran beside him through the crowded streets of Trujillo; but he made no answer to their jeers and insults. Still with the calm smile on his lips, with the pinched look about the grey eyes, the boyish Walker went to his death. About a quarter of a mile beyond the town, at the ruins of an old garrison, the soldiers halted. In the angle of a broken wall they placed their enemy, themselves lining up on three sides of a square, Walker and his wall making a fourth side. Then they fired at him, first one squad, followed by the next, but greaser marksmanship never could kill little Walker. He fell, riddled, yet living. So a greaser officer went over, put a pistol to the filibuster's ear and shot his brains out.

And that was how he died, how the brave dream went.

XI
Ruffians' Hall Stands Open

THERE was, in truth, nothing noble in Walker's dream. We can admire his courage while deploring his ambitions, for he is the dictator who would rule not for the good of the people but for the satisfaction of his own insane arrogance. He was a splendid fighter but a bad soldier, an heroic leader but a poor general, a childlike politician who underestimated his adversaries, his vanity being so great that he misjudged the abilities of others, he scorned to confide in his friends, he refused advice, and if it were given him would stubbornly do the opposite. He could not realise the mighty power of Vanderbilt, and continually he insulted Great Britain and the U.S.A. When Sir Robert McClure, of H.M.S. *Esk*, noticed the filibuster flag on Walker's navy—one schooner—he sent a boat to inquire what it meant because he couldn't find it in any of his books. Her commander, Fayssoux, courteously replied that it was the ensign of the New Republic of Nicaragua and that this ship was the Nicaraguan schooner-of-war, the *Granada*. Sir Robert, outraged in all his British proprieties, ordered the insolent Fayssoux to come on board the *Esk* at once and bring his demmed commission with him. Fayssoux told him to go to the devil, and when Sir Robert threatened a broadside, he beat to quarters all his twenty men, loaded his two six-pound carronades, and patiently waited to be blown to splinters. But there was a U.S. man-of-war cruising nearby, and Sir Robert probably suffered from the stupid delusion that she might join in if she saw her countrymen massacred, for he even went to the extent of being polite to Fayssoux and asking him over for a drink. Later, when Sir Robert sailed up to Rivas to demand an explanation from Walker about his officer's insolence to the British Flag, he found that small, angry man thin and weary, yet with grey eyes that seemed to bite at him with rage. " I presume, sir," said Walker sternly, " that you have come to apologise for the outrage offered to my flag and to the commander of the Nicaraguan schooner-of-war, *Granada*? " Sir Robert was so astounded that he could only gape. "If they had had another schooner," he was heard to mutter afterwards, "I believe they'd have declared war on Great Britain!" And he was probably right, for once.

Walker's arrogance was lunatic, but that was only because he had no guns or army to support his threats, threats no different from those which Hitler and Mussolini use to-day in their systematic abuse of democratic nations. He was such a secretive man that it is difficult to estimate Walker's ambitions beyond his intention to grab all five Central American states, not to bring them into the U.S.A., but to create a second U.S.A. under his own personal domination. The desires of the people did not matter, his own desires were paramount. One of the few glimpses we get inside his mind is given by Doubleday who was so shocked by the truth that he insisted upon immediately resigning his commission. He writes: "Conquest was the end, and by the simple method which is epitomised in the saying, 'Nothing succeeds like success.' This was to be the talisman to draw to his standard not only the bold spirits ever ready to follow without asking questions, but also the more timid who courted safety by an adhesion to power in any shape. The impediments of constitutional law were, of course, considered as mere cobwebs to be brushed aside by the power which, like Louis the Fourteenth, could declare, ' I am the State.' Such was the policy outlined by this bold and capable, but not sagacious man; not sagacious, inasmuch, as he took no account of a factor in modern politics all powerful now, however insignificant it may have been anterior to the first French revolution—that of popular ideas. As his scheme included the re-establishment of slavery in a population the majority of which were of mixed African blood, and an affiliation with the Church in a time when freedom of thought had made progress, it came at too late a date with the world's history. I listened to this conspiracy against the popular liberty, for which I had entertained a romantic attachment, and my heart was sad. He was ambitious of power while I was merely philosophic."

Unfortunately, the rise of Mussolini and Hitler has proved that Walker was more sagacious than Doubleday realised, but Walker's material was poor. He had a courageous and tiny army of adventurers with no interest in the country for which they fought, and the Central American is too good-humoured a fellow to want to be bullied into hard work for ambitious foreigners. Walker had no real backing. If he had come to an agreement with Vanderbilt, the exploit would have had a different end, we cannot doubt that he would have succeeded.

He was a cold-blooded devil, this Walker, with apparently no weakness towards women or drink, for the greatest ruffians are commonly the most ascetic of men. That is half their power, it gives them a feeling of superiority. Others must rely on alcohol to bring them courage or must seek the consolation of a woman's love, but the ruffian despises all who are not ruthless and lonely. In his own eyes he remains the one perfect creature, the one infallible god who must be worshipped.

And realising his own godhead, he is naturally fearless. This is not to say that the ruffian is necessarily anti-social. A wise government can control this arrogance, can direct it towards worthy ideals. Many a soldier worshipped by the people would most likely have been hanged had not a war broken out. You will find quite a few ruffians in every army. Take Craufurd, for example, one of Britain's heroes. I consider Craufurd, in his way, almost as great a ruffian as Sir Henry Morgan. During the magnificent Peninsula retreat, he halted the troops when the French were but a few miles behind, merely that he might hang some stragglers. Rifleman Harris in his memoirs shows the giant figure of Craufurd ever present, stern and angry, unconquerable with arrogance. " The Rifles liked him," writes Harris, " but they also feared him, for he could be terrible when insubordination showed itself in the ranks. ' You think, because you are Riflemen, you may do whatever you think proper,' said he one day to the miserable and savage-looking crew around him in the retreat to Corunna; ' but I'll teach you the difference before I have done with you.' " It was this very ruffianism, his unflinching arrogance, that kept the men on their feet. Remember, he commanded the most dangerous post—the Rifles were the men who kept the French back, they were the rearguard. " An iron man," Harris calls him: " nothing daunted him—nothing turned him from his purpose. . . . If he stopped and halted his horse, to deliver one of his stern reprimands, you would see half a dozen lean, unshaven, shoeless, and savage Riflemen, standing for the moment leaning upon their weapons, and scowling up in his face as he scolded; and when he dashed the spurs into his reeking horse, they would throw up their rifles upon their shoulders and hobble after him." On the second occasion when he commanded the Light Brigade, he addressed them briefly: "When I commanded you before," he said, "I know full well that you disliked me, for you thought me severe. This time I am glad there is a change in yourselves." And once, so the story goes, when a commissary complained to Wellington that "General Craufurd, my lord, says that if the provisions for his division are not ready in time, he will hang me. What do you advise me to do?" The Duke calmly, and quite truthfully replied, "I strongly advise you to obtain them; General Craufurd, I observe, keeps his word."

No, you cannot tell a ruffian by the cut or colour of his coat. You can tell him by only one thing, by the contemptuous arrogance which, no matter how he attempts to conceal it, will be revealed in some phrase or gesture. He may appear to be a mild and inoffensive little man leaning on the bar shiftily eyeing the barmaid's rump, but you have only to touch some little weakness to see the eyes brighten, to hear the tankard pounded on the counter, and the voice rise in defiance. The easiest method of getting at this arrogance is in some way to belittle the man—a jest is most effective, for few ruffians possess a sense of humour—and his thin skin will react at once. He will justify himself, and call on every customer in the bar to hear his justification: his arguments won't be logical, but you can be sure that they'll be noisy and probably vituperative. This trick of the ruffian, one of the most important facets in his character, of having to justify every dirty deed must not be passed over too quickly. It must be underlined, because it is important in our estimate of his mentality. Captain Bellamy, the pirate, once shouted at a prisoner: "Damn ye, you are a sneaking puppy, and so are all those who will submit to be governed by Laws which rich men have made for

X

their own security, for the cowardly whelps have not the courage otherwise to defend what they get by their knavery. But damn ye altogether. Damn them for a pack of crazy rascals, and you, who serve them, for a parcel of hen-hearted numskulls. They villify us, the scoundrels do, when there is only this difference, they rob the poor man under cover of Law, and we plunder the rich under the protection of our own courage." An even better illustration of this colossal good conscience and the need to prove the ruffian's honourable intentions, is given in the memoirs of the Notorious Stephen Burroughs of New Hampshire. His friend—whom he discreetly calls Lysander—cajoled him into the art of coining with this superb and most convincing argument. " Money of itself," says he, " is of no consequence, only as we, by mutual agreement, annex to it a nominal value, as the representation of property." He continues in this strain, with the same senatorial sentences, proving beyond all possible doubt that paper money is only paper and not money, and concludes with this unanswerable argument: " That an undue scarcity of cash now prevails, is a truth too obvious for me to attempt to prove. Your own observation will convince you of it. Hence, whoever contributes, really, to increase the quantity of cash, does not only himself, but likewise the community, an essential benefit." He convinces Burroughs, at any rate, and being a thoroughly good ruffian, weeps on his shoulder, insisting that he only counterfeits for the sake of his wife and children, and never for himself. Burroughs, carried away by this altruistic philosophy, passes some coins, is instantly arrested and shoved into jail by an ungrateful community. The description of his prison experiences is truly heart-rending: he reveals to us the tragic portrait of a persecuted honest man. He tries to murder the jailers, he tries to burn down the jail: all with the utmost smarmiest good conscience.

Dangerous men indeed, untamed and ravenous, they are always waiting to pounce upon you with a hard-luck story or a knuckle-duster. There seems no protection for us ordinary cowardly men. All we can do is to run as fast as possible when we meet a man who looks us steadily in the eye and talks about his good conscience. If we can't run, we must keep calm, we must not lose our nerve. Stare him back in the eye, and see who flinches first. Stay calm. He can do nothing then. Wyatt Earp knew that. He was a U.S. marshal in the bad old days of the two-gun cowpunchers. When he went to make his first arrest, he walked calmly into the street, hands loose at his sides. He knew that if he made one move towards his gun he was a dead man. He walked steadily towards the group of angry ruffians, and the man he wanted, Ben Thompson, held a shotgun against his stomach. Wyatt kept his eyes fixed on Thompson's wrist, ready to shoot the moment he saw the muscles move; the muscles did not move. Before that quiet, determined figure, never faltering in its pace, the gunman lost his nerve. " What do you want, Wyatt? " he asked. " I want you," said Wyatt, never pausing in his step. Once Thompson had started parleying, Wyatt knew that he had won the battle. He had. The man came quietly to the calaboose. The courage of Wyatt Earp was such that one can almost venerate the man. He feared nobody. He never got excited even in the most dangerous corners. Once, riding a little ahead of five companions, he blundered into an ambush. Nine men suddenly rose before him from behind a bank. Each man had a rifle at his shoulder, and each rifle opened fire. Even in that moment of surprise, Wyatt noticed that his old enemy,

Curly Bill, was one of the nine and found himself wondering: "Well, there's Curly Bill. I'm a little surprised to run on to him out here on the desert. He looks natural. Hasn't changed a bit since that night in Tombstone when Marshal White was killed. I wonder what old Curly's been doing all this while. . . ." Then realising that his horse might jump and disturb his aim, he clambered leisurely out of the saddle, slipping one arm through a bridle rein. In his own words: " As I stood there by my horse's head, cocking my gun, I looked the nine men over. They struck me as pretty busy fellows, all with their heads down on their rifles, and all firing away. I noted with surprise that every rifle seemed aimed at me. I rather resented that. I wanted to kill Curly Bill. . . . I seemed suddenly to be praying, and my prayer was that I shouldn't be killed before I had killed Curly Bill. So I raised my shotgun to my shoulder and drew a careful bead on Curly Bill. As I sighted at Curly Bill, he was sighting at me. I could see the deep wrinkles about one of his eyes that was squinted shut. His other eye, held down close to his gun, was wide open. I noticed with curious interest that this one eye, blazing murder at me over his rifle barrel, was blacker than I remembered his eyes to have been when I saw him last. Then I pulled both triggers. Curly Bill threw up his hands. His rifle flew high in the air. He gave a yell that could have been heard a mile as he went down. I saw him no more. I knew he was lying dead behind the bank. Each one of my shotgun shells was loaded with nine buckshot. Both charges struck him full in the breast. Three seconds possibly had elapsed from the moment the outlaws rose from behind the bank till Curly Bill was killed. . . . Bullets were now singing songs all around me, soprano bullets, tenor bullets, bass bullets, a regular Hallelujah chorus of bullets. My shotgun was empty. I reached across my saddle to get my rifle, hanging on the other side of my horse. But my horse, trembling and wet with the sweat of terror, began to rear and plunge, and I was unable to draw the gun from its long scabbard. I jerked out one of my six-shooters and, shielding myself as well as I could behind my horse, fired under the animal's neck. . . . But my comrades' guns were not roaring in my ears, and I saw none of the outlaws fall except Curly Bill. This struck me as strange. . . . Sheltered behind my horse, I shot a quick glance to my rear. Not one of my bold companions was in sight. Every mother's son, including my old pal Doc Holliday, one of the bravest men I ever knew, had turned tail at the first volley. . . . No wonder the bullets were shouting a Hallelujah chorus around me. The whole outlaw bunch was shooting at me. There was nobody else to shoot at." Wyatt calmly got back on his horse, the eight men still firing at him, and galloped after his friends. "One grand little fight you made, Wyatt," said Doc Holliday when they met; "let's go back and finish the job. Come on." But Wyatt had had enough. His friends' generosity in wanting to fight for him brought tears to his eyes. "You fellows go back in," he said, "I've had a bellyful." He was unhurt, miraculously. "My hat," he writes, "had five bullet holes in it, two in the crown, and three in the brim. Bullets had ripped ragged rents up and down the legs of my pants. The bottom of my coat on both sides, where it had been held out by the holsters and the handles of my six-shooters, had been torn into strings and shreds. But, as by a miracle, I had not received a scratch."

There, now, is a lesson on how to act when faced by a ruffian—by nine ruffians—and written by a ruffian.

Study it carefully. Wyatt never lost his nerve. While the outlaws were excitedly blazing away with erratic aim through over-eagerness, he thought coldly and logically and concentrated on one man, on Curly Billy whom he believed had helped murder his brother Morgan and wound his brother Virgil. Wyatt got him. He kept his head and came off unhurt with his enemy slain. Nor do we see any false heroics. No charging shouting back beside his comrades. He had had a bellyful, and anyhow, revenge was purposeless, Curly Billy being dead. It is useless to argue with the ruffian, as Wyatt knew when he strode out to arrest Ben Thompson, the moment Ben began to talk to him the man was weakened, it was a proof of his uncertainty. Distrustful though he is of words, they yet can sometimes sway the ruffian, not intellectually but emotionally, for he is himself the victim of his own egoism, and is tortured when he considers the opinions of others. He may despise these others, yet he is always desperately eager to earn, if not their love, at least their respect or fear. And that is one of the few ways by which one can sometimes deflect him from his brutal path. Take this from the delightful memoirs of William Hickey. During 1771, he was in the Piazza Coffee House when a roaring ruffian called Hamilton arrived. Hamilton was extremely drunk, and when he learned that there was a stranger waiting alone upstairs, determined to see what the man wanted. Hickey, knowing the fellow's murderous activities, thought best to follow, and " upon entering the room," he tells us, " I saw Hamilton standing in a boxing attitude, whilst a genteel-looking young man of slight form, and apparently of bad health, was striking at him without effect, as he met every intended blow before it could reach him with a severe stroke from himself under the assailant's arm.

I directly stepped between them, saying to Hamilton: 'Is this a proof of your valour? Such a Herculean fellow as you to attack such a man as this! For shame, for shame, Hamilton, you deserve to be scouted from the society of gentlemen.' Instead of any expression of anger at this address, he immediately answered: 'By God, it is very true, Hickey! I am ashamed of myself,' and, turning to the gentleman, he continued, 'and, sir, I beg you ten thousand pardons. I have behaved scandalously, and will make every concession you demand. Can you forgive me? Again I beg your pardon.' In the moment of this conciliatory speech in came Frederick, who instantly exclaimed, 'What's this I hear? Zounds! Hamilton, do you beg any man's pardon!' Hamilton, in a moment, replied: 'No, by God, not to any one breathing,' and turning to the stranger, he added, 'I have beat you, and I'm damned glad of it. You are a damned scoundrel. However, if you wish for it I'll give you satisfaction whenever you please. Hickey knows me; everybody knows Hamilton, you scoundrel.'"

That is quite an illuminating glimpse of the simple ruffian's mental reflexes, dominated by his mighty arrogance, the determination to figure always in the bravest light. There is no other way of hurting or convincing the man, save through his vanity, a vanity easily pricked and very swift to seek revenge. Even murder is to him justification for any betrayal of this vanity

Listen to the bullying Alonso de Contreras, knight of that glorious military Order of St. John: "We remained married with great content for more than a year and a half, in love and amity together; and sure it is that so great was the respect I had for her at that time, on our walks aboard, I would not wear my hat in her presence, so greatly did I esteem her. To make a long story short,

I had a friend, to whom I would have trusted my very
soul. He came in and out of my house as if it had been
myself. But so base was he, that despite the great friendship which there was between us two, he began to cast
his eyes upon my wife whom I so greatly loved. . . . A
page of mine said to me: ' Sir, do people in Spain kiss
the wives of their relations? ' ' Why do you ask? ' said
I. And he answered: ' Because So-and-so kisses Madam,
and she has shown him her garters.' Said I: ' It is the
custom in Spain, for if not, So-and-so would not have
done it ' (for I do not wish to mention either him or
her by name), ' but do not speak about it to any other
person. If you see him do it again, tell me, so that I
may speak to them about it.' The boy spoke to me
about it once again. And in short, though I could not
sleep for it, I managed by an effort to appear uncon-
cerned; until, as fate would have it, I found them one
morning in each other's arms—and they died. May God
keep them in heaven if in that hour they repented.
There were many other details, but I am loath to write
about it." That is a really delightful picture of egotism.
(The translation, by the by, is Catherine Alison Phillips'.)
He will even take off his hat in her presence, having
obviously married her for her money—although he boasts
that he didn't touch a penny after the murder. He probably didn't dare to—and upon killing her, concludes with
a fervent prayer hoping that God will forgive them,
although he rather doubts it. God, as we have seen, is
extremely popular with the ruffian, nor is it any explanation to dismiss this religious chatter with the bland charge
of hypocrisy, for hypocrisy, after all, means that the man
is consciously lying, deliberately trying to deceive people,
and this is not true of the average ruffian. He is
definitely schizophrenic, he has two distinct personalities,

as with Jekyll and Hyde, and each personality when it comes to the front dominates his thoughts and his acts. They do not conflict because they never mingle. Some of the most cold-blooded murderers in history have been also the most devout of Christians.

William Palmer, of Rugeley, doctor, racing-man, and poisoner, could never look you in the eye, which is unusual with ruffians, yet he was popular and even loved by some. His mother was fanatically religious, and William, from extreme childhood, was soaked in prayers, hymns, and Bible readings, yet after he had married Annie Brooke and discovered that her fortune was to be doled out only in small quarterly chunks, he calmly insured her life and murdered her. Having succeeded with this speculation and having spent all the profits on the racecourse, Palmer next decided that his drunken brother George was useless to society and would be best out of the way; but this time he miscalculated: the investment did not come off, for the insurance companies, suspicious of two sudden deaths in the Palmer menage, investigated and refused to pay. The astounding part is that they did not carry their investigations further and have Palmer arrested, for apart from brother and wife, there is a suggestion of at least two previous killings. He decided now to broaden his activities, and murdered a wealthy young racing-man called John Parsons Cook. To read the evidence in court of this murder truly makes one shudder; the description of the wretched man's agonies under the serene ministrations of his murderer, the body so twisted by quantities of strychnine that the heels met the head, makes one put the book down with a sickish feeling. Yet strangely, at the post-mortem, no evidence of strychnine was discovered in the corpse, and Palmer might have got clean away but for his own stupidity in attempting to bribe the messenger who was carrying the jar containing the stomach to smash it before it reached the analysts. This remorseless poisoner has been damned as a hypocrite because of his continual church-going; immediately after his wife's death he partook of holy communion with every evidence of pious zeal, and his mother was later to declare to the inevitable mob that hung around her house to gaze upon the parent of the notorious murderer: "Yes, I am Dr. Palmer's mother. I had seven children, and my saintly Bill was the best of the lot, but they hanged him."

To say that Palmer was a hypocrite is to beg the question. He was unquestionably sincere in his three different personalities, as a Christian, as a jovial companion on the racecourse, and as a methodical poisoner. He needed money with which to bet, and he had no method of obtaining that money except by murder, therefore to him murder was perfectly justified. It was the fault of society that William Palmer couldn't have all the gold he needed, therefore he obtained it from society, which had given him a good training for the job, by the only way he knew, poison, and in his vanity he would feel quite assured that God would understand. The Middle Ages give us glimpses of women seeking priests as lovers, not only because for his own sake the priest would not boast of the conquest, but because he could deliver absolution immediately after sinning. Modern times offer us a splendid example of this schizophrenia, of double personality so powerful that it convinced not only the man himself but his victim. This is Father Hans Schmidt of St. Boniface Church, New York, who arrived in the States during 1910 to help administer religion to a large German community. He was most deeply devout, an untiring worker, loved by his flock and

respected by his colleagues, until he noticed young Anna
Aumuller, a servant in the clergy house, and seduced
her.

The affair tortured Schmidt, not because of his religious
scruples, not because he, as a priest, was sleeping with
the girl, but because he, as an unmarried man, was committing the sin of fornication with an unmarried woman.
Here we see the mental split very clearly. As priest and
as lover Schmidt was two entirely different people, and
he decided to make this break even clearer by marrying
Anna. He married her to himself. Father Schmidt
being the servant of God was above blame, but Hans
Schmidt, the carnal man, was living in sin, therefore
the Father would absolve the man of his wickedness by
marrying him to Anna. Thus united, they rented a flat,
and the morning after the bridal night, Father Schmidt
was solemnly celebrating Mass while Mrs. Anna Schmidt
was cleaning the nearby clergy house. Being a good
Catholic, Hans Schmidt did not hold with birth control,
so that when the inevitable happened, he became desperate. An abortion too was against his creed, and he
grew afraid that when Anna would be forced to resign
from her work the truth would be exposed. He had but
one solution: he cut Anna's throat. Then remained that
nightmare of the murderer, a corpse with apparently
inexhaustible supplies of blood, so Father Schmidt, to
conceal the sin of Hans Schmidt, dismembered the remains, running off to attend Mass in the middle of his
task, then returning to hack the body into as many small
pieces as possible. Three times a day for three consecutive
days he entered and left the flat with his parcels which he
threw into the river, nor did this task interfere with his
religious duties, he remained the good and conscientious
father, the beloved of his congregation. He had,

however, blundered badly, for he had forgotten to weight the parcels, and soon numerous scraps of female flesh were bobbing up in the river, until the police began to investigate. Schmidt was arrested in December 1913, and his one explanation was that "the Lord commanded me to do it." Naturally there was a mighty uproar, and the New York Roman Catholics agitated furiously for his release on the plea that so saintly a man could not have committed so ghastly a crime unless he were insane; they might have got him off, too, had he not dismembered the body. For some reason this natural attempt of a murderer to get rid of the remains always horrifies people to an incredible extent. The agitation, however, kept Schmidt from death until February 1916, when he was electrocuted in Sing Sing. He probably died convinced of his own innocence and the injustice of the sentence, for as he once remarked, "I loved Anna, but I loved my Church better, and she had to die." A simple and straightforward statement of fact, there was to Father Schmidt, as a sincere Christian, no other solution to his problem.

It is when we come to cases like Joseph Smith, the founder of Mormonism, that we find it difficult to judge the man's sincerity. But after all, his sincerity does not matter, and it would seem after examining the evidence that, while faking the golden plates of the Book of Mormon, he was at the same time convinced of their authenticity. Having written them himself they must have been genuine, they were his own creation and therefore infallible. From the age of fifteen he saw visions and it was on September 22, 1827—he was born in 1805—that the angel of God appeared at Cumorah Hill and revealed to him these golden plates written in peculiar hieroglyphic symbols. Together with the plates,

Smith was given a pair of spectacles called the Urim and Thummim, and through these spectacles he was able to interpret the heavenly characters. A friend, Martin Harris, helped with the work, sitting behind a curtain and taking down Smith's dictation. It appears that Harris's wife had little faith in this divine revelation, for she managed to get hold of the first 116 pages of the manuscript, and evidently burned the lot, to the despair of Harris and the horror of Smith, who was unable to remember all he had dictated; God, however, came to his rescue, by reassuring Smith not to bother about the lost portion, but to carry on from page 117. Thus was written this great work of faith, and the plates were returned to the angel, never to be seen again. Smith was a man of enormous energy, finely built, tall and handsome, and his strong personality alone was sufficient to convince the doubtful. Soon he had a large following of worshippers, but he had a weakness in him which no true ruffian should possess. He once stated: " Whenever I see a pretty woman I have to pray for grace," and it was because of this sensuality that the principle of polgamy was added to the church's rules. Smith's wife, Emma, according to her photograph, was a pugnaciously unattractive creature, sufficient excuse for any man to seek consolation elsewhere. Emma was very much against this new pronouncement from God, particularly when Joseph in his enthusiasm wedded twelve new ladies; Emma threw them out, then reluctantly she agreed to have two rivals, on condition that she chose them herself. Luckily, she picked on two whom Joseph had already secretly married, two sisters aged eighteen and nineteen, but after a few months even they became too much for Emma, and out they went. Meanwhile Joseph was frenziedly trying to inspire the same zeal in his followers, they had to agree to taking further wives if only to convince Emma, and strong men wept at the thought, although later, on the whole, they took eagerly to the creed. Smith, inspired by this demon lust, could not remain satisfied even with his wives, and he attempted on one occasion to seduce a married woman while her husband was recruiting in England. On his return, the husband was unable to appreciate the holy honour of such cuckoldry, for Brigham Young notes in his journal on August 8, 1842, that with others he " spent several days labouring with Elder Orson Pratt, whose mind became so darkened by the influence and statements of his wife, that he came out in rebellion against Joseph, refusing to believe his testimony or obey his counsel. He said he would believe his wife in preference to the Prophet. Joseph told him if he did believe his wife and followed her suggestions, he would go to hell," which evidently convinced the unfortunate Pratt. It is probable that Mormonism, like so many other of the strange sects of the period, would have vanished had not Smith been martyred when a mob shot him in 1844. He was not a great man, he was clever and convincing in talk, but he lacked the genius of Brigham Young who led that superb exodus across the desert to the Salt Lakes. Young was the St. Paul of Mormonism, a superlative ruffian, a magnificent organiser.

Religion throws up quite a few of these confidence trickster ruffians whose first victims are themselves. There was James Jesse Strang, a schismatic Mormon, who inaugurated a colony on Beaver Island in Lake Michigan with sixty-two followers, only seventeen of whom were men. Here he was crowned King Strang on July 8, 1850, and issued dictatorial edicts against alcohol, tobacco, tea, and gambling. His end was brought about by the royal command that all women must wear bloomers. This impropriety so shocked his disciples that two of them, Thomas Bedford and Alexander Wentworth, rather than permit their wives to wear such sinful abominations, rose in rebellion and were publicly flogged. Later they shot their king in the back and beat his skull and face to pulp with their guns. To-day we have examples of this type on every hand, but the U.S.A. with its vast conglomerate population naturally gives us the best examples, for here have settled many of the most illiterate Europeans beside semi-savage negroes. It is a strange country, half-barbaric and half ultra-civilised, for it can give us a man who is probably the greatest statesman alive, Franklin Roosevelt, and also the queer tubby little negro, Father Divine, step-dancing with his angels on the other side of the Hudson. But lest England feel superior with its more pure-blooded population, it must not forget its charlatans of the past—and to-day, in comparative secrecy, London has many magical churches—it must not forget Johanna Southcott with her dropsical belly that was to bring forth the Prince of Peace, or Henry James Prince with his Abode of Love at Spaxton near Bridgwater. He called his followers the Agapemonites, and everything was blissful until one of the chaste sisters was tactless enough to produce a child in Eden. Prince swore he would never die, yet all the same his body decided differently: it started on the road of corruption on March 8, 1899.

But these petty hangers-on of Ruffians' Hall are scarcely worth our consideration. All the same there have been men of deep Christianity, men living pure and unselfish lives, who have created genuinely great churches, and who would yet be given their entrance-tickets into the Hall. I am myself an atheist, but if I should ever consider believing in Christ, there is only one church I should choose, only one church that to my mind is based on the New Testament—the Quakers. Yet my respect for this religion does not restrain me from accepting George Fox as a ruffian, as a noble ruffian, if you wish, but as a ruffian nevertheless, because it was his arrogance, his belief in his indestructible godhead, that carried him through all perils and sufferings. Strangely enough, unlike Bunyan and most other profoundly religious leaders, he never suffered from any doubts, from any torment at the thought of original sin, he was quite certain of his divine mission. A huge powerful man, he tells us that when he was in Falmouth gaol, a bully was sent into his room and, says Fox, " he walks up and down the room, and I bid him fear the Lord, and he comes upon me and struck me with both his hands and clapped his leg behind me and would fain have thrown me down, but he could not; but I stood stiff and still and let him strike." His courage was immense because he knew, being the symbol of God, that he had naught to fear. At Warwick in 1665 " the town," he writes, " rose up against us in the open street and one laid hold upon my horse's bridle; my horse being a strong horse turned his head and turned the man under his feet and so he hung upon the bridle and so there came another man or two to throw stones at my horse's bridle, and so as we rode through the streets people fell down upon us and much abused us, and so when we were ridden quite through the market, I was moved by the Lord to go back again into the street to offer up my life among them . . . and so I passed up the street, and people fell upon me with their cudgels and abused me, and struck me and threw the horse down, yet by the power of the Lord I passed through them and called upon the town and shopkeepers and told them of their immodest state, how they were a shame to Christians and the profession of Christianity."

What difference is there in this courage of Fox in returning to possible death and in the courage of Drake sailing boldly into fortified Cadiz? Both men were assured of their own immunity from the swords or guns of the enemy. Drake may have been inspired with the desire to loot or to protect his country from invasion and Fox by a complete faith in God, yet both were armoured in an arrogance which refused to believe that lesser men could possibly injure them. That is why the ruffian is so powerful and can prove so dangerous. This terrific belief in himself might be used for worthy objects as Fox used it, or it might become the inspiration of some poisoner like William Palmer, of Rugeley. I insist that the impulse guiding both men is roughly the same; good or bad may ensue, but that will depend largely on the ruffian's environment or hereditary make-up.

Let us return to William Walker. If, shall we say, the United States had at that time been waging a legitimate war—if any war is really legitimate to anybody except financiers—he would probably have gone down in history as a patriotic hero. There was that dirty smuggler Jean la Fitte who was eager to become respectable and would have sided with the United States if he had not been snubbed in society because of his boorish manners. Walker naturally reminds us of the dictators, for it was his ambition to become sole master of Nicaragua, no matter what the natives desired; but when we come to dictatorships, and so-called dictatorships, we must step warily, we shall have to spend time with men who were not ruffians so that we may point more clearly at those who were and are.

Our history has been written continually from false

Y

angles, on the exaltation of class. England shudders at
the guillotining of fat Louis and his silly, vain wife and
speaks with abhorrence of the alleged Terror under
Robespierre, but it does not mention the even greater
terror that struck the people when the émigrés returned
for vengeance; it does not tell us of the ghastly public
executions under the royalty which Robespierre swept
aside, executions to which the fashionable would come as
to a play to watch greedily men having hot lead poured
into their veins or their flesh snipped off them with
white-hot pincers. Napoleon sadly contemplated the
sacking of the Tuileries when the loyal Swiss guard was
massacred, and he records: "I saw well-dressed women
indulge in acts of the utmost indecency towards the
corpses. I visited all the neighbouring cafés; everywhere
passions were violent; rage was in all hearts; it was
visible on every face, although they were far from being
the common people." Here we see not the bloodthirsty
half-naked *sans culotte*, so popular with cheap novelists,
but fashionable well-bred ladies dancing amongst the
corpses. To keep the middle-class conscience intact, such
things are rarely repeated, only is upheld the dripping
head of a worthless Marie Antoinette in the filthy arm
of a proletariat as warning of the dangerous people who
must at all costs be kept under. We do not hear of the
political executions decreed under the merry monarch
Charles II, of the decomposing bodies of Cromwell,
Bradshaw, and Ireton pulled from their coffins and hung
to stink at Tyburn, we forget that the poet we reverence,
John Milton, had to run to hiding on the restoration and
that it was decreed that his immortal works should be
" publicly burnt by the hand of the common hangman."
We are shown a lying portrait of King Richard II
promising the commons to be their leader, we forget that

the result of this alleged courage of a fourteen-year-old boy was followed by the appalling slaughter of those very commons he had promised to lead. Before the spectacle of a stupid Czar and his wife going to execution we shut our ears to the awful screams of peasants flogged to death for centuries. In a newspaper to-day columns are given to some drunken scallywag who breaks his neck at the vicious sport of fox-hunting, and it will be spoken of sadly over the tea-cups, but, save for a passing insincere shudder, the deaths of miners are soon forgotten. Frankly, I cannot see the difference between man and man. All lives are surely valuable no matter whether born in palace or hovel? That is my creed. I believe in liberty of thought and action, and when the day comes for the frightened reactionaries to employ the fascisti for their protection, physical coward though I am, I shall be standing with a rifle in the people's armies, no matter what name they give themselves, whether it be liberals, socialists, democrats, communists or anarchists.

First, I suppose, in modern times our example must be Oliver Cromwell. If you ask the average Englishman about Cromwell he will probably shrug him aside as a kill-joy puritan in slovenly dress, and exalt the alleged merry-making under Charles II. What has confused him about Cromwell is, not only the religious fervour of some of his supporters, but many of his own semi-mystical pronouncements. He was a deeply religious man, but he was certainly not narrow-minded. He adored music, and personally employed some of the king's performers after the royal household was disbanded, while under his protectorate English music was at its highest since the days of Elizabeth; it was during this period that Henry Lawes published his *Books of Ayres*, Playford his *Dancing Master*, while Byrd, Bull, and Orlando Gibbons were all at work. Nor can we damn as intolerant a man who can write this to Major-General Crawford for dismissing an officer: " Aye, but the man ' is an Anabaptist.' Are you sure of that? Admit he be, shall that render him incapable to serve the public? Sir, the State, in choosing men to serve it, takes no notice of their opinions; if they be willing faithfully to serve it—that satisfies." Other of Cromwell's enemies, such as Hilaire Belloc, insist, on no evidence whatever, that he was a savage beast, but Clarendon who knew him well states that he was " not a man of blood," while Marvell, after viewing his corpse, wrote sadly:

" Those gentle rays under his lids were fled.
Which through his looks that piercing sweetness shed."

It is true that he behaved abominably at Drogheda, but that is the only black mark against him, and unquestionably later he regretted his command, yelled in the heat of battle, of No Quarter. During the Civil War he was always considerate to captured towns, and the same cannot be said of the Royalists: we hear, for example, that " Campden House, the stately mansion built at the expense of £90,000 by King James's silk mercer, was burnt by Rupert's orders lest it should afford a shelter to the enemy." One who knew him writes that Cromwell was " naturally compassionate towards objects in distress, even to an effeminate measure," and again and again he tried to bring the stupid, stubborn Charles to reason until he could argue no further and had to agree to his execution. Nor was he a solemn creature, his humour was largely horse-play, but he liked laughter, and was an ideal husband and parent. The more we examine Cromwell the less reason can we find to give him passport into Ruffians' Hall; he did not desire the dictatorship, and he refused the crown. In his last speech, looking back upon a confused attempt to create order, he said, "Misrule is better than no rule, and an ill government, a bad government, is better than none." He had striven to create a democratic order, actually calling three parliaments within five years, but the parliaments could never agree, while the rump he had to dissolve because it attempted to pass a law that would practically have abolished free election; he never acted on his own, being always, as protector, controlled by his council of state. He was the leader of the middle-class, of the tradesman, the yeoman, but the oppressed people saw in him, in his tolerance towards religious arguments—he even tried towards the end to be tolerant towards such vindictive political enemies as the Roman Catholics—a beginning of socialism. But the time had not come for socialism, and deep though his sympathies must have been towards the communistic Levellers and Diggers, although politics drove him into attacking them, Cromwell was yet statesman enough to realise that he could not force advanced idealism on the nation while so many ancient abuses remained to be removed. The question of religion is vital to our understanding of the period, for the people's revolt had become transmuted into a religious revolt, the Bible being taken symbolically as a socialist indictment of wealth. Cromwell himself was touched, like Bunyan, with this confusion of politics and theology, but always he struggled for the freedom of the people, and finding his path blocked by intolerant self-seekers on every side, he despaired of a solution. In this maze he cried despairingly: "Every sect saith, 'O give me liberty!' But give it to him and to his power he will not yield it to anyone else." He once asked Ludlow what he wanted. "That which we fought for," said Ludlow; "that the nation might be governed by its consent." " I," answered Cromwell, " am as much for a government by consent as any man, but where shall we find that consent? " That was the point: in this hurly burly, which voice was the voice of the people? The din was such that he could not hear and therefore sought instead the still, small voice of God, his conscience. He grappled with the most obvious abuses, with the strangling of trade by crown impositions, and he fought to destroy the reactionary out-of-date gild system which strove to keep a monopoly in the hands of an intolerant group. He attempted to bring freedom to an oppressed people, even inviting the Jews to return and thereby converting much of Antwerp's trade to England and starting our present monopoly of world-markets. It is strange that this man, in many ways a socialist—" If there be any one that makes many poor to make a few rich, that suits not a commonwealth," said he to the Speaker in 1650—should, while advocating free-trade, have started not only imperialism, but the British Empire itself. Parliament unfortunately could not control its excitement at being given open speech; the Barebones parliament of 1653 was probably one of the most enlightened in our history, but its very enlightenment was its own destruction. It demanded too much, and each man tried to shout the other down. Cromwell was forced to institute what was more or less a dictatorship if he did not want to see the republic killed by its own strength, and his superb and impossible dream became a Protestant union of Europe against the union of the Catholic countries under the control of Rome. The dream was hopeless because of that domination of Rome, for the Protestant churches were divided and fought amongst each other, they could not be brought into cohesion even by a Cromwell. And as with Walker with his tawdry ambitions, money dragged down the splendid aspirations of Cromwell: his fight against the Papacy brought war with Spain, and for trade reasons the City of London was opposed to such a war. The middle-class now fully on its feet, thanks to revolution, was eager to see that revolution go, for corruption is more easily obtained under a monarchy than under a democratic government. The merchants and moneylenders could afford to have their king back, for they knew that they could control him. Cromwell had done his job, and therefore his platform could be discarded: better a tame autocrat than the people in power, and the City proved itself correct: twenty-eight years later it had no difficulty in kicking an obstreperous James out of England.

No, Cromwell cannot enter Ruffians' Hall. He never strove in the totalitarian fashion to exalt the state above the people, and the few poor scraps of freedom we possess to-day in England have been given us by men like Pym and Hampden, and interpreted by Cromwell. He was never a tyrant, but attempted always to hold the balance between his red-coated army—the British red-coat was instituted by Cromwell for his Ironsides—and parliament, to control the turbulent army and at the same time to protect parliament.

It is now, when we approach Robespierre, that we see how distorting has been the historical mirror shown the middle-class to raise the bogy of the people, as to-day is raised the preposterous howl of the Red Terror whenever there is a proletarian demand for freedom. Robespierre was no tyrant, no dictator. A little man, five feet three inches tall, he was on the surface cold, inhuman, with his green-tinted spectacles and his harsh voice, and his vanity about his appearance, about the elaborate powdering of his hair; but there was affection in him, affection controlled by a strong will, for in childhood he had lost those he loved and was determined never to let his emotions again betray him into weakness. Yet he struggled hard at first to keep Danton and Desmoulins from the guillotine because they had been his friends, and there can be no question about the corruption of Danton.

The common charge against Robespierre is that he instituted the Terror, and he cannot be entirely exonerated from this. He afterwards stated that he did not know what was happening, but that is obviously absurd, and he added that he could not go against the trend of public opinion. There is probably more truth in the latter remark, for Robespierre had an almost childlike determination to obey the people. That was his one criterion: was it the will of the people? To understand the situation, however, you must rid yourself of the common idea that Robespierre was a bloodthirsty dictator, he remained in power only by force of popular opinion. It had been entirely against his will that Brissot, leader of the Girondins, had started that world war which was eventually to destroy the work of the revolution. Four magnificent speeches did Robespierre make against this policy of converting the world to republicanism; sanely, he recognised the truth, he pointed out that an invading army could never bring freedom, that it would unite oppressors and oppressed under the flag of patriotism. But his sanity could not stand against the illogical jingoism of Brissot, who stirred the emotions while Robespierre appealed to the intellect, and war became inevitable. It was now, when France was menaced by the bayonets of Europe, that the panic resulting in the Terror was created. Marat, in a sense, may be blamed for this shame upon the revolution, for while a man of great culture—he was too sensitive when a doctor to attend even a post-mortem—he wrote violent articles advocating massacre. " I believe in the cutting off of heads! " he cried. " He was a little man," we are told, " slender but well made. Of a yellow aspect, he had a quick eye. He had a great deal of motion, seldom keeping his body or legs still. He was thin." This yellowish complexion was mainly the result of his theatrical passion for lurking in cellars under the belief that he might be assassinated; such an unhealthy existence brought on him also a revolting skin-disease. Suffering from persecution mania, he scribbled violent articles, urging a dictatorship and the execution of all enemies of the people, while he skulked in dirty cellars with the lovely, gracious Simone Evrard, to whom he was the most devoted of husbands—they were married only in the civil, scarcely recognised fashion—and in her turn, she worshipped him, surrendering her fortune with her compassionate love. He was incredibly generous—every farthing was given to those in need. He acted the part of leader of the people, wearing a handkerchief about his head and keeping his shirt open at the neck, a costume that must rather have shocked the fastidious Robespierre. Marat admired Robespierre, seeing in him the ideal dictator, but the Incorruptible had no sympathy with either dictatorship or bloodshed, although he recognised and approved of the sincere faith of Marat. The two men tried to understand each other, and one of the accusations brought against Robespierre on the 9th Thermidor was his refusal to accept Marat's programme of violence. Disagree though they might, they respected each other, Marat writing, after they had met: " The interview confirmed me in the opinion I had always had of him—that he combined the wisdom of a wise

legislator with the integrity of a truly honest man and the
zeal of a staunch patriot, but lacked the breadth of
vision and the audacity of the statesman."

France was desperate, Brissot's insane war, as Robespierre had prophesied, was draining the country of men
and money and inspiring traitors to undermine the revolution. Panic-stricken, the people turned upon all whom
they suspected of being in sympathy with *émigrés*. A
revolutionary tribunal was set up and Robespierre was
elected president, but he refused the post. He had declared against capital punishment, and when as a young
man he had been appointed judge of the ecclesiastical
court of Arras and had had to sign a murderer's death
sentence, for two days he had not slept or eaten but had
walked up and down, muttering, " The man's a villain.
He deserves to die. But to kill a man! To kill a man!"
That sentimentalist still lived in Robespierre; although
experience had taught him that traitors must suffer, he
could not agree to a system that sought not only justice
but revenge. Yet he made no efforts to rescue the poor
wretches, many of whom were innocent, when the terrified leaders of Paris, hemmed in by an armed Europe,
sought a vent to their fears in blood. Robespierre did
not move; it is true that he could have done nothing to
stop the savage slaughter, for you cannot stem that
dangerous, unreasoning force, public opinion, but at least
he could have revealed his thoughts, have made some
gesture to express his disgust. That is the only stain upon
his memory; by his silence he appeared to condone the
Terror.

Then France began to win the war, for as Spain to-day
has proved, the armies of democracy have an inspired
courage unknown to the trained soldier. Brissot became
the most powerful man in the convention with well over

a third majority, Robespierre had about the same number, while the remaining deputies were more or less on Brissot's side. Efforts were made to discredit Robespierre, childish scandals invented, and when he strove to answer his enemies he was shouted down. But the Girondins made one bad tactical error, they agreed to give him eight days in which to prepare his reply to the accusations, and eight days are a long time, passions are easily cooled, and when Robespierre appeared again in the convention his dispassionate analysis of the attacks was irrefutable. The Girondins had lost.

It was Saint-Just who, on November 13, 1792, demanded the head of Louis. He was twenty-five years of age, tall and handsome with a heavy chin above the frilled white stock, with straight brows that almost met when he frowned, with large bright eyes and soft, sensuous mouth. He faced the convention: " Kingship itself is a crime! " he said. Saint-Just remains one of the truly great figures of the revolution. Had he not died with his friend, one cannot doubt that he would have carried the revolution to victory, that there would never have been an Emperor Napoleon. As incorruptible as his master, so deeply inspired was he by the principles of freedom and morality that when his mistress followed him to Paris, he refused even to see her. The French success in battle was mainly because of his organisation, he knocked the army into shape, shot any officer whose troops fell back, sabred any soldier who ran; officers and men were commanded to sleep in their clothes, the whores were driven out of camp, and he led the men again and again into battle. A man of terrific energy, remorseless towards traitors, untouched by pity, believing in naught but the principles of the people, he was executed when he had not even reached the age of twenty-seven. After his beheading, amongst his papers, these words were found: " I pray for death, as for a boon from heaven, rather than that I should be any longer a witness of crimes, committed against my country and the human race." Always he lived up to his own statement: " The only rest for a revolutionary is in the grave," and now he stood in the convention and demanded the death of Louis without trial. This may seem unjust, yet the verdict of any trial must have been guilty, otherwise the people would have risen in a second Terror. Robespierre and Saint-Just wanted to avoid the inevitable excitement of a trial. There was no question that Louis had to die; while he remained, there would be continual attempts at restoration, he was the centre of intrigue, nor can I understand why such excessive sentiment should be wasted on this stupid man and his vain wife simply because they happened to be a king and queen. As I have already stated, I consider all lives valuable unless they work deliberately to oppress humanity, and the regime of Louis had been a regime of oppression.

We will not go in detail through Robespierre's life because it is outside our thesis, and is only stated here to show the difference between an honest man and a ruffian in power. It is often urged against him that he abolished religion and set up reason in its place. This is utterly untrue. The opposition party, the Hébertists, were the creators of this idiotic pantomime, and during the famous Feast of Reason on November 10, 1793, Robespierre left in the middle of the proceedings. As a matter of fact, one of the main causes of his downfall was this reaction, for he knew that you cannot uproot religion by decrees, and as a counterblast to Hébert he instituted his Feast of the Supreme Being on June 4, 1794, when he attempted against violent opposition to bring Christianity back as a state religion. Six weeks later his enemies, the corrupt who feared the exposure of their corruption, entered the City Hall and tried to murder him. One story goes that he attempted to commit suicide, but to blow one's jaw away is a queer method of trying to kill oneself, and the more likely tale is that the assassin, Merda—although his boasted story later cannot be accepted—was sent to destroy him before he could speak while the place was being stormed. We do not know the truth, for Robespierre was given no chance to defend himself. On the scaffold of the Place de la Révolution, he stood on July 28, 1794, the last to die. His wounded brother and Couthon were first carried up to the guillotine, then Saint-Just, contemptuously, not bothering to speak, laid his head beneath the knife, before Robespierre walked up the steps. The executioner, a royalist, Samson, wrenched the bandage from his victim's shattered jaw, and a low cry of pain was jerked from him while they pushed him down.

No, like Cromwell, Robespierre will find Ruffians' Hall closed against him. He hated ostentation, he was angry when called the Incorruptible, saying that it was a fine state of affairs when men were honoured merely for not betraying the revolution, and when an enthusiast tried to put the red cap upon his head, he tore it off and threw it to the ground; he lived in philosophic quietude, eager to show mercy, inflexible in giving justice. Before him always remained the thought of the people; for them, as he once said, he was ready to die, and it was the ruffian who destroyed him: Fouché, Tallien, Barras, these little men were all eager to scoop gold for their own pockets, not caring for the revolution that was to have brought equality and fraternity. Robespierre loved the idea of liberty, he insisted on the freedom of the Press and would not censor plays, saying, "Public opinion is the sole judge of good taste," and as we have seen, he had no hand in the Terror. The one blame here is that, disapprove of the massacre though he did, he showed no glimpse of that disapproval save in personal letters.

These men loved the people, not the state, that symbol of themselves as God, and it would seem that their work died with them, but that is not so. Cromwell made parliament a force stronger than the king, and Robespierre gave, not only to his country, but to the whole world, an ideal of freedom that yet exists. His policy even affected the man who did so much to kill the revolution—without Robespierre, Napoleon could never have become so great. Here we are given the spectacle of a noble youth gradually losing his nobility when the lust for power takes hold, we see almost the evolution of a ruffian. On the fall of Robespierre, Napoleon was imprisoned as the friend of Robespierre's brother, Augustin, and although soon freed, he existed miserably on half-pay, an object of deep suspicion when the *émigrés* returned to set the money-wheels spinning again so that wealth should not be distributed throughout the country but into the pockets of a few. He even contemplated suicide when he saw the hopelessness of ideals, the smashing of that splendid dream of Robespierre in which he had profoundly believed; then Barras employed him to attack a royalist mob, and that was a task he liked. His revolutionary faith did not hamper him when he could turn guns on aristocrats. But the dream gradually faded, he had Barras's mistress Josephine for wife, and she was also in the pay of Fouché, chief of police; seeing how those around him rose to power by corruption, he freed himself from the shackles of idealism and strode brutally ahead.

He was to tell Las Casas on St. Helena that "he had been very warm and sincere at the beginning of the revolution; that he had cooled by degrees as he acquired more just and solid ideas. His Jacobinism had sunk under the political absurdities and monstrous domestic excesses of our legislators. Finally, his republican faith had vanished." Nor were those "legislators" Robespierre and his friends, but the greedy politicians around Barras, for Napoleon always spoke of Robespierre with respect, and gave a pension to his sister, Charlotte. It is unnecessary to repeat the rise of Napoleon, we all know so well how from a sincere revolutionary he became the emperor who kept his credit alive by seizing gold through war, and who killed free speech—on the day he departed for the campaign that was to end at Marengo, sixty-one Paris newspapers were suppressed—and he left behind him nothing but a bankrupt country. His reign shows the uselessness of a ruffian dictatorship, the Code Napoleon we have certainly, but that was not his creation, he merely sanctioned it, and the few ideas of liberty he permitted to grow were those left over from the revolution.

Yet, strangely, there have been ruffian dictators who nevertheless have brought good to the people. There was Mustafa Kemal of Turkey, but it must be remembered that he was attempting to impose liberty on a backward nation, his urge certainly was personal power, but, being a man of the people, he loved the people, and their needs came before the selfish lusts of a bureaucracy. His efforts to bring a parliament into force by creating a government and an opposition almost ended in tragedy; for the Turks were not civilised enough to achieve the Englishman's conviction that all politics are crooked, anyhow, and they attempted to slaughter each other with guns as well as argument. Mustafa Kemal was, of course, lucky to be born in the right age, as Lenin, Mussolini and Hitler were lucky, for revolutions are rarely successful save after a war when a dispirited nation is eager to fight to regain its ego. Just as Hitler raised the war-cry of the Red Terror, Mustafa Kemal raised the cry of the English Terror, and with it he rallied Turkey to his side. He smashed the corrupt sultan, he drove religion from the country and nearly destroyed himself with it, but the cry of the English Terror came in useful here, and between the threat of no religion or the grip of England, the Turks quickly agreed to having no religion. One can only judge these men by the contentment of the people under them, and Mustafa Kemal did not work for his own aggrandisement, he worked for the people and created a contented nation. He was a ruffian certainly, he has been given the key of Ruffians' Hall, but he was a noble ruffian who, while worshipping all principles of ruffianism, nevertheless used those principles for a noble end.

He is the opposite to Mussolini who, in truth, gives us one of the most perfect examples of ruffianism we will find, for he is ruffianism gone mad, spinning with flaying arms in a desperate momentum that dares not stop lest he fall, whirling to nowhere, whirling to dizzy himself from thinking, screaming to deafen himself from hearing the voice of truth. And by his very fury, his apparent menace, he has astounded the world, and blinded many. He who shouts loudest is heard by most and believed by most, that is the principle on which Mussolini and Hitler work, and if by any chance a small, brave voice should rise in protest, there are always clubs and bayonets and concentration camps to silence it. Let us examine Mussolini, this man who shouts of "blood

BENITO MUSSOLINI

baths " and heroic revolutions: he is really most instruc-
tive, almost the apotheosis of our theory.

Son of a blacksmith, he was bred on strong socialist
principles. He and his father, in his own words to Emil
Ludwig, had " passionate discussions " together and
" when my father died a thousand comrades of the party
followed his coffin." Strange boasting this would seem
for a man who was later to put a stop violently to any
passionate discussions and who would turn machine-guns
on those thousands of the Socialist party behind his
father's coffin, but this is a small contradiction to what
follows. All Mussolini's life is contradiction. He fled
to Switzerland to escape military service, and there was
befriended by the revolutionary, Angelica Balabanoff,
who, pitying him in his misery and loneliness, befriended
him, helping him translate a German pamphlet because
he did not know the language. She it is who tells us
in *Sawdust Cæsar* that he was afraid even to go home
alone at night, and would implore her to accompany
him; this charge of nameless terror, this shrinking from
the unseen spirits of night, is substantiated by Armando
Borghi, who remarks that when Mussolini was being
treated for syphilis he was too scared to visit the doctor
by himself and would always insist on some friend going
with him. This, one would think, is not the stuff of
which ruffians are made, nor the petty theft of a watch
from a comrade who had taken him home, nor his vague
confused ideas of Marxian philosophy and his incitings
of the people to revolt. Cowardly, a pitiful revolutionary,
he might seem, but as yet his will was distracted, he
knew not where to turn, for that huge arrogance of his
gazed jealously upon an indifferent world, urging him
to boldness which the spirit feared. It was later, after
he was expelled from Switzerland on the charge of a

z

faked passport and had spent a wandering existence as teacher of French, journalist, and inciter of strikes, that he becomes of definite importance and his character takes shape, it is not until after the 1914 war. Already he was known as a dangerous socialist, and had been one of the foremost in the Red Week of June 1914 when a general strike ran through all Italy; but despite the applause of his admirers, he did not particularly distinguish himself in the trouble, although acting as one of the leaders. His main importance was the fact that he edited *Avanti* with the help of Comrade Balabanoff. This was the party's official organ, and Mussolini's journalism if slightly verbose and grandiloquent was powerful; even if his ideas were occasionally confused by reading ill-digested philosophies, even if he should sometimes contradict himself, he wrote with rage and conviction. Then war came, and the country was split into three parties: into the nationalists demanding that Italy fight for Germany, into a kind of liberalism calling on the nation to side with the Allies, and into the socialists who insisted on neutrality. As Benito himself put it, " Even in case of a European conflagration Italy can adopt only one attitude, if she wishes not to be dragged into the final ruin: ' absolute neutrality.' " Then suddenly, for no apparent reason, *Avanti's* policy began to change. In wonderment the socialists now read that Italians should side with the French to end the war; so sudden a *volte-face* could have but one explanation—Mussolini had been bought. Mussolini himself has always remained extremely vague about the matter, talking patriotic abstractions to explain his amazing change of front, but his worshippers have not been so discreet, they actually speak of his conversion as sent by God, and compare his realisation of the holiness of the Allied cause with Paul's vision of Jesus. The truth, however, has been clearly stated: the *Italia del Popolo* on May 3, 1919, openly accused Mussolini of having "cashed cheques from the French Government. Cagliostro wishes to bring an action, and that is his duty. We shall do ours by nailing to the pillory this vulgar adventurer, at the cross-roads of his folly and his crimes." No action was brought. Then in Paris in 1926, a certain Bonomini was being tried for the murder of one of Mussolini's friends, Buonservizi: Maitre Torres defended Bonomini, and in court he definitely stated that Mussolini had entered the Allied cause because he had been bought by France. Later, Armando Borghi wrote asking Maitre Torres for details, and received the following statement which was published in many newspapers: "There was a moment quite at the start when the Italian socialist party was unanimous against the armed intervention of Italy. The French Government was concerned, and considered the matter in a cabinet meeting. They examined the question to see if there were not some means of converting some of the socialists to the cause of war— financial means. The name of Mussolini was mentioned. The first payment was 15,000 francs, and after that they allowed him 10,000 francs monthly. It was Guesde's secretary, Dumas, who brought him the money. It was then that *Il Popolo d'Italia* was born, immediately Interventionist. That is the exact story, which no one will dare to deny, for fear of more crushing documentary evidence." No one has dared to deny it.

The violent Socialist, the hero of the Red Week, he who had bellowed in the columns of *Avanti* that Italians must never be sacrificed for the cause of international finance, did one of his characteristic pirouettes and now howled lustily for Italian intervention, for the blood bath to end blood baths. In fury the socialist party ejected him, and they would not even listen to him, they screamed with outraged horror at this treachery, and an eye-witness tells us that " Mussolini left the meeting, very pale and trembling with rage, his finger to his mouth; he seemed to say: we shall meet again." He was never to forget; the strongest impulse in him was the impulse to hate, to seek revenge, for such is the ruffian principle; his tortured thin-skin shrivels at a note of laughter or a word of contempt. The revenge he took at last was complete and terrible. But first, on May 24, 1915, Italy declared war on Germany, and as Mussolini was the supreme jingoite, it was thought that he should prove himself not afraid to face the perils he incited his fellow-countrymen to endure. He had to go to the front, but to a very quiet sector of the front where there was no possibility of so valuable a patriot getting himself hurt: the only shots aimed at him were from cameras, he was photographed more often than a film star, posing in innumerable patriotic attitudes with his bulbous jaw projecting pugnaciously. And then he was wounded. They were trial-firing with a trench-mortar when in Mussolini's own words, " the firing went off without the least incident until the last round but one. But this round—and we had fired two casefuls—exploded in the barrel. I was hit by a shower of splinters and hurled several yards away. I cannot say any more." It was scarcely heroic enough for him to say any more; one of his own shells during practice blew him up with a peppering of metal in the backside. The myths bred from this inglorious end to his military career have been astounding; it has actually been said that he was wounded more than thirty times—that was possible, thirty wounds at the same moment and in the same place—and the truth is that he was laid up far longer than would seem necessary because the syphilitic condition of his blood delayed natural healing.

When he was ejected from the socialist party Mussolini had cried, " You will pay for this! " That dream of vengeance dominated all his thoughts, all his actions after the war. He had to justify himself, to prove his worth, even if he had to kill to prove it. After Caporetto, when the troops ran like frightened women before the Austrians, the comic-opera poet d'Annunzio suggested to Mussolini that his paper gather around it all the disgruntled returned soldiers eager to redeem their reputation; and thus began the fascist movement. It became a kind of symbol of a re-inspired Italy, patriotism gone mad. Then after the war, three heroes stood out: d'Annunzio, who had been flown by a pilot over Vienna so that he could rain bombastic leaflets on the city; Mussolini, who from his editorial chair had thundered warnings against the enemy; and Rossetti, who alone had sent a torpedo into an Austrian flagship. There was argument as to which country was to possess Fiume, and d'Annunzio with an army of soldiers who could find no place in civil life marched and took the port, after which he ruled in hysterical ecstasy, yelling involved flowery speeches, waving a stiletto, and leading innumerable parades. Mussolini remained in Milan and decided to run for parliament. Money was pouring into his hands, money intended for the army in Fiume, and later he was forced to confess that he misappropriated a great deal of these funds destined for soldiers and women and children. He confessed it indirectly by stating that " certain contributions, some ten thousands of liras, served to pay the legionnaries arrived in Milan from Fiume and from other Italian towns, and who formed what were called ' armed bands,' who stood at my orders." Yet even with these armed bands to bully the electors the mighty patriot could barely get a thousand votes and spent a day in prison for his illegal methods of electioneering. Again, we find Mussolini accused of being a traitor. He had appropriated the Fiume funds and when d'Annunzio suggested marching on Rome he protested furiously against the idea. He was in the midst of the elections and wanted no trouble with the government; in fact it cannot be doubted that he was now more or less in the pay of that government under Nitti, and later under Giolitti, who were determined to destroy the aspirations of the working class. Mussolini had been the leader of that class, but now, still wriggling furiously at the memory of his ejection from the party, he was eager for revenge. Giolitti decided to uproot that nuisance of a d'Annunzio, and Mussolini made no attempt to stand by his friend. He let him be thrown out of Fiume with scarcely a protest, but struck at those he hated, at the socialists. As one of his ex-comrades wrote: " One must also note that it was after the crash of d'Annunzio's Fiume enterprise that there began the fascist expeditions against the labour exchanges, the co-operatives, etc.— expeditions which multiplied to the point of creating a veritable terror."

Mussolini was keeping his word, he was demanding blood for the insult the socialists had placed upon him. He sent out his armed bands to massacre his one-time comrades, while he himself remained secure, safe from the fighting, in Milan. There was a general strike in Italy, and at first Mussolini backed it, hoping perhaps to raise his price with the reactionary government. He called it "a creative strike," and by his enthusiastic propaganda actually earned for himself the title of " the Lenin of Italy "; there is also proof that he attempted to steal back into the socialist ranks. He had to have his self-esteem bolstered. If those who had ejected him now confessed their mistake and agreed to accept his hand his ego would have been satisfied; but the socialists would not touch him. He was, in fact, playing two cards, offering fascism to the highest bidder. Whichever side had bothered to put up the most money could at that time have made the famous March on Rome either a communist or a reactionary march.

It became a reactionary march. He who had upheld the stay-in strike as a magnificent blow for freedom now suddenly denounced it. He sent his armed bands against the workers. The massacres that followed are too revolting to re-tell; suffice it that Mussolini was now marching towards power and at the same time wreaking bloody revenge upon the socialists—all from the safety of his editorial chair in Milan.

Then came the elections, and the fascists found themselves with a mere thirty-two seats, fifth on the list of parties, only the communists being lower with eighteen seats. Realising that alone he could do nothing, his party being so unpopular, Mussolini decided to compromise with his enemies: he signed a truce with the socialist and catholic parties, swearing to " defend with all my forces this treaty of peace," and promising that should a follower of his not obey, with " the rods of my oath, of my courage, of my passion, I will either correct him, or I will make his life impossible." Logically he should have used that rod upon himself very soon afterwards, for his gangsters objected to living tame lives, and anti-Mussolini songs were shouted at meetings. His throne again was rocking, and he actually resigned; he became no longer the Duce. But this noble gesture did not last for long; to return to life as a tame newspaper editor was impossible to his ruffian pride. He rejected the peace treaty and swore a crusade against socialism, liberalism, catholicism, and democracy with shouts of "Down with parliament!" and "Long live the dictatorship!" The industrialists had stepped in and now controlled the movement: the financiers, the men of wealth who were determined to see a rebellious working-class beaten if necessary into toiling for practically no wages. It was the same situation that was later to bring Hitler into power. But the short-sightedness of these industrialists, driven to panic-stricken terrorism under the bogy of Bolshevism, little realised that in creating an army to beat down all threats of revolution they were creating an army that would in time turn also upon them.

The same process seems to be beginning even in England, but Italy was the first of modern states to employ the gangster in organised battalions. The U.S.A. have attempted it on a small scale, but there the industrialists have, at least so far, been intelligent enough not to let their thugs grow too powerful. In Italy they gave these thugs unlimited power and placed Mussolini at their head, and one of his first acts was to destroy his rival newspapers, wrecking *Avanti*, for he, more than most men, knew the iconoclastic strength of the press.

At this time, even Mussolini could not have realised the possibilities ahead; he was merely a paid strike-breaker and newspaper-man. In *Popolo d'Italia* he wrote on July 2, 1921: "The Italy of 1921 is essentially different from the Italy of 1919. This has been said and demonstrated several times. Fascism must not have the air of having arrogated to itself the sole credit for the profound change in the national situation. Thus limited our merit cannot be contested by any party. To say that a bolshevist peril still exists in Italy is to want to change into reality certain fears that are not to be acknowledged. Bolshevism is vanquished." Later, when he realised the necessity of resurrecting the Red Terror to draw help and sympathy from the terror-struck industrialists of other countries, he must have regretted that admission. But can Mussolini regret anything? It is so easy merely to ignore what one said yesterday. And, anyhow, the trick worked. It still works. The wealthy classes of England and France and the U.S.A. still cling pathetically to their little scraps of property in fear of a revolution that will never come and applaud Mussolini and Hitler. They actually prop them up with loans which they know will never be repaid, under the preposterous belief that they are their one bulwark against a world-wide conspiracy engineered by the totalitarian U.S.S.R., which is rapidly growing as capitalistic as any other country in the world.

Now comes the glorious March on Rome. There is one figure here that must not be forgotten, the Duke of Aosta, cousin of King Emmanuel III, who thought to use Mussolini's gang and, after seizing power, himself command the movement, for he had the official army behind him. First of all he approached d'Annunzio to take control, but d'Annunzio had suffered enough treachery to refuse. General Peppino Garibaldi was next asked, and he also refused. Finding no other ruffian to his hand, Aosta turned to Mussolini, who accepted on the understanding that, the King being overthrown, Aosta should become regent. The King, however, knew of the scheme. He feared his cousin, " but," as Francesco Ciccotti writes, " there was a way to get rid of the Duke of Aosta, to isolate him and force him to renounce his leanings towards seditious plottings, by making his possible ally and future generalissimo (that is Mussolini) on that same day Prime Minister to King Victor Emmanuel." Whereupon the famous telegram was sent to Mussolini in Milan asking him to form a ministry.

A revolution is no revolution without fighting. While his gangs were leaping on trains (refusing to pay the fare) and commandeering motor cars, shouting " To Rome! to Rome! " their heroic leader was bellowing from his newspaper office, " To the barricades! to the barricades! " There was nobody likely to attack him, but it sounded in the grand tradition, and outside the Milan offices of the *Popolo d'Italia* tables, boxes, and distribution carts were piled high while the fearless revolutionaries defied the world. " I put on the black shirt," wrote Mussolini. " I barricaded the *Popolo d'Italia*. In the livid and grey morning Milan wore a new and fantastic appearance. Pauses and sudden silences gave one the sensation of great hours that come and go in the course of history. Frowning battalions of royal guards scouted the city, and the monotonous rhythm of their feet sounded ominous echoes in the almost deserted streets." Later he tells us that as he stood, armed with a rifle, behind the barricades, with his loyal newspaper staff beside him, " bullets whistled around my ears." But the only bullets fired that day were fired by him and his comrades, and the only near casualty was himself when an excitable enthusiast shot from behind and almost nipped him in the ear. The poor devil was nearly lynched, but Mussolini nobly pardoned him: that was rather a pity—one corpse would have been something for that day of glory to record. Then came the telegram from the King, and soon Mussolini was steaming comfortably in a pullman on his glorious March on Rome while his armies in the city were beating-up anyone they thought might possibly oppose them. The Duke of Aosta was forgotten as Mussolini met the King, having first donned his black shirt in the train. " I beg your Majesty to forgive me for appearing in your presence in uniform," he said, kissing the royal hand, " I have just come from a bloodless battle which had to be fought."

Now Mussolini had to form a ministry, for as yet he dared not aspire to complete dictatorship, and he had no programme to offer. All parties attacked him and he fretted like a bull under gnats while the deputies clamoured to know his policy. He had no policy except power for himself and hatred of the socialists, based on a philosophy derived from those two irreconcilables, Karl Marx and Machiavelli. Unable to retort, he organised the Cheka, the secret police, on Russian lines, and sat sweating and muttering impotently beneath the assaults of the socialist Matteotti. Matteotti tortured Mussolini, he brought against him his pack of lies and evasions; day after day he tormented him, jeering, mocking the fat traitor who could find no answer to the truth. Mussolini strove to rally the world with the inevitable cry of the Red Terror from which he said he was defending Italy. But you have already told us that bolshevism is dead, laughed Matteotti, " You would not whip a corpse, would you? " And to all this, Mussolini could answer only insults, vague epithets that clouded his own bad conscience.

" How do you explain," asked Matteotto, " that fascism, playing the adulteress, has passed from the bed of the working-class to the bed of the capitalist class, betraying each in turn, at its whim, at its fantasy? " Mussolini could not explain, nor could he explain how one day he had boosted the stay-in strikers and the next day wished to slaughter them; he could not explain how one day he had said that the King was useless, and the next had kissed his hand; how he had attacked financiers, the army, the clergy, and denied God, and then calmly

turned round and exalted them. He could explain nothing, he was a ruffian, ruthless, revengeful, spurred by
scarcely articulate resentments, and he knew only that
he wished to destroy so that he could exalt himself. In
desperation he offered a programme that was practically
word for word the programme of Karl Marx, whose
doctrines he had sworn he came to exterminate. Then
frenziedly he began to murder those against whom he
had sworn vengeance, and Matteotti threw the murders
up against him in parliament, deaths of men who were
avowed enemies of fascism. Mussolini again could not
explain. He threatened Matteotti in the Press, calling
him a " vulgar charlatan, notorious scamp, and ruffian
of the worst sort; he will do well to look after himself :
for if one day he finds himself with a broken skull, but
fractured in a good cause, he will not have the right to
complain after all the ignominies he has written and
signed." Matteotti promised to prove that the fascists
had faked the elections with about a million and a half
fraudulent votes, but before he could produce the evidence, he disappeared.

This was the moment when Mussolini could have been
destroyed, for all Italy rose in horror at the crime, but
democracy deserves the contempt with which the dictators
speak of it. Torn by antagonistic parties each determined
to show its humanitarian beliefs in contrast to the enemy,
they let that enemy escape and grow so powerful that
they are themselves eventually destroyed: so it was in
Germany when a feeble government permitted Hitler to
bludgeon it helpless: so too it was in Spain when the
liberal parties forgave the traitor generals and let them
go to conspire and rise with borrowed troops against
them. Now, in Italy, while the whole country was
appalled by the disappearance of Matteotti, while Musso-

lini was in terror, beaten, they gave way. Mussolini
denied all complicity, he almost wept in parliament,
crying, "Justice will be done, must be done, because the crime is a crime that is anti-fascist and anti-
nation. It is more than horrible, it is of a bestial
humanity." He swore to be a good boy, to give freedom
to the Press, to abolish his gangsters, and the democratic
parties believed him, they let him continue in power until
he could reorganise his terrified followers who had fled
at the first sign of revolt, and before long he could
announce boldly again: "If fascism is an association of
evil-doers, I, myself, am the chief of these evil-doers, and
I boast of it."

It is time we paused in this recital of the bloodthirsty
rise of the greatest ruffian of modern times, but a brief
excursus into his private affairs might throw a little
further light upon his character. He began as a drunkard
and a lecher, and he has remained a lecher, but there is
no longer any need for alcohol to give him a false idea
of greatness, he has examples enough of that on every
side. His treatment of women is apparently as callous
as his treatment of friends. Armandi Borghi gives an
illuminating tale of his behaviour with one Irene Desler,
who made the following statement before a notary, and
the document still exists: "I declare that I lived for
about two years in marital relations with a certain Benito
Mussolini, to whom I bore a son, legally recognised by
his father, and inscribed at the office of the civil depart-
ment of Milan, where I registered him. I attest that at
the time when Mussolini resigned from *l'Avanti* we
found ourselves in such poverty that we made our plans
to go to America—a project which we abandoned soon
after. At this period I spent the little bit of money which
I personally possessed in order to meet our needs. After

the founding of *Il Popolo d'Italia* our circumstances were not appreciably improved, and we continued to live in embarrassment; but suddenly after Mussolini's return from a trip to Geneva in January 1914 or 1915 (I cannot say exactly [it must have been 1915]) they were completely changed, Mussolini told me he had a lot of money, and I remember having seen him handle important amounts. . . . I asked him on his return if the money he showed me came from the source of which he had spoken. He answered that it came from France. He offered me a brilliant which I refused. I remember that Mussolini was much preoccupied with the fact that his trip to Geneva had been severely criticised in socialist circles of Milan. He said to me: 'I am lost; they have noticed something.' . . . I am ready to repeat these declarations in no matter what circumstances, and before no matter whom, even on sacred oath."

During this period Mussolini was married, but for a time he left his wife Rachel for this Irene, and then in her turn he deserted Irene when she had helped him through his period of poverty, when the French money was beginning to arrive. But Irene Desler knew too much, and was therefore arrested in 1917, and without a charge being preferred against her was pushed into jail with her three-year-old son. Later she was apparently released, for Borghi saw her in 1919, but after that she disappeared, and it is likely enough she was put into an insane asylum, for that was how Mussolini attempted to get rid of Maria Rygier, and would have succeeded had not the doctors refused to certify her. This Madame Rygier tells us that she knows of one early mistress of Mussolini's now in an asylum, and she probably refers to Irene Desler, but of the son nothing whatever is known.

Mussolini is, strangely enough, still alive and is so very close to us, while so much is hidden, that it is difficult to form a complete estimate of him. Yet I doubt if many could read the above brief recital of his rise without instantly offering him the throne and crown of Ruffians' Hall.[1] Napoleon, enemy of the world though he was, began with splendid ideals that gradual megalomania destroyed, but Mussolini from the very beginning has been so complete a ruffian that he would sell himself without the least qualm. It is rather frightening, this good conscience of the ruffian. We ordinary people wonder if men like Mussolini can sleep at night; surely they must wander, tortured, screaming, " Out damned spot! " when they see the accusing dead stir around them in the dark? But we feel this because we are ordinary men; people like Mussolini have so absorbed the idea of the superman that they would no more consider themselves answerable for their actions than we would think of demanding our accounts with God, for they themselves are god unto themselves. This is ruffianism utterly uncontrolled, and the terrible terrifying thing is that this man is worshipped, not so much by his own people as by the selfish, frightened little creatures of democratic lands who kneel before any violence that will protect them from the threat of the working-class.   Both communism and fascism

---

[1] There may be some who doubt the truth of this outline of Mussolini's treacherous history, and I therefore refer them to two easily obtainable and excellent works where all authorities will be found : *Sawdust Cæsar*, by George Seldes (Barker, 1936), and *Mussolini Red and Black*, by Armando Borghi (Wishart, 1935). The common retort to attacks on Mussolini is that, ruffian though he may be, he has done wonderful things for his country, and the same preposterous claim is even put forward for Hitler. To dispel fully this myth about Mussolini the reader should consult that exhaustive work, *Under the Axe of Fascism*, by Gaetanio Salvemini (Gollancz, 1936).   The so-called and much boosted achievements of fascism were all well under way before Mussolini seized power.   That glorious triumph of getting the trains to run to schedule, for which American and British tourists are so grateful in their hurry to run through the art galleries of one city in time to reach another city, was begun immediately after the war, for the confusion of the war had naturally completely disorganised the service. Mussolini merely carried

will seize their goods, but at least under fascism, even though they are beaten to their knees, they will retain the superiority of class, and that they feel is something.

Of Mussolini's pupil and later his master, Adolf Hitler, there is no need to speak so fully. His methods are so akin to Mussolini's that the recital would become tedious. He too attained strength on the pretence of a revolution with the same powerful catch-cry of the Red Terror, he also was leader of a minority of gangsters called into power by a weak government in fear of the working-class, and he too treated the working-class as serfs to be beaten and kicked and starved. Both boast of having risen through bloodshed, yet both attained power by allegedly legal methods, both have murdered most of their early comrades who threatened to become powerful, both have created a totalitarian state, based on terrorism and leading to moral and financial bankruptcy. But as a ruffian, Hitler shows a different side from Mussolini. Mussolini is the opportunist ruffian with no ideals, but Hitler is a fanatic, almost a lunatic. Both are eminently suited to their countrymen, for the Italian is an easy-going realist while the German is a sadistic metaphysician, the German likes uniforms, he likes marching humourlessly in step, he likes bands and violent, empty words full of sound and fury: all this

on with superb self-advertisement where the government left off. It was the same with his noisy achievement of draining the Pontine marshes: the truth is that during the first years of fascism work on this was actually slowed down. The disappearance of the Mafia and Black Hand gangs is also spoken of with awe, but the explanation is simple: those who had not emigrated to the U.S.A. to join their pal Capone, were recruited by Mussolini for the ranks of his fascisti. As for the corporative state, the union between employer and employee, it just doesn't exist, it is a pretty fairy tale to deceive enthusiastic foreigners. The half-starved workers dare not confess the truth of their slavery, while the rise in the cost of living and the heavy drop in wages is appalling, even according to official figures, and the way that Mussolini proudly balances his budget is an example of how figures can be made to lie (for this see particularly *Sawdust Cæsar*, as also for Mussolini's comic efforts to nationalise culture).

ADOLF HITLER

Hitler can give with an hysterical mysticism that has no foundations in any logic whatsoever. But the German never has been a logician. Those who talk of the blood kinship between England and Germany have no knowledge of history, and so far as our different attitudes towards life and politics are concerned they are as distant from us as are the Chinese or the Esquimaux. What is one to say of a country that exalts a man who went upon his knees and thanked God that war had broken out? A complete paranoiac, Hitler is blind to everything but himself. All newspaper correspondents I have met endorse Vernon Bartlett's opinion in his autobiography that interviews with Hitler consist of being shouted at and, if, those newspaper-men say, they had left the room while Hitler ranted, they are quite certain that he would not have noticed their absence.

During Hitler's trial for treason in 1924, Reichswehr General von Lossow summed up the Fuehrer completely: he thought himself, said Lossow, a combination of Mussolini, Gambetta and the Messiah in one. The godhead complex has him more fiercely in its grip than it has Mussolini, but he is the true fanatic in that he is apparently entirely sexless, spurred on only by a loathing of his father and a passion for his mother. He confesses that he could never hold a job, and in the war this heroic leader rose no higher than a lance-corporal. His advance to power has been as easy as Mussolini's, he has never suffered. When he was sentenced to five years for high treason he served about nine months in the Landsberg Fortress and had a comfortable enough time, living on the finest foods, with a delightful chamber for a cell, and was presented with a secretary and a typewriter. It was here that he wrote *Mein Kampf,* although it has been suggested with what truth I know not, that Hess was the

2 A

actual author, Hitler but providing the ideas. *Mein Kampf* is an interesting book, and in it he actually implies that he suffered from supernormal premonitions and heard voices inspiring him. There is the story, for example, of how once in the trenches while eating with a score of his company he heard a Voice whisper: " Get up and go to the other end of the trench." He obeyed the Voice, and a moment later those whom he had left were blown skyhigh. As he states that all were destroyed, it is unfortunately impossible to check this story; but there is a second tale which is so astounding that one is merely bewildered to think that the German people can possibly accept it, a miracle to equal any of those of the Christian saints. He tells us that one evening he was flying from Hamburg to Kiel with other members of the party on an electioneering trip. Night fell, fog swathed them, and for hour after hour they flew on and on, the pilot steering by compass. At last Hitler grew uneasy, and said to the pilot, " You have passed your destination. Turn back." The pilot objected, naturally enough, to a layman's interference, and Hitler asked him how much petrol he had left. The pilot told him that he had enough for another half-hour's flying. Hitler thereupon ordered him to turn round and fly in exactly the opposite direction, and when the pilot obeyed, the clouds opened and they descended on Kiel with five minutes' petrol in hand. But for Hitler's intervention, we are told, the plane would have gone on blindly till it fell like a tired bird into the dark sea. God was in that plane, says Hitler. Altogether this is an extraordinary story. It is approximately seventy miles from Hamburg to Kiel, and a passenger plane could make the journey in half an hour or less. How could any pilot fly for hours and hours by compass when he must have known that he would normally reach his destination in half an hour? It is of course possible that he was cruising round in the hope of finding an opening in the fog or that the fog would disperse. But it is extremely unlikely that he would continue doing this for hours and hours, and if he had been doing so, he could scarcely have argued with Hitler, affirming that he had not passed his destination, and the fact that he turned directly back and reached Kiel is another argument against the circling theory. Besides, a glance at the map shows that the romantic touch about the plane falling like a tired bird into the dark sea is preposterous. On such a course the pilot could easily have landed in Denmark or Sweden. If one assumes that the pilot was insane, Hitler inspired, and that God was performing a first-class miracle, this story might be accepted. But not otherwise. Hitler himself, however, is obviously convinced of its truth, innumerable Germans accept it without a protest: the god-complex is here in full maturity.

His belief in his own ordained triumph was such that twice Hitler wept and threatened to commit suicide at party meetings because he could not impose his will upon his followers. A fanatic, indeed, living only for the ambitious ego, disdaining the simple pleasures of the flesh, for he has no interest in women, eats no meat, drinks no alcohol, and plays at no sport, all his energies being concentrated into the messianic desire for power. The hypnotised Germans have at times come near to proclaiming him a god, but in spirit, their Leader, has been before them. They may not be altogether unanimous about his godhead, but it is perfectly obvious according to *Mein Kampf* that Hitler has no doubts. Long before he came to power he voted himself ruler, and, allowing no others to vote, had in that election an absolute majority of One. Hence his contempt for democracy, a hatred second only to his hatred of the Jews, that symbol of fatherhood, being the children of Jehovah. His detestation of democracy is maniacal, he calls it the "forerunner of Marxism," speaks of "the absurdity of that institution called parliament," and makes wild flourishes of meaningless nonsense such as saying that democracy "by its denial of the authority of the individual and its substitution of the mass present at any time, the parliamentary consent of the majority, sins against the aristocratic principle in nature." There is no attempt at logic in his arguments, there is only an uncontrolled hatred expressed in wild insults: "A majority can never be a substitute for *The Man*. It has always been the advocate not only of stupidity but also of cowardly policies, and just as a hundred fools do not make one wise man, a heroic decision is not likely to come from a hundred cowards. . . . There must be no majority making decisions, but the *decisions* shall be made by one *Man*."

Mein Kampf is spattered with such futile abuse. Being uneducated, Hitler refers with admiration to the Roman Empire, but he ignores the fact, probably through ignorance, that this Empire was founded on the conquests of the Roman Republic; he also seems never to have read of the Greek democracy defeating the Persian aristocracy, or of the success of the Dutch and American republics, or of the fact that a more or less democratic England managed to isolate Napoleon on St. Helena. This obsession, this hatred of any semblance of democratic freedom, is forcibly demonstrated by his objection to committees in the early days when he was struggling to rise in his party. He states: "In the years 1920–21 the Movement had a committee

in control of it, elected by the members in assembly.
This committee, comically enough, embodied the very
principles against which the Movement was most keenly
fighting, namely, parliamentarianism. I refused to continue such folly. I refused to attend the meetings of the
committee. I made my own propaganda for myself. I
refused to allow any ignoramus to baulk me into any
other course. As soon as I was established as Chairman
of the Party all such folly came to an immediate end.
The chairman is responsible for entire control of the
movement." Always, the man, the god; the people are
but dumb worshippers—for them he has only contempt.
"The German," he writes, "has not the slightest idea
of how a people must be misled if the adherence of the
masses is to be gained." Ruffianism can go no further:
verily now has the ruffian become God.

But let us pause, for there came recently in the history
of the world a genuine revolution, a revolution of an
exhausted brutalised people turning their bayonets upon
their flogging leaders, a revolution that rose like a
spiritual dawn upon the world, and we, we lovers of
freedom, looked with hope towards a New Russia and
saw the great figure of Lenin standing there beside the
angular Trotsky with his spectacles and jutting beard.
At last, here rose the people against the ruffian, at last
the ruffian seemed enchained, the Lilliputians had
turned upon a tyrant Gulliver. There was nothing of
the ruffian in Lenin: in the first place he had a sense
of humour, fatal to a ruffian, and he truly loved the
people, he hated bloodshed. When Dora Kaplan fired
into his chest while he was leaving a factory meeting,
he insisted that she should not be executed. How vastly
different from the later Mussolini who wears a bullet-
proof shirt, and who, in defiance of the King's protests,

passed a law reinstating capital punishment for attempted assassinations of those in authority. We were a little suspicious perhaps of Trotsky; he was so excitable, so enthusiastic, there was a possibility of ruffianism in him, but the logical, gentle philosophy of Lenin none could doubt.

Those shots from Dora Kaplan, however, were gradually to kill Lenin, and with his death the revolution seems to have been destroyed, it seems to have been destroyed subtlely, for that is often the ruffian's way when he dares not step immediately into the open. It is impossible to know the truth, so many lies have been spewed over the history of post-revolutionary Russia that we can only sit back dazed and in despair. We see an exiled Trotsky shouting in fury at the betrayal of the people, we see a mysterious Georgian with low forehead and heavy moustaches, dressed in shaggy clothes, being worshipped as a " golden sun," as the " wisest and best-beloved of fathers " and retorting to Trotsky that he is in league with fascism, but we cannot shut our ears to the rifle-fire as the old guard of bolshevism is shot down by the orders of Stalin, we cannot forget that scene in the central committee in 1927 when the Stalinites howled Trotsky into silence as the racketeers of Tallien and Fouché screamed down Robespierre years ago; we cannot forget the defiant Trotsky striving vainly to speak above the uproar while he reads his impeachment of Stalin and his gang. No, we who love liberty, we who have faith in humanity and the peoples of the world, must, I fear, turn from this country of which we held such hopes. Trotsky has gone, luckier than other comrades of Lenin who faced the gun so that Stalin and his bureaucrats could seize all power. . . . It seems that we must turn from this spectacle in disgust and fear. Lenin cried,

"We shall see the progressive withering away of the state, and the Soviet State will not be a state like the others, but a vast workers' commune." But like another Hitler or Mussolini, Stalin has crossed out the brave words of that ideal. He has stated, "We advance towards the abolition of the state by way of the strengthening of the state." The democratic workers' soviets have under Stalin apparently become a bureaucratic dictatorship upheld, like the regimes of Hitler and Mussolini, by a remorseless and ubiquitous secret police; free speech and newspapers are dead, even literature is strangled, and André Gide tells how in the U.S.S.R. he was not allowed to send a telegram to the leader of socialism unless he addressed him by a title more suitable to the Emperor of Japan; equality of the people seems to be more the oppression of the people under a tyrannical group, a privileged minority. . . . Those who fought with Lenin, those who loved him and believed his faith, are mostly either dead or in exile.

Can the ruffian never be controlled? Will this, the revolution of Russia, be the last effort of a despairing mankind to enchain the arrogant enemy? Will Spain too fall under the hammering of that agent of Mussolini's, the petty ruffian Franco with his hordes of Italians, Germans, and Moors? Is this the end? Must we look forward to a future of ruffianism, of Hitlers and Mussolinis and Stalins and Francos? Surely man will tire of it, will throw wide the prisons to release the victims of ruffianism and enchain the mad creatures of egoism, the enemies of us poor, frightened folk crying like children in the dark for liberty, for a little peace and happiness?

The armies have marched from Ruffians' Hall. The temples of art and love and freedom are broken beneath the lightning of these terrible creatures, we stand appalled before them, whimpering, not knowing how we can unite against a handful of humourless godlike beings blind to all but their own satanic ambitions. We are afraid, weak, tortured by conscience and a horror of bloodshed, yet united there is no greater force than the armies of democracy. When democracy first struggled against autocracy at Marathon, Athens against Persia, centuries ago, Herodotus wrote: "Liberty and equality of civic rights are brave and spirit-stirring things; and they who, while under the yoke of a despot had been no better men of war than any of their neighbours, as soon as they were free became the foremost men of all; for each felt that in fighting for a free commonwealth he fought for himself, and whatever he took in hand he was zealous to do the work thoroughly."

Let us pray that those words are prophetic; and at least to give us courage we have to-day the inspiring spectacle of a starved civilian Spain fighting magnificently against the might of organised ruffianism. Perhaps, timidly we hope, this present insane world, this deification of the ruffian, is but a final madness, the bursting of the ulcer, after which freedom will return and the great door of Ruffians' Hall will close for ever.

Pray God that that be so!

Index

AGUIRRE, LOPE DE, madness of, 117–20

Ahearn, Danny, author of *The Confessions of a Gunman*, 117–20

Allen, Ethan, 140, 141, 142, 143, 144

André, Adjutant-General John, 174, 175, 176

Arnold, Benedict, American invasion of Canada headed by Arnold, 1775, 136; Natanis, the Indian, guides them, 136; tramps from Lake George to Connecticut, 137; sets off to save America, 138; recruiting in Massachusetts, 139; Ethan Allen and his Green Mountain Boys forestall him, 140; joins Cambridge army as volunteer; fall of Ticonderoga, 140; sends resignation to Provincial Congress, 141; joined by Oswald and sets out for Crown Point as colonel, but Allen already had captured it, 141; captures St. Johns with Allen, Arnold takes command at Ticonderoga, 142; Allen captured by English at Montreal, rumours of disappearing stores, Arnold resigns, 143; charges dropped against him, 144; follows Schuyler to Canada through Maine wilderness, 145–51; Canada reached, 151; on the Heights of Abra-

Arnold, Benedict—*contd.*

ham, 152; withdraws from Quebec at approach of Carleton and waits for Montgomery, 153; attacks Quebec and fails; Congress makes him Brigadier General, and he continues futile blockade of Quebec, retires to Montreal, 155; investigations about stores in Montreal, is exonerated, 156; builds navy and attacks British fleet, 156–9; abandons fight and treks back to Ticonderoga, 159; made Major General, 159; resigns again, 161; relieves Fort Stanwix, 162; helps to fortify Bemis Heights with Kosciusko, 163; mutinies against Gates and holds up British attack, 162–3; resigns again, but implored to remain with army, 164; is shot, but victorious against Fraser's army, 165; Gates claims honour and Arnold kept in bed with wound, 166; given military governorship of Philadelphia, 167; makes profits on merchandise, incident of *The Charming Nancy*, 167; marries Peggy Shipper, 169; gets into debt, 170; charges brought against him, 170–2; offers to buy Colonial soldiers for Clinton, 174; meets André secretly to make ar-

377